ALIEN CONTACT

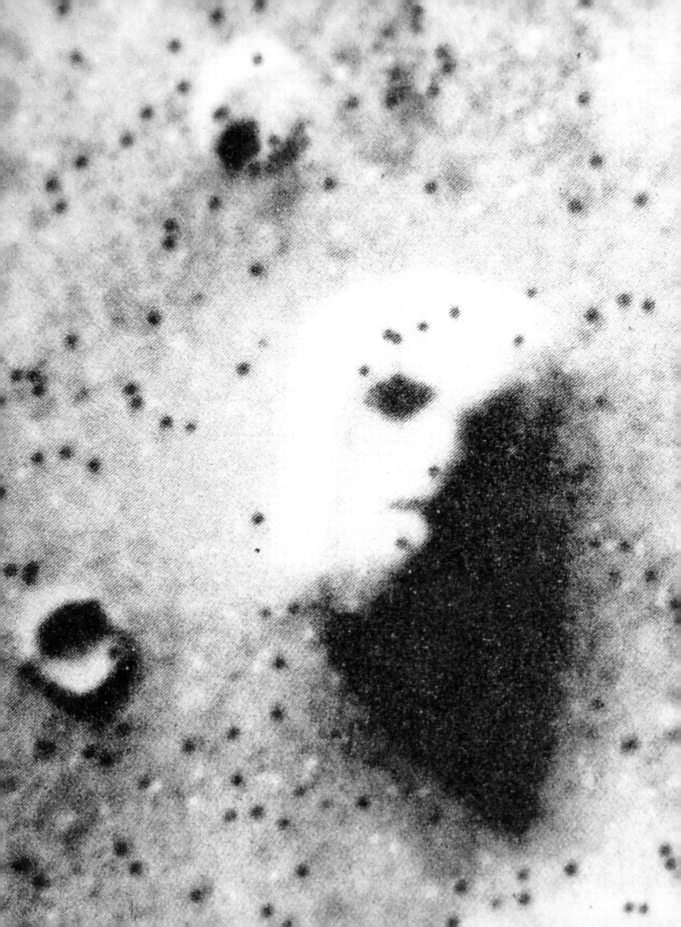

Jenny Randles
ALIEN CONTACT
The First Fifty Years

Sterling Publishing Co. Inc.   New York

Picture Credits
Front cover: Spiral galaxy (courtesy of Spectrum Colour Library).
Opposite title page: The 'face on Mars', as found by NASA landing missions,
a highly-debated issue of 1993.
Pages 17, 27 © Roy Sandbach; page 33 David A. Hardy/Science Photo Library;
page 51 © J. P. Templeton; page 53 NASA/ Science Photo Library page 63 NASA/Science
Photo Library; pages 87, 93 BFI Stills, Posters and Designs; page 94 David Parker/Science
Photo Library; page 103 © 1982 Starchild; page 123 (right) NASA/Science Photo Library.

Conceived, edited and designed by Collins & Brown Limited

Library of Congress Cataloging-in-Publication Data Available

10 9 8 7 6 5 4 3 2 1

Published by Sterling Publishing Company, Inc.
387 Park Avenue South, New York, N. Y. 10016

Originally published in Great Britain by
Collins & Brown Limited

Copyright © 1997 Collins & Brown Limited
Text copyright © 1997 Jenny Randles

Distributed in Canada by Sterling Publishing
c/o Canadian Manda Group
One Atlantic Avenue, Suite 105
Toronto, Ontario, Canada M6K 3E7

Reproduction by Centre Media, London
Printed by Midas, Hong Kong
All rights reserved.

Sterling ISBN 0-8069-0476-3

CONTENTS

Introduction   6

1947: The Aliens Arrive   8
1948: Crash Landing   10
1949: Secret Invasion   12

1950: Little Green Men   14
1951: Standstill   18
1952: From Another World   20
1953: The Men in Black   22
1954: Aliens in Europe   24
1955: Contact   28
1956: Aliens v the Earth   30
1957: Sexperiments   32
1958: Alien Colonists   36
1959: Hello Earth   38

1960: Close Encounters   40
1961: Abduction   42
1962: Under Wraps   46
1963: It's Out There   48
1964: Time Bandits   50
1965: Aliens in Orbit   54
1966: Star Trekking   56
1967: Science and Aliens   58
1968: The Invaders   62
1969: Alien End Game   64

1970: The Aliens Return   66
1971: Under the Skin   68
1972: Fading Vision   70

1973: Mark of the Aliens   72
1974: Euro Rendezvous   76
1975: Global Encounters   80
1976: The Alien Armada   84
1977: Investigations   86
1978: We Are Not Alone   88
1979: Angels or Demons?   92

1980: Back with a Bang   94
1981: Alien Interlude   98
1982: The Oz Factor   100
1983: Alien Rejects   102
1984: Star Children   104
1985: Strange Energies   106
1986: Big Bad Aliens   108
1987: Spacenapped   110
1988: Alien Revelations   114
1989: Tell the World   116

1990: Extraterrestrial TV   120
1991: New Frontiers   122
1992: Under the Influence   124
1993: The Alien Oscars   126
1994: Not Going Mad   130
1995: Proof at Last?   132
1996: Alien Artefacts   136
1997: Are We Ready?   138

Further reading   139
UFO organizations   141
Index   142

INTRODUCTION

Fifty years of UFO reality has just elapsed. Now it is time to assess where this has led us. However, this book focuses not so much on UFOs although, of course, they are hardly incidental to our story. Rather it examines the whole concept of alien contact. I do this chronologically, so that you can follow the main cases and the debates that have surrounded them. You can see the way in which trends and patterns have appeared and developed to create the legends of today's conspiratorially-minded UFOlogists.

Just as importantly, I have contrasted these events with other strands that contribute towards the fuller picture. These help us to figure out how these patterns may have come into being.

There has always been the world of political intrigue. We must look at the whys and wherefores of its involvement with this mystery. How have governments around the world reacted to the prospect of alien visitors? Did they capture solid proof many years ago, as some people allege? Have they invented stories to confuse and deceive us? What is the real motivation for investigating these phenomena?

We also see how science fiction has been 'loving the alien' for a very long time. Do novels, television series and movies imitate reports of UFOs or stimulate them? In other words, is there a symbolic relationship between the grand masters of fantasy and those people who claim that they really have encountered aliens on a dark and lonely night?

Finally, we see how science has striven to turn this science fiction into reality, pushing outwards towards that frontier in space and seeking some faint sign that we are not alone in the universe. Researcher Paul Devereux perceptively calls it 'the cry of a lonely species' and it is a most powerful cry, compelling us not only to build rocket ships to reach the stars, but to seek out that tiny voice that might prove once and for all that there are other lifeforms somewhere beyond earth.

All these threads weave together to form the complex tapestry that is alien contact – making the story you are about to read a fascinating one. But unlike a novel by Agatha Christie, this is not so much a whodunnit, as a *what*dunnit.

Will the answer to the mystery of alien-contact sightings be found within our subconscious, as some psychologists suggest? Is the desire to have intergalactic neighbours so powerful that we are forced to invent them, like a planet-wide version of the child's imaginary friend?

Is the earth, as some scientists contend, a living dynamo seething with energies that we comprehend only dimly, but whose forces can distort the bio-mechanical computer that we call the brain? Do these energies make us see things that are not really there? Are the aliens that we meet nothing more than the space-age equivalent of demons and dragons?

Are other lifeforms living here within our own environment, beyond the grasp of our ordinary senses? Do they rule a planet that our towering human arrogance makes us call our own? Is our consciousness not yet sufficiently advanced for us to see the truth that lies around us?

Or are we really being visited by a space-faring race from somewhere, out there, in the seemingly eternal ocean that is the universe? Science far from repudiates that possibility. Indeed, most astronomers believe that life 'out there' is a certainty. The only doubt they entertain is whether it is possible that this life could be coming to earth right now.

The answer to the riddles posed by this book may lie in one of those areas, or in some prospect that we have not yet even dreamed of. That is what makes it so exciting. Everyone has an opinion – but no one yet knows the truth.

Public fascination with the question of alien contact has never been greater. With the birth of *The X Files* the idea has grown that secret government departments are hiding proof about visitors from another world.

According to such popular culture, which entrances millions of viewers, the governments of NATO know the truth. They have landed and we are mere playthings in their presence. The conspiracy of silence is maintained, even withheld from prime ministers and presidents at the behest of some top-secret body, so as to prevent our world from descending into a madness of panic and instability.

Of course, this idea is not new. Even HG Wells pre-empted the concept of invading aliens more than a century ago when he wrote *The War of the Worlds*. The 1996 smash-hit movie *Independence Day* updated the imagery. This time it was not a failure to be protected against earthly disease that spelt doom for the alien marauders. They had to contend with the action-hero US president and a secret government base known as Area 51 which houses the carefully garnered proof of alien contact first captured in 1947. That movie was fiction, but Area 51, also known as Dreamland, really does exist.

In the murky world of UFOlogy, it can be difficult to know whether to take some things as fact, speculation or downright disinformation. Frankly, to some intelligence operatives this mystery is a powerful tool that can be used to manipulate public opinion. If you want to test fly some secret aircraft without shipping it to a remote island, the UFO phenomenon provides a perfect smokescreen. People will report what they see as an alien spaceship. Most of the world will dismiss that as a possibility – and you

have successfully hoodwinked your opponents. It is even better if you can be sure that some story-hungry journalist or over-eager UFO buff will blame the unfortunate aftermath of your mistakes on an alien power. You accidentally release radiation into the environment: drop a hint that a starship from Alpha Centaurei was responsible and nobody bats an eyelid. You test a new weapon and it starts frying the brain cells of an unfortunate passer-by: no problem, just make sure word gets around that ET was seen near by and pretty soon nobody who matters will be questioning what you are up to.

The cover-up exists, but not always (if ever) to hide the truth about alien visitors. Often, I fear, those same alien visitors serve as extraterrestrial scapegoats for some very terrestrial goings-on.

Unfortunately, this has serious problems for those of us who sense there is some kind of truth behind the sensationalism, jokes about little green men and the bluff and counter-bluff of the powers that be. 95% of all UFO sightings can be explained in terms of ordinary things. But there are still 5% that cannot be satisfactorily explained, and these can be highly intriguing. Many cases of alleged alien contact are hard to interpret, as they rely upon the isolated testimony of a hill-farmer or a huckster. But there are plenty of others in which the evidence builds towards an impressive argument.

Sorting out the truth about this whole phenomenon is a bit like wading through a minefield surrounded by treacle. You must be constantly on the alert for false leads, deliberate disinfomation, hucksters and charlatans out to make a buck and, of course, the many people who are telling the truth as they really observed it.

This book provides a fascinating detective story just waiting to be resolved. So sit back and join a magical mystery tour through 50 years of truly extraordinary alien contact and see if you can figure out what is really going on.

1947: THE ALIENS ARRIVE

The first 'flying saucer'

The UFO mystery officially began on June 24, 1947, when American pilot Kenneth Arnold had a close encounter above the Cascade mountain range in Washington, USA.

While flying across the north-western states on a routine business trip, Arnold's attention was caught by a flash in the afternoon sky. After ensuring that it was not a reflection off the canopy of his small aircraft, he watched in astonishment as a formation of crescent-like objects streaked across his path. As an experienced pilot, Arnold was able to judge their speed and knew that they were travelling much faster than any aircraft that he knew about.

At the time Arnold concluded that the objects he had seen must have been secret American aircraft on a training flight. However, his brief report to ground control created more fuss than he imagined. When he reached his destination at Yakima, he was greeted by journalists eager to hear his amazing story. It was a slow news day and Arnold offered the perfect antidote. He told reporters that the objects moved 'like a saucer skipping across the water' – meaning that they bounced through the air like a flat stone skimming across a pond. He certainly did not mean that they were saucer-shaped.

Unfortunately, or perhaps deliberately, his words were misappropriated and a pressman coined the phrase 'flying saucer'. It was a headline writer's dream and the media line – not believed by Arnold at the time – was that these craft were 'not of this earth'.

Until then UFO sightings had been sporadic, consisting of vague reports of lights in the sky. Arnold's handy phraseology changed all that.

The next day, all America gazed skywards searching for some sign of these phenomena.

Many observers thought they had seen a 'flying saucer'. Aircraft reflecting sunlight, meteors and even odd clouds were all mistaken for UFOs. Newspaper offices and radio stations were inundated with callers. The UFO mystery had well and truly arrived.

UFO crash at Roswell

The two weeks after Kenneth Arnold's sighting were filled with dubious stories about 'flying saucers'. However, sensational news broke on July 8, 1947, with a press release from Roswell Army Air Force Base in New Mexico: "The many rumours regarding the 'flying disc' became a reality yesterday when the Intelligence Office of the 509th Bomb Group of the Eighth Air Force, Roswell Army Airfield, was fortunate enough to gain possession of a disc. The object landed on a ranch near Roswell some time last week."

The ranch owner, William Brazel, heard an explosion during a storm one night in late June

Cover-up
An obviously embarrassed Major Jesse Marcel of the Intelligence Office shows off the remains of a weather balloon at Carswell Air Force Base in Texas on the afternoon of July 8, 1947. This had been substituted for the real wreckage found at Roswell, New Mexico. On orders from the Pentagon, Marcel was acting out his role as a stooge to get the media off the US government's back.

and next morning found a gouge cut through the earth with metal fragments at its end. The strange metal was flexible yet tough, and wood-like material with odd symbols was also present. It looked as if an object had crash-landed.

Local journalist Johnny McBoyle arrived at the scene a few hours before the press release and before officials from the Intelligence Office went to collect the rest of the wreckage and seal off the area. He sped from the crash site and called the KOAT radio station in Albuquerque. They had a teletype machine, enabling his first-hand account to be dispatched across the nation. McBoyle had just scooped one of the greatest stories in history.

The aliens

McBoyle's story was the first to associate 'little men' with UFOs. It was not followed up at the time, because the Roswell case was effectively squelched by higher authorities. They had panicked as soon as the press release hit the wires. Calls came in to the Pentagon and Roswell base from all over the world. The 'flying disc' story was fast getting out of control.

Major Marcel had loaded the wreckage onto a B-29 to ferry on to Wright Patterson Air Force Base in Dayton, Ohio – location of the US government department known as the Foreign Technology Division. The FTD is where top military and scientific experts analyse any weaponry or aircraft captured from an enemy power to assess the strengths and weaknesses of the technology. The fact that this destination was chosen for the 'disc' makes it clear just how seriously the US Air Force viewed the Roswell debris.

Marcel never got to Ohio. The plane stopped at Carswell Air Force base in Fort Worth, Texas soon after the Roswell press release. By now, the Pentagon had issued instructions to clamp down on the story. Lydia Sleppy recalls how McBoyle's call from Roswell stopped mid-sentence. She heard him arguing in the background. Then the teletype burst into life: 'Attention Albuquerque: Cease transmission.

Repeat. Cease Transmission. National Security Item. Do not transmit. Stand by.'

Another New Mexico radio station, KGFL, even reports how it got a call from Washington that afternoon threatening to revoke its licence unless it complied with the orders to scupper the story. They assumed that this meant that the wreckage had been identified as some sort of US experimental craft. Yet if this was secret US technology, it would be in a museum today.

Nor does this account for the claims of those who saw the debris or McBoyle's story about 'little men'. He was supported by a nurse from the air base who claims she saw a dead alien brought there. The pilot of the B-29 also says he was told he was taking little alien bodies with metal wreckage on their journey to the FTD at Wright Patterson. Such accounts claim the aliens were child-sized, frail, with large heads and big eyes but no body hair.

At Fort Worth a hastily convened press conference was held under the orders of General Roger Ramey. It was a mistake, he said. The 'flying disc' was a weather balloon that nobody had recognized. A clearly embarrassed Major Marcel was paraded with the debris from an actual balloon to show just how it did resemble a silver dishpan. He was obviously stunned at being made to look like an idiot.

Of course, a balloon has none of the properties described by the eyewitnesses who saw the Roswell wreckage. It is implausible that trained military officers at a top US base would not recognize one. In any event, those officers present at that press conference have since insisted that none of the recovered fragments was ever put on show. The balloon ruse was just a cover-story to make the press lose interest. As the reporters were shown balloon fragments, the Roswell wreckage was continuing its trip to Wright Patterson where the best minds in the US government would try to fathom out this 'foreign technology'.

This was not the end of the Roswell saga. 1947 was but chapter one in a 50-year mystery.

1948: Crash Landing

Alien bodies

This year was to prove extraordinary. Two separate UFO crashes allegedly took place – both in south-western USA and both involving the supposed recovery of dead alien bodies.

The first report emerged from Aztec, New Mexico, and was promoted by Frank Scully during lectures and writings. He said he heard about it from one Doctor Gee – a specialist in magnetic anomalies for the US government working at Los Alamos.

The doctor was supposedly flown out by helicopter to the desert on a 'secret mission' in April 1948 to study the wreckage of a disc-like craft that had impacted in the area. Dead bodies of small human-looking beings just over 3 feet tall were found. They had no body hair, soft downy skin, and two of them had even reputedly survived the impact for a short time.

The alien craft had used some kind of magnetic propulsion system to fly – hence Gee's

association with the case. It had been constructed of a light but durable metal and pictorial symbols not unlike hieroglyphics were found inside.

The dramatic similarities between this description of the felled object at Aztec and the stories about events at Roswell are intriguing. The Aztec case is a close match not only in details of the craft observed, but in its representation of the first evidence of the 'little gray men' that have become a regular feature of UFO lore.

While many UFO researchers have long argued that Scully invented this story, Dr Robert Spencer Carr, an expert in non-verbal communication at the University of South Florida, disagreed. He claimed to have inside knowledge of the incident through his contract with the government. According to Carr, the object was tracked on radar as it fell. The recovered bodies were taken to Wright Patterson Air Force base and frozen in cryogenic suspension. Carr added that they were unexpectedly human – with only their small stature, over-large heads, rounded eyes and oriental appearance in any way distinguishing. They even had O-type human blood, which most scientists find preposterous for beings from another planet.

The second crash appears to have more substance. Several UFO researchers were approached by witnesses, including Len Stringfield, a specialist and dedicated investigator of so-called 'crash-retrieval' stories. Their sources, usually anonymous, were relatives of military personnel who had been involved in the affair.

This new story said that a large craft had come down just inside the Mexican border near Laredo, Texas. Some reports said it had been

Stranger in the sky
An unidentified, early photograph of a UFO, typical of those submitted during the 1940s when the subject first came to the fore.

SPACE SPECTACLES

At the end of World War Two, it was discovered that Nazi scientists had been surprisingly well advanced in rocketry experiments. The technology that would eventually take man into space had been used to create the V-1 and V-2 unmanned rocket-propelled bombs that were launched against London in 1944–45. Longer-range transatlantic models were under test as the war concluded.

Sensing the importance of this work, both for military and scientific purposes, the US Government offered facilities to some of the leading rocket engineers, many of whom had worked under duress for the Nazi regime. They were led by Dr Werner von Braun and were taken into the USA and relocated in New Mexico.

Secret tests of V-rocket technology continued during 1946 and into 1947, by which time some of the experiments were public knowledge. They could hardly be covered up as many of the launches went disastrously wrong, causing rockets to explode on the launch pad. In one case in May 1947 a rocket veered off course and exploded onto a graveyard across the border into Mexico. Thankfully nobody was injured, but some of the more sensitive research was kept under wraps after this serious mishap.

Even more secret work involved the use of 'pilots' in the rockets. From early 1948 monkeys were used to test the stresses and strains of this new kind of technology. It seems more than possible that the Laredo shoot-out story might, in fact, be an exaggerated version of the crash of a prototype rocket on launch from New Mexico. It may have carried a 'pilot' on board, but a monkey rather than an extraterrestrial. This would explain the use of an air crash photographer and the apparent ease with which the Mexican government appear to have allowed the Americans into their territory to 'clean up' the mess.

However, there is one further point about the 'dead alien' photograph from 1948. The photo appears to show some rounded wires amidst the wreckage that look remarkably like spectacle frames. If this is indeed what they are, then it suggests that the body may be that of a dead human pilot, as it seems rather improbable that either monkeys or extraterrestrials would wear spectacles!

pursued by jets from Dias Air Force base and may have been disabled in a shoot-out. A massive recovery operation checked over the debris and a badly burned, hairless being about 4 feet tall was rescued.

The case took a dramatic twist in 1979 with an admission by a retired photographer from the secret government test facility at White Sands that he had been taken to the site to film the aftermath of an air crash. Although he was told that it was just a secret aircraft, the object appeared to be out of the ordinary. The body recovered from the wreckage had a large head and claw-like hands. He overheard doctors saying that the being's skin was smooth, there was no muscular structure, and a sulphurous odour permeated the body.

An alien pilot
One of the photographs taken at the Laredo 'UFO' crash site in 1948. It was said by the photographer to show the burnt body of the alien pilot – but note the spectacle frames on the lower left of the photograph.

The photographer had duplicated a few of the 500 photographs taken at the crash site. Kodak confirmed that the film dated from around the right time, but could not comment on the pictures' content. They appeared to show a small burnt form inside twisted wreckage, although the horrific burns masked much of the being's features.

Had the stories of recovered alien bodies from UFO crash sites finally been proven?

1949: SECRET INVASION

Aliens: the movie

By early 1949, stories of crashing UFOs were becoming improbably common. Possibly the most extraordinary of all the reports came from Death Valley in California, a desert hell where temperatures during the day get so high that human beings can die within the hour.

On 19 August, as the hot rays of the Mojave sun baked the landscape, two prospectors described seeing a disc-like craft in trouble in mid-air. It fell from the sky and made a rough landing onto a sand dune but remained more or less intact. It was at this point that the most astonishing thing occurred – two creatures leapt from the wreckage and stared dumbstruck at the men.

The beings were described as the size of dwarves, but otherwise human in appearance. This description is extremely typical. Upon seeing the witnesses, the entities scuttled away across the desert and vanished over a sand dune. The prospectors tried to catch up with them but by the time they reached the dune the beings had gone. When they looked back the UFO had also disappeared.

Increasing tales of alien encounters and UFO crashes led, by the end of 1949, to strong rumours that Hollywood was hard at work on a movie (*The Flying Saucer*) that would stun the world. The rumours insisted that it would use film evidence of captured UFO wreckage and real extraterrestrials in the possession of the US government.

This amazing claim came to nothing in 1949, but it was a story that reappeared throughout the years – until in 1995 the world was agog when it seemed to come true!

Why are they here?

One question was buzzing around the US government in connection with the rising numbers of close encounters that were now being reported. If these were not advanced aircraft from another power on earth, then was it possible that the UFOs had come from another planet? If so, why had they chosen this precise moment in time to make their presence felt?

That very problem was addressed in February 1949 by astronomer Professor George Valley, acting as a member of the Air Force Scientific Advisory Board. In a top-secret report he told the Pentagon his theories about the alien civilization that might well be coming to the earth:

'Such a civilization might observe that on earth we now have atomic bombs and are fast developing rockets. In view of the past history of mankind, they should be alarmed. We should, therefore, expect at this time above all to behold such visitations.'

Watching brief
Oval lights typical of the kind seen over sensitive sites in New Mexico in 1949.

TOP-SECRET UFO

Throughout the year there was serious concern amongst the scientific community about the number of close encounters and UFO crashes that were occurring in the American south-west. This was no academic interest, for here was the home of the most secret technology being perfected by the world's most powerful nation. Someone was paying undue attention and engaging in surveillance.

At Los Alamos and White Sands in New Mexico, the nuclear industry was under development, with particular emphasis on atomic weapons. The first steps towards rockets to the stars were being taken in the same area, albeit with the intention of creating an inter-continental ballistic missile. The sites were heavily guarded from any potential spies, but there was no obvious way of protecting them from the invasion of UFOs.

As a result, top-secret conferences were frequently held. These discussed the UFOs and involved some of the world's top scientists such as physicist Dr Edward Teller, one of the key people in the construction of the atom bomb. Data about the conferences was kept secret for 30 years. At these gatherings scientists reported seeing UFOs all the time. Leading meteor expert Dr Lincoln La Paz, from Albuquerque, managed to take a spectrographic reading of one. He noted the UFO's high copper content and this caused him to suspect that such objects were not natural, but possibly probes sent by an alien intelligence.

On August 20 Dr Clyde Tombaugh, the only astronomer this century to have discovered a planet, had a close encounter. He had discovered Pluto in the outer reaches of the solar system, but his encounter with a UFO is less well known. Indeed, scientists to this day still erroneously claim that astronomers never see UFOs, thereby emphasizing their non-existence.

Tombaugh made his sighting along with his wife and mother-in-law. They saw greenish-yellow lights in a circular formation that moved across the sky near his home at Las Cruces, New Mexico. At the time he was working at the White Sands missile site and stated later that he knew there was no US aircraft or technology that could behave as these objects did. He added that he was 'so unprepared for such a strange sight that I was really petrified with astonishment'. The matter was reported to the FBI and the astronomer himself requested secrecy.

Against Tombaugh's wishes, the sighting later became public and as a result he decided not to report two later sightings that he made. He is by no means alone amongst his scientific colleagues in fearing the public ridicule that might result from such encounters and he chose to remain silent. But the events that Tombaugh described, along with the growing number of encounters in New Mexico, started to make the US government a touch apprehensive.

It was based upon disturbing statements such as these that the concept of alien contact was first taken really seriously within the American halls of power.

Of course, the implication of Valley's report was not lost on the Pentagon. If an alien civilization was watching us, then its primary target might well be the technology at the heart of all the scientific research into atomic weaponry and space flight. And this was precisely where all of the early UFO activity was being focused.

Vital intelligence

One of the then top-secret reports of the security conferences that took place in 1949, when there was deep concern over the UFO sighting over top scientific research centres such as Los Alamos, New Mexico.

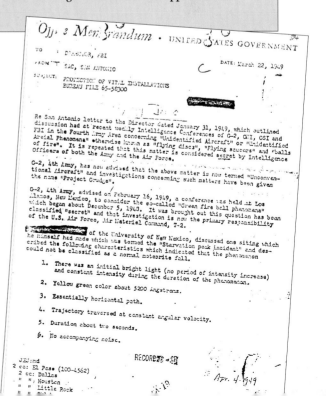

1950: LITTLE GREEN MEN

Alien close-up

Bruno Facchini became one of the first people to have a really close-up view of aliens in a landing case that occurred on April 24 of this year. The incident took place in the late evening near Varese, Italy.

Facchini was first alerted by some sparks near his house which he assumed were lightning. As he went to investigate he discovered a disc-like craft hovering beside a telegraph pole. Four strange beings surrounded it, seemingly engaged in some kind of repair work.

Each was of normal human height and wore a gray one-piece suit with a transparent face mask. A breathing tube came from the front of each mask.

The sparks were pouring out from pipes or tubes which one of the aliens appeared to be working on with some kind of device. Even the inside of the craft could be partially seen through an open vent. There were lots of dials and cylinders, which Facchini assumed held oxygen. The air surrounding the UFO was

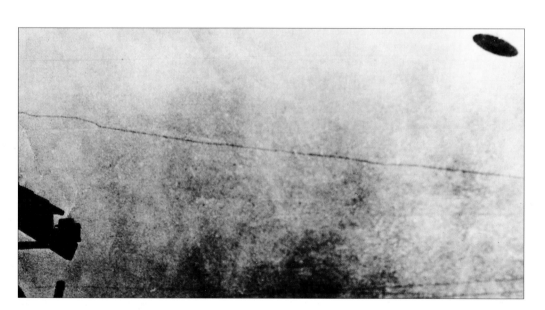

THE REAL THING

May 1950 produced what is widely believed to be one of the best photos of a genuine UFO in existence. Taken by farmer Paul Trent and his wife at McMinville, Oregon, USA, it has passed all the tests to which it has been subjected and appears to show an object far too big to be a model.

PROJECT TWINKLE

Throughout 1950 American scientists mounted the first investigation into UFOs, codenamed Project Twinkle. Unlike the US Air Force investigations which had begun in 1948 and had gone through a variety of names (settling eventually on Project Blue Book), this was not primarily a debunking exercise operated by low-grade military staff. Twinkle was a serious attempt by physicists and astronomers to find out what was flying over the space technology sites of New Mexico, often observed in the form of 'green fireballs'.

Twinkle was a failure, but for rather interesting reasons. Every time the complex measuring equipment and cameras were set up in a location where the fireballs had been sighted, the sightings stopped and moved elsewhere. With new resolve, the team of scientists and military men moved to a different location, only for the UFOs to take off and appear in yet another spot. It was as if the phenomenon was toying with the researchers and this was one of the many reasons that suggested an intelligence lay behind the reports.

As a result of these events, a top-secret 'estimate of situation' report had been submitted to the highest levels of the Pentagon. This had insisted that UFOs showed signs of being extraterrestrial visitors. But it was not known if they were friendly or hostile. The focus of the sightings around atomic and rocket development centres suggested to the scientists that these visitors might have come now because of our twin discoveries of atomic energy and the rudiments of space flight. The question was asked: Are we now a threat to these aliens in their own backyard? General Hoyt Vandenburg demanded physical proof of these arguments.

Of course, all this was carried out in secret. Even today, the full 'estimate' report has never been released, only summaries of it through the US Freedom of Information Act introduced in 1977.

Another intriguing top-secret memo was penned on March 22, 1950, by an FBI agent in Washington. It was written to the director, J. Edgar Hoover, and its subject matter was the reports of UFO crashes and alien beings that had been occurring in New Mexico. These were virtually unknown to the general public at the time.

The FBI agent explains that the USAF had reported how 'three so-called flying saucers had been recovered' and that bodies had been retrieved 'dressed in a metallic cloth of very fine texture'. The beings were only about 3 feet tall and were precisely like those being reported in many of the UFO sightings and from witnesses to the crash retrievals (although almost none of these sightings had yet been reported in the public domain). According to the FBI memo, the crashes occurred in New Mexico because of the technology positioned there and the intense radar coverage in the area. It was speculated that radar beams caused the UFOs to malfunction.

Whatever the truth, the claims of crashing UFOs and recovered alien bodies were now firmly out of the realms of purely unsupported stories from occasional witnesses. They were finally being debated in the archives of both the intelligence and the scientific community. This dramatic real-life 'X file' had set a precedent that still provokes discussion half a century later.

An early 'X' file
The FBI memo that first brought to notice the US government's interest in both crashed UFOs and bodies supposedly recovered from them.

unusually warm and a buzzing sound like a giant beehive was constantly heard.

Facchini watched this alien performance for some time and then decided to offer his assistance to the strangers. They responded by talking to each other in guttural language. One being then pointed a tube towards him, out of which emerged a beam of light. Facchini was knocked back several yards and this was followed by a blast of air, which felled the witness.

The beings got back into the object, which took off skywards. Facchini went back to the site in daylight and found scorch marks, imprints seemingly left by landing legs and pieces of metal. This debris was handed to the police who brought in the Ministry of Defence. Scientists who examined the samples said that they were comprised of heat-resistant metal that would be ideal in space flight to face the burn-up as the capsule entered the earth's atmosphere.

The first abduction

Shortly after the Bruno Facchini encounter, the world's first attempted alien abduction occurred. Although the incident was investigated in detail at the time by the gendarmerie and Dr Jacques Vallee procured a report in 1967, it is virtually unknown within UFO circles.

It happened on the afternoon of May 20 in the Loire Valley, France, and the witness was a young woman heading home to prepare the evening dinner. Suddenly her cheerful whistling was interrupted by a brilliant flash of light and two dark arms appeared from above, grabbing her

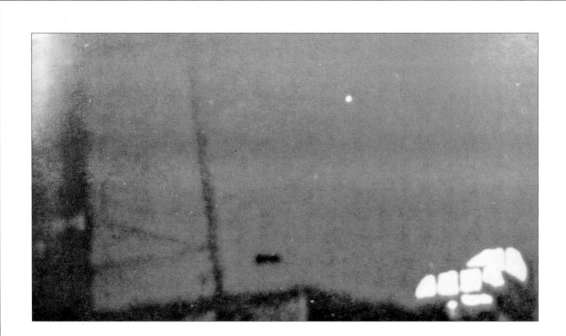

UFOs in Motion

A still from the first movie footage of a UFO that is considered genuine, taken by the manager of a baseball stadium at Great Falls, Montana, USA, in August 1950. The identity of the objects remains unknown.

by the face and neck. She only had time to notice their yellowish caste before she began to lose consciousness.

The woman recalls being dragged through bushes. Everything seemed to be happening at speed around her and she heard a voice from above saying, 'There she is. We've got her'. She was taken into a clearing when, for no apparent reason, the pressure ceased and she collapsed onto the ground. Her bag and its money were laid out as easy prey for any robbers, so this was obviously no ordinary attack.

After spending a few moments regaining her composure, the woman heard a noise like a whirlwind and a blinding light trailing wind shot across the sky above her, vanishing into the distance. A calm then fell over the riverside.

The terrified witness stumbled to a lock keeper's cottage, where she was cared for and the police were called. Her body showed the clear physical evidence of the attempted kidnap, including the indentations from two hands – each with five fingers – embedded into her face.

In conclusion, the gendarmerie wrote this off as an utterly puzzling abduction attempt but could not reconcile its bizarre features with any human attacker. In more recent times alien kidnapping has been much more common and, whilst this case has a number of peculiarities, there is enough about it to be immediately recognizable by today's UFOlogists.

This was possibly the first attempt by aliens to abduct a human being as she went about her everyday business. If so, it failed, and may have led to a desire to perfect less crude methods.

Water, water everywhere

Several early cases reported aliens apparently desperate for water – pleading for it from an engineer in the Drakensteen Mountains of South Africa, for example. Among them was a case from Ontario, Canada. On July 2, 1952, a mining executive and his wife had just beached their boat at Sawtooth Bay to have a picnic when they noticed an object on the surface of the lake. They described it as looking like two plates stuck together. As the couple watched in amazement some small beings, under 4 feet tall and wearing silver clothing, stood on the rim of the craft and proceeded to suck up water with a hose amidst a loud humming sound. When they had 'topped up' their UFO it climbed skywards. A slight glow was left on the lake where the craft had been.

At the time there was speculation as to whether Mars was an arid planet populated by aliens in dire need of water. Captain W. E. Johns (who had previously written the Biggles stories but now penned tales of space adventures involving UFOs and aliens) adopted this theme in a series of children's books in the 1950s. Interestingly, although the kind of aliens that appeared in Johns' books, and in other fictional works of the period, bore no resemblance to those described in the Ontario case, little figures in silver suits were reported in other real-life cases worldwide.

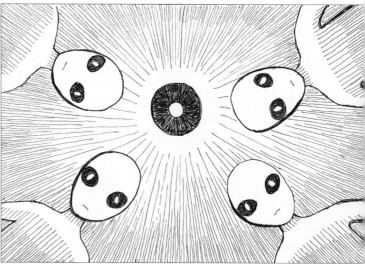

Watching over us?
By 1950, stories of aliens as small humanoid creatures with large eyes – as drawn in this cartoon by artist and UFOlogist Roy Sandbach – had become commonplace. The image still endures in UFO lore today.

1951: STANDSTILL

Landing site

On August 14 a farmer at Veghenza in the north of Italy had a fright early in the afternoon when a strange object came down on his land next to the town cemetery.

Walking towards the craft that had now come down on the open ground, he got to within a few feet and had a perfect view. The object was about 20 feet in diameter and looked like two pie cans on top of each other. It was made out of a white metal that resembled aluminium. It sat on legs and had stairs at either side leading up into the machine. A line of blue portholes surrounded the centre.

As the farmer stared at the object he did not notice the arrival of half a dozen aliens. They were inspecting the cemetery almost as if they

were curious tourists. When they saw the farmer they seemed amused by his appearance. The creatures looked very odd, being not much over 3 feet tall and dressed in white one-piece coveralls that reflected the sunlight. Their faces were white and almost resembled the faces of monkeys and their eyes were large, round and blue.

The beings never spoke, communicating with one another only by gestures. They wore cylinders or oxygen bottles on their backs, with tubes leading towards their mouths. They also had belts in which various transparent objects like multi-coloured glass lenses were carried.

After the farmer had watched the entities for a time, they seemed to panic. It was as if they had suddenly acknowledged the threat posed by the

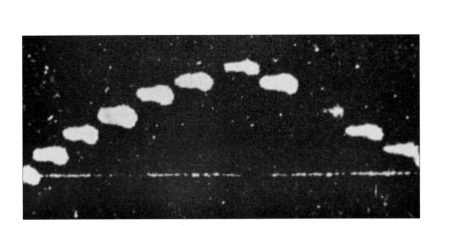

DUCK SHOOT, TEXAS STYLE

On August 30, 1951, a formation of glowing objects was seen passing over Lubbock, Texas, USA. This photo was taken by Carl Hart and shows the lights seen by many witnesses. The official explanation from the US government is that the lights are ducks with shiny underbellies. The witnesses reject this theory.

CINEMATIC CAR STOP

There are people who suggest that the alien contacts that were reported during the late forties and early fifties were dreams or fantasies that built upon the science fiction of the day. This argument is difficult to sustain because the typical images of aliens in the comic-book novels that were around at the time were more bug-eyed monster than little gray man.

Indeed, the human appearance of the aliens was one of the most obvious features of these early cases and yet was hard to find in the traditional monster fiction of the era. Hollywood was also slow to respond to the wave of UFO sightings. In 1951, however, the first classic movie of the UFO age appeared and it generated plenty for the sceptics to get their teeth into.

The Day the Earth Stood Still was a fable of alien contact in a modern setting. Its aliens looked human; not the little men of the real cases, but more human still than that. Where the film did draw upon UFO imagery was in the depiction of the saucer-shaped craft. This itself was a problem; UFOs were not – and never had been – particularly saucer-shaped. It was always a media myth which this movie, and several that followed, helped to preserve.

In the movie, the aliens are concerned about the aggressive nature of humankind and seek to demonstrate their superior technology by causing all electrical power to cease functioning. As a result, the earth does quite literally stand still for a time.

Before 1951 there were no cases where such an effect had been reported in real UFO cases. However, it would not be long before the 'car stop' or 'vehicle interference' effect was a common feature of reports. In today's alien abductions, the first a witness usually knows about the arrival of the aliens is when their car engine and lights fail to operate in the presence of a UFO – as if some sort of inhibiting field of energy is at work.

Did these cases occur because of the popularity of *The Day the Earth Stood Still*? Or was it simply a coincidence? Had there already been incidents of 'car stops' that had simply not been recorded? This debate rages on to this day and there seems to be no easy answer. In any case, reports of vehicle interference have established a life of their own and there is considerable hard evidence to back them up. It would be difficult to dismiss these as simply a figment of the imagination in the wake of this epic movie.

But then perhaps aliens watch our movies too! Could they have borrowed a trick from Hollywood in order to demonstrate their superior abilities?

farmer. One of the beings picked up a tube and pointed it at him. There was a flash of light but nothing happened. However, the farmer was understandably stunned and when he recovered his composure the entities were heading up the ladders back into the UFO.

When they were all inside, both the ladders and legs were pulled inside and the outer edge of the craft began to rotate. A noise like a vacuum cleaner was heard and a reddish-green flame spurted out from underneath the craft. The UFO rose upwards, stopped at rooftop height and tilted at an oblique angle. It then shot away at phenomenal speed without leaving a shock wave.

This case typifies a number of trends that, by 1951, were beginning to appear in alien-contact cases. The seemingly pointless behaviour of the entities, wandering around aimlessly looking at the sights, is fascinating. Also noteworthy is the way the craft took off as this, again, has often been reported. In fact, when descending, the craft are also often said to float from side to side, like a leaf falling in a breeze from a tree. Indeed, this flight motion is referred to by UFOlogists as 'falling-leaf motion'.

Although it is unlikely that farmers and other non-scientific witnesses would realize it, they are actually describing the perfect aerodynamics for an object that has somehow made itself almost gravity-free. This may well teach us something about the propulsion system involved. Do UFOs somehow control gravity and make themselves almost weightless?

1952: From Another World

The monster

The first alien encounter in the classic science-fiction mould occurred on September 12 in Flatwoods, Virginia, USA. It remains highly unusual and is not easy to dismiss as just a hoax. It featured an out-and-out monster in true Hollywood style.

Three boys were playing on a field when a red ball of fire crossed the sky in a majestic arc and dropped behind the crest of a hill. The youths set off for the crash site, thinking that a meteorite might have fallen, and along the way gathered quite a collection of people, including a woman and her two sons and other local townspeople. A dog accompanied them and ran ahead, barking furiously at the unseen danger.

By the time the meteor-hunters reached the barking dog, they confronted a thick, pungent mist. The red ball was positioned on the ground.

Soon they were less interested in the UFO and more in the strange creature seen in a nearby tree; it had a huge head and two glowing eyes staring fixedly out. Beams of bluish light appeared to emanate from them.

The monstrous form had no obvious lower body or legs.It glided towards them silently, creating mass panic amongst the intrepid explorers. The dog collapsed and had to be dragged from the path of the approaching beast – it had apparently fainted. The humans were deeply shocked and fled from the hillside. When they reached town, most of the observers were still unable to talk coherently and several required treatment for shock. This, probably more than anything else, persuaded the people of Flatwoods that the monster they had seen was real.

The next day, evidence of the previous night's encounter was clearly visible. The grass gave off a foul odour and was crushed flat in places; there were also marks on the ground at the spot where the red ball had landed.

Few people ever doubted that a real sighting occurred. Even sceptics have usually tried to explain the events as misidentification rather than fabrication. The US Air Force reputedly sent investigators to the site (dressed out of uniform and not identifying themselves), but concluded that the story resulted from mass hysteria together with the sighting of a meteor and an owl!

However, there were other cases. A week earlier a woman at Weston (only ten miles away) saw a similar creature and was so disturbed by it that she was in hospital for several weeks. Her sighting was never reported in the media.

There are also links between this smelly monster and sightings of 'Bigfoot', which have rarely been reported in the area. During the mid l960s, a not dissimilar figure known as 'Mothman' provoked reports throughout West Virginia.

Red mists and strong odours also featured in another case from the southern United States. On August 19 'Sonny' Desvergers, a scout master at West Palm Beach in Florida, was driving some of his troops home when they saw an odd light. Entering the bush he found himself staring up at a hovering object with a red vaporous glow. This engulfed his body and emitted an ozone smell.

Desvergers collapsed and was found by police at the scene. His cap had a set of 'electrical spark holes' and the soil beneath the UFO's hovering spot showed curious traces. A USAF lab revealed that the grass roots had been 'cooked' from below ground, but exposed leaves were unaffected. An alternating magnetic field seemed to be the likely cause, generating electricity and forming ozone whilst rendering the witness briefly unconscious. But where had this energy field come from?

WHITE HOUSE WHITEWASH

This year was a turning point in official interest in UFOs. On July 19 and 26, Washington DC was 'invaded' by UFOs. They were seen from the ground, crossing closely protected air space that guarded the White House and Capitol building. Aircraft saw them and both civil and military radar recorded them. Jet interceptors were, after some delay, sent up in pursuit, but nothing was ever proven.

Officially, the US Government accepted claims by a meteorologist that unusual radar 'inversions' and mirages were to blame. However, none of the radar operators who tracked the objects agreed and an investigation by Professor James McDonald, an atmospheric physicist, showed that this theory was impossible given the prevailing conditions and the behaviour of the objects.

There is evidence that defence strategists were concerned by this wave of sightings. Secret data from the time shows that some had noted the way in which the UFOs, after seeming to study US technology in New Mexico, had now moved on to the country's seat of power. The press conference offering the 'inversion' theory had achieved its aim – 'to get the press off our backs,' Privately, panic had set in.

Sceptics often say that they will believe in UFOs when one lands on the White House lawn and this almost happened in 1952. The wave persuaded many scientists and government officials that UFOs had to be taken seriously. In Britain, Prime Minister Winston Churchill penned a memo demanding to know from his Air Minister what 'all this stuff about flying saucers' meant. We know from data available at Britain's Public Record Office that an official UFO investigation procedure was

then set in motion and RAF pilots were ordered to keep quiet about their own encounters. We also know from US records that Churchill sent intelligence officers to Washington armed with dozens of questions to enable Britain to create its own UFO monitor.

There was not long to wait. On September 19–21, a NATO exercise, Operation Mainbrace, was intercepted by UFOs. Jets chased objects across the skies of Yorkshire. An aircraft carrier taking part in the exercise in the North Sea was buzzed by a large daylight disc. Naval staff on board photographed the UFO, which was kept secret until many years afterwards.

In the wake of all this, nations now had to take UFOs seriously. This may have been the year when the truth about UFOs was finally embraced.

What's it all about?
The famous memo penned in July 1952 by Winston Churchill – then British Prime Minister – asking for a report on UFOs from the Air Ministry. This was in the wake of the extraordinary Washington DC encounters.

Alien invasion
In July 1952, Washington DC was 'invaded' by UFOs. This photograph purports to shows UFOs over the Capitol building. The 'UFOs' are, in fact, ground lights surrounding the building flaring in the lens of the camera.

1953: THE MEN IN BLACK

The government hits back

Albert Bender from Connecticut was one of the first people to set up a private UFO group. This was in 1952 and he gave it the grand title of the International Flying Saucer Bureau. Because of the growing fascination with the phenomenon, the bureau soon swelled in numbers and, indeed, the British Flying Saucer Bureau (set up as on offshoot of the IFSB in Bristol) still exists today as the oldest surviving UFO group in the world.

However, Bender was to have a much more dramatic role in the story of alien contact. He had begun by trying to send a message to the aliens that his group could be their friends. He ended up running for his life, the victim of a series of events that came to be known as the 'Three Men' or the 'Men in Black'.

Bender was heavily into horror fiction and had an obsessive personality. Even so, people were stunned when, in September 1953, he quit the group and UFOlogy, saying only two things to close friends: he was afraid for his life and that he now had the answer to the UFO subject. This had been provided when speculations he had made had attracted the attention of the US Government. They sent three 'agents' dressed in

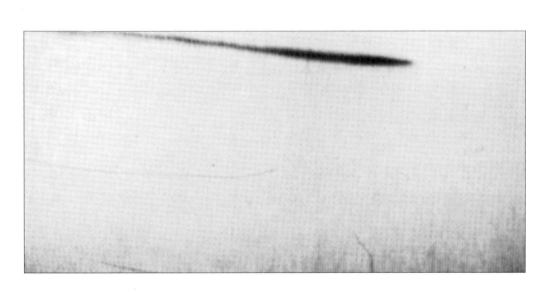

GUN-CAMERA ACTION

By 1953 jet aircraft were sent in pursuit of UFOs on a regular basis.
This flight from Luke Air Force base in Arizona, USA, captured proof
of the UFO on its gun camera in March.

OPERATION DEBUNK

In January l953, the US government responded to mounting pressure. The CIA set up a panel of top scientists, headed by atomic physicist Dr H P Robertson. They met in Washington to analyse the evidence that an alien intelligence was surveying the USA.

Robertson's team included some prestigious scientists who made a number of decisions, including that the subject was to be debunked out of public existence. Fearing that the USSR might use the UFO hysteria as a cover for a sneak attack, public concern had to be defused. To combat this, the CIA team suggested several methods, all of which were implemented. These included employing cartoonists to make silly UFO films and mounting surveillance operations on prominent civilian UFOlogists.

Soon after the CIA panel had met, one of the best documented UFO crashes occurred. It was also the last of this early spate of reports. The case took place on May 20 near Kingman, Arizona, and four independent accounts emerged as the years went by – each achieving no publicity and one being a death-bed confession. The reports told how individuals were taken to the crash site in buses with all windows blacked out to prevent them from recalling the location. Each person had a specific job to do and was then taken away again. Alien bodies were recovered and taken to Wright Patterson Air Force Base (home of the Foreign Technology Division) where they were also seen arriving packed in dry ice.

Descriptions of the entities were extraordinarily consistent. They were 4 feet tall with a yellowish-brown cast to the skin. They had egg-shaped, hairless heads with large rounded eyes. Once more this is a very familiar account. Can all of these similar reports be untrue?

black suits to visit him and announced that they knew the truth about alien visitation and had done so for two years. He must not tell anyone what he had learnt and should trust the government to inform the world within four years.

The sinister story was published three years later by Bender's friend and confidant, Gray Barker. The book, *They Knew too Much About Flying Saucers,* created the Men in Black legend and inferred that Bender and several other UFOlogists who quit suddenly had all been silenced.

Bender was thought to have become disillusioned with the failure of the US Government to keep its promise and reveal all it knew. After several years of pressure from Barker, he agreed to write a book on his story. This came out as *Flying Saucers and the Three Men*, but even Bender's friends found it hard to believe. Some felt he was still 'under threat' and so had to lie. Others say he just made the new story up. Either way, it was Bender's final word.

He claimed that the Men in Black were really aliens in disguise; their true appearance was like the Flatwoods monster (see page 20). They were on earth to extract a substance from sea water and return it to their home world, known as Kazik. In l960, the mission ended, they flew home and Bender was free to tell his tale.

Although no more was to be heard from Albert Bender, it was far from the last word on the Men in Black.

War of the worlds

Indeed on November 23, 1953, death occurred at the hands of a UFO in a way that seemed to mirror Bender's dire warnings.

An object was tracked by air defence radar over Lake Superior on the borderland between the USA and Canada. A USAF F-89 interceptor was scrambled from the Kinross Air Force Base in Michigan. At 8000 feet above Keeweenaw Point the jet closed in on the UFO. Radar showed two blips come together, merge and disappear.

No trace of the aircraft was ever found. The pilot and radar operator on board had become casualties of what the growing band of amateur UFOlogists viewed as a war of the worlds.

1954: ALIENS IN EUROPE

The French connection

Before 1954 there had been waves of localized UFO activity. Alien-contact cases had occurred sporadically throughout, most of them from the USA, but some from Italy. In the autumn of 1954 an entirely new event struck – a wave of encounters where nearly all cases involved humanoids. The focus was Europe, and France in particular.

One of the earliest cases, on September 10, happened at Quarouble, a village near the Belgian border. It involved an object hovering over a railway track. As local resident Marius Dewilde went out to investigate, he noticed two small beings, just over 4 feet tall and wearing diving suits. They projected a light beam that seemed to paralyse him. By the time he could move again, the beings had returned to the craft which then disappeared.

The police investigated the incident, as did the French defence ministry. Indeed, they were especially concerned by the physical evidence of the incident – crushed railway tracks and burnt rocks found at the spot where the UFO had been. Whatever resulted from this scientific study was never made public. In fact, the police later complained that even they were being denied access to the evidence by the ministry. When Dewilde had a second encounter with a landed craft a few weeks later, he chose to remain silent. Did he speak only with the defence authorities? Are we looking at an example of a French 'Men in Black' attempt at silencing a witness?

If so, nothing could stifle the flood of reports that followed. One of the most impressive occurred on a construction site near Marcilly-sur-Vienne on September 30. Foreman Georges Gatay reported a strange tiredness coming over him. Before he knew it, he was walking away from his men towards a brilliant dome-shaped object that was hovering above the ground. In front of it stood a small man wearing a diving suit. A beam of light – which we might today recognise as a laser projection – was coming from his midriff.

Suddenly the figure vanished and a high-pitched whistling sound was heard. The object climbed skywards and was immediately surrounded by an eerie blue glow. It then vanished.

Gatay rushed back to his workmates who confirmed that they too had felt 'strange' and had seen the whole thing as well. Over the next few days the witnesses could not eat, felt light-headed and suffered from insomnia. Although these symptoms were not recognized as such in l954, today they are hints that a deeper experience may hide behind the conscious memory – possibly even an abduction. The apparitional image that seemed to be the form of both the UFO and entities, and the way in which they simply disappeared, were also to become common features of alien-contact cases in coming years.

The wave spreads

As sightings continued throughout France, the pattern remained much the same. Little men came face to face with witnesses, projected light beams at them, caused them to become paralysed and in some instances to have vague feelings that something deeper had happened.

Throughout October the reports increased and spread out to encompass much of Europe. An incident on October 20 near Como, Italy, was typical. The witness had just parked his car in the garage when he saw a strange creature about 4 feet tall and dressed in a one-piece luminous suit. The being fired a light from its midriff which

LYING SAUCERS?

In 1954, contactee stories were receiving huge publicity. King of them all was George Adamski, who supported his claims with spectacular photographs like the ones shown here. **Above:** Adamski claimed that this photograph showed a 'Venusian' spaceship, but later, when more sophisticated analysis became possible, many UFOlogists came to suspect that this was simply a small table-top model. **Inset:** This photograph purports to show a 'mother ship' surrounded by smaller 'baby' crafts.

froze the terrified man mid-track. However, as he clenched his fist, the force of the garage keys still in his hand seemed to break the spell. He then tried to attack the alien, but the creature reacted swiftly by floating vertically upwards in defiance of gravity. A strange whirring noise was heard.

Once again, this case was subjected to a detailed investigation by the local police, who could find no fault with the story. The witness also became physically ill and was bedridden for some time afterwards.

On October 23 a detailed account was made by a farmer in Tripoli, Libya, who watched an egg-shaped object land. It had various protuberances, including wheels and ladders, and made a noise like compressed air escaping. Inside the UFO he was able to see several humanoid creatures wearing yellow coveralls. They were using various kinds of equipment, including a radio set with earphones. Although this may have been state-of-the-art in 1954, it seems curiously antiquated from our current perspective. Indeed, this is true of many of the fairly rare occurrences from the 1950s where the witness had a close view inside the UFO. The machinery is often modern for the era, but given the pace of our own scientific progress in the past 40 years, it has aged very quickly.

Yet would not alien equipment be centuries ahead of our own, rather than mirroring what we have? This feature of alien-contact stories is known as 'cultural tracking' because the UFO technology tracks what our culture has but rarely exceeds it by a great deal.

However, there are several instances where what we now know as lasers and holograms were apparently used by aliens in a decade when they were yet to be invented.

Three young women from Torpo, Norway, also got a view inside a UFO which hovered only a few feet above their heads on November 23. The small, but otherwise human-looking, being inside was moving levers and dials and seemed to do this in a hurry to escape their attentions. The alien actually piloted the UFO straight into some over-head power lines, resulting in a massive shower of sparks. However, unlike the cases of UFOs felled by more innocent radar waves, this one kept on flying to complete its getaway.

National aliens

The 1954 wave offered us the first real clues about another puzzling feature of alien contact stories – why did they seem to manifest in different ways, accord-ing to the country from which they emerged?

Take me to your leader
An alien captured and in the hands of security guards. This is widely believed to be an April fools hoax by a German newspaper.

As you have seen, the American stereotype was already well established – small, egg-headed, grayish skin and rather egocentric and scientific. The term 'gray' has become attached. Over 75% of cases from the USA represent such aliens. This percentage has, if anything, steadily increased over the years.

French cases feature dwarves, but they are more impish, like elves or goblins of folklore. In case after case they plague witnesses, laughing as they paralyse them with light beams and running

about in almost absurd splendour. The word 'trickster' has been applied to such cases.

Elsewhere in the world the situation is differ-ent again. In South America, for example, hirsute dwarves with what might be termed a macho tem-perament crop up regularly. On December 10 at Chico-Cerro de las Tres Torres in Venezuela, four of the hairy beings, barely 4 feet tall, attacked two hunters and tried to drag them towards their UFO. One man fainted, the other fought back by clocking an alien with his gun. The butt broke in two as if it had struck iron. By the time the two men had escaped they were badly bruised, scratched and in a dishev-elled state as a result of the alien aggression.

The first well-attested alien contact in Britain occurred amidst this huge autumn wave on October 21. The location was a farmhouse at Ranton in Staffordshire, and wit-ness Jessie Roestenberg described to me how a disc-like craft circled her home and caused her and her three children to hide under a table. This was not before they had an excel-lent view of the two occu-pants. Human-like beings, slightly smaller than nor-mal, with long blond hair and wearing blue ski-suits were staring out of the transparent dome, obviously watching the scared witnesses with a curious expression. Jessie Roestenberg said it was not quite curiosity, not quite pity; it was a sort of detached fascination.

The British aliens frequently followed this pattern – tall, blond-haired, rarely aggressive or even directly interfering with a witness. They are perhaps the most human of all entity types. Witnesses often say you could walk past one in the street and few people would bat an eyelid –

ALIEN VOTES FOR JFK

Probably the first truly intelligent UFO-related movie appeared this year with *This Island Earth*. It told of scientists being recruited to take part in an experiment only to discover that its instigators are human-like aliens. The earthlings are being taken to assist with problems which the aliens have on their distant home world.

Aside from the exploration of a less gung-ho approach to alien invasion that had dominated all other movies, this film adapted well into UFO mythology and introduced a theme that was virtually unknown in 1954, even to seasoned UFOlogists – 'spacenapping', the kidnapping of humans by extraterrestrials for their own purposes.

UFOlogists would not encompass the idea of alien abduction for more than a decade, although the evidence was there in obscure cases that few people knew about; such as the French woman grabbed by flailing hands (see page 16) and the Venezuelan hunters viciously attacked. These crude methods clearly did not work and were not repeated. In any case, when abductions did begin in earnest, the aliens had updated their approach.

A different form of science fiction came in the form of contactee stories. These were frequent during 1954 and would increase in popularity. Contactees such as café owner George Adamski went one step beyond claiming to see aliens. He said he actually conversed with them, was taken on rides in their spaceships and in some cases became part of the intergalactic community of space brothers. Some of these people spun harmless yarns of goody-goody space philosophy, backed by evidence that did not fit. Others launched cults to back them up with numbers and money, with some still thriving today. One contactee even ran for US President but withdrew when the aliens asked him to support John F. Kennedy instead!

There are those who suspect that some contactee tales were planted by the CIA to debunk serious interest in UFOs. They were certainly silly enough to ensure that many scientists who might have been impressed by the growing strength of the alien-contact evidence were disinclined to take their interest further. Even Captain Edward Ruppelt, head of the USAF Project Blue Book and author of a book expressing a belief in alien UFOs, changed his mind after meeting the contactees.

A CIA memo in 1954 referred favourably to the contactee literature without stating that it had a hand in its flourishing agenda. The CIA did, however, note that the (unstated) policies adopted after the Roberston panel met the year before were achieving their goals. Make of that what you will.

Alien monsters
By 1954, descriptions of aliens ranged from goblin-like creatures seen in France to hairy dwarves that feature prominently in stories from South America. Both types, however, are greatly outnumbered by the American grays.

hardly a statement one could make about the egg-head grays or the hairy dwarves. Because of their Scandinavian appearance and aura of civility, the British aliens (also seen quite often in other parts of northern Europe) are referred to as 'Nordics'. They were a common sighting in British cases in the thirty years after 1954 until the American grays made a determined takeover bid for the entire world.

These nationalistic images – technocratic American grays, macho South American dwarves and civilized Nordics in northern Europe – suggest a surprising link between an area's culture and the aliens who visit. Have different alien races really divided up the planet, deciding 'you take America, we'll have France?' Or is this a hint that psychology and sociology are somehow at work?

1955: Contact

From the Vienna Woods

In 1955, Josef Wanderka claimed to be one of the first to have established direct contact with the occupants of a landed UFO. The incident took place in the woods around Vienna in Austria, where Wanderka had already spotted a silver cigar. A group of Russian soldiers stationed near by had assured Josef that they had seen the machine quite often; it was, of course, one of their newest aircraft, a secret Soviet weapon.

This assessment was to be overturned in early September, when Wanderka found himself within a few yards of a silvery egg-shaped object about 15 miles south west of the city. The only visible opening was a ramp leading into the craft, with soft lighting coming from within. Wanderka rode up it to find himself surrounded by half a dozen human-type beings of above average height but with beautiful, child-like faces. They wore one-piece gray coveralls and had blond hair tied in a bun at the back. He quickly realised that these were certainly not Russians.

There was nothing inside the UFO, not even seats or instruments, and no indication of how the craft could fly. Wanderka apologised to the entities for the intrusion and introduced himself by name. The beings spoke fluent German in a female voice, even though there was no indication that any of them were female. Wanderka reported that they did have a slight accent, similar to that of an English person speaking German.

The aliens said that they had come from Cassiopeia, a distant star system, and Wanderka then talked about the lack of justice on earth. They told him that he must be appointed leader and should rule out all privilege and inequality

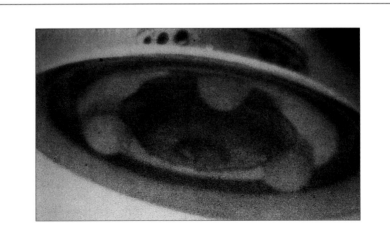

A Model Case

Contactee George Adamski took many photographs of the alien craft he claimed to have encountered. The authenticity of the photographs is questioned by many UFOlogists, but they are certainly graphic images.

ROCKET MEN

Radio stations were becoming excited by the slow but steady progress towards space flight that was being reported from White Sands and the team of scientists based around Los Alamos. The dream that the USA would send a craft into orbit in the near future led to all kinds of space fiction such as *Journey into Space* and *Rocket Man*. These took the story onwards into the future where space travel was expected to become commonplace. Comic books were filled with the adventures of Buck Rogers and Dan Dare meeting evil aliens and fighting intergalactic wars.

There is little indication from these dramatic tales that alien contact was proving an influence. Indeed, the space fiction itself was clearly not creating these true stories through some kind of cultural link as the nature of the depictions seemed very different.

However, one social movement that was prominent in 1955 was the campaign for nuclear disarmament, known as CND. Huge marches across the United States reflected the widespread concern about the Superpowers' race to amass the largest nuclear arsenals possible, arsenals that might eventually lead to the destruction of humankind. The fear of this new weapon ran deep within the human collective unconscious and this fear bared its teeth through the contactee stories.

Many of these escalating yarns were even wilder than the stories from Austria and Sweden and referred to the alien visitations having first been triggered by the two advancements of nuclear weapons and our quest to reach space. Without either of these we were an isolated, war-like planet. With both at our disposal we could now export mass destruction to the universe and this had suddenly become a threat that had to be taken seriously.

It is true that many of the messages told via contactees were riddled with tales about ending nuclear warfare. One blossoming movement in Europe, the Aetherius Society, was even given warnings about nuclear accidents at the newly built power stations, allegedly before they even happened. A book entitled *You are Responsible* was typical of the literature of the day. Amidst philosophies of peace and love, warnings relayed in contactee episodes were not unlike an alien version of the CND movement.

Was this alien association with nuclear technology a response to public concerns – suggesting, perhaps, a psychological force at work creating both – or were the wide-scale cultural efforts to change the direction of humankind's power struggles manipulated by the aliens via the contactee movement? This question was not discussed at the time, but can be seen in better focus with hindsight.

on the planet. They then wanted an explanation of how his moped worked!

Once Wanderka had given the explanation, the beings turned the machine through 180 degrees as if it were on a railway turntable and sent the witness back outside. He left, determined to fight for the cause he believed that they had now set before him.

An alien's last words

An even more astonishing story came from a lumberjack at Vestra Norrland in Sweden, who claimed to be the first person to see a UFO crash from the sky and to reach the occupant before it died. Along with two colleagues, he saw a silvery cigar plunge earthward, observing

a brilliant flash of light followed by a terrific suction force that knocked the lumberjacks unconscious and dragged them into the base of some trees.

When they awoke, no craft was visible, but on the ground they discovered a strange being that looked dead. It was only 4 feet tall, with a large head, peach-like skin with a yellowish cast and a soft fuzz covering its body.

Although it was barely alive, the creature communicated telepathically for two hours before dying, explaining that several different alien races were on earth. The body was placed in the river and dissolved. Its final words were, 'You have come without any wish to and depart against your own wish. Our life is like vapour.'

1956: ALIENS V THE EARTH

Battle in the skies

Although the official US Government position in 1956 was that UFOs had virtually disappeared, this was mainly down to the CIA's debunking policies. The truth was that close alien encounters were continuing around the world.

In the UK, on the night of August 13-14, 1956, radar stations throughout East Anglia picked up unusual targets moving from the North Sea across Suffolk. One object was tracked on a steady course westwards. The crew of a USAF transport plane saw a yellow oval below. The UFO was buzzing NATO defences at only 4000 feet. At around midnight, Squadron Leader Freddie Wimbledon at RAF Neatishead Command HQ launched an interceptor from standby alert at RAF Waterbeach. The two-man Venom took off in pursuit of the target and maintained radio contact with the USAF crews who had been chasing the UFOs from the ground for the previous two hours.

In 1996 I managed to talk with the crews of this Venom and of a second Venom launched a few minutes later who had remained silent for 40 years. The first Venom locked onto a stationary radar target near to the USAF base at

BAY AREA WONDER

This photograph of a UFO high above San Francisco's Bay Area was taken on October 10, 1956. It typifies a growing dilemma. If UFOs can appear on a photograph above such a densely populated location, why did thousands of witnesses not report each sighting?

COSMIC CONSPIRACY

Ironically, as these episodes were occurring in real life, one of the first movies to try to reflect the UFO mystery had been released with the title *Earth Versus the Flying Saucers*. It was based upon a book by Major Donald Keyhoe, a retired US marine who had become the first crusading UFOlogist to insist that there was a cover-up on the subject of aliens visiting earth.

The movie reflected the idea that the aliens might have vastly superior technology to our own. Scenes show earth defences useless against the alien onslaught.

Keyhoe had compiled some impressive evidence from his sources within the US Government. It would be 20 years before the files on these cases were released through the new Freedom of Information bill and thus prove that he was right. He wrote about USAF planes trying to shoot down UFOs and failing, and USAF jets crashing in mysterious circumstances after chasing UFOs. Time proved that these were not myths. They had happened and the authorities had hidden the full story for fear of public reaction.

Keyhoe and a whole generation of UFO investigators that followed him believed that the cover-up was imposed because the truth about the alien 'invaders' was fully known and the Pentagon did not wish the powerlessness of the United States to be exposed. Today this idea is more in dispute. The mood seems to have changed and there is an impression that the authorities could not really comprehend the alien-contact phenomenon. Whilst they may well have suspected that it hid some terrible truth, they may not, with the exception of Roswell, have had any actual proof. In the absence of this they would have to continue to investigate and monitor the situation and just hope that the proof would one day arrive.

In the meantime, silence was paramount to maintain control of the situation. If technology was up for grabs, each major power must have wanted to get to it first. In that regard, movies that proclaimed an alien invasion of earth and a conspiracy of silence on the part of world governments were not exactly helpful.

Lakenheath in Suffolk. They circled it but could not pin it down. Despite claims by the USAF in 1968 that the crew saw the UFO, the navigator denied this. After the first plane ran low on fuel, the second attempt at an intercept followed, but that aircraft was equally unsuccessful. The aerial battle was then aborted.

Operation intercept

In the same month as the battle over Lakenheath, an encounter took place in daylight between the Isle of Wight and the British mainland and involved two Javelins taking part in a mock dogfight. A strange, unidentified blip was picked up on the secret radar installation at Sopley near Bournemouth on the south coast. Ordered to investigate, the two aircraft sped towards the object and both achieved radar lock-ons. The target was stationary in front of them and the pilots were told to intercept.

Closing at speed on the target, the object was now visible to the crews as a silvery oval hovering over the sea. At just a few miles range, a collision looked imminent, but the UFO then turned on its edge, sped upwards at an astonishing speed and disappeared off the radar. An RAF Canberra on a high-altitude test flight later in the year had exactly the same experience.

Within months a similar incident occurred over several RAF bases in south-west Scotland, an object being tracked on radar and explained away to the public as a balloon. Documents from the British Ministry of Defence reveal that the explanation had been fed out to the press to put them off the trail and that they viewed the matter far more seriously.

Such brazen displays of superior technology by the aliens had shocked the authorities. It was as if they were warnings not to attempt to enter into combat with the UFOs.

1957: SEXPERIMENTS

Inside view

If the events of 1956 were a warning, the following year would see the tenth anniversary of the UFO mystery celebrated in style. The events of l957 began a new phase of overt activity in which aliens sought to abduct humans for their own purposes.

A little-known case in April occurred at Cordoba in Argentina and was a preview of things to come. A young man riding his motorcycle came upon a landed UFO and was allowed to enter to examine the interior without interference from the dwarf-like aliens. He noted the curious way in which the light from the UFO filtered out across the room from no apparent source. Indeed, his encounter was very similar to that experienced by Josef Wanderka in the Vienna Woods a year earlier.

However, it is difficult to know whether the episode involving James Cook can be viewed in quite the same light. At 2.15am on September 7, Cook responded to a mental impulse and climbed a small hill near the River Mersey at Runcorn in England. A multicoloured light appeared and turned into a disc-shaped craft that eventually came to rest a few feet above the rain-sodden ground. He was informed

A Cloudy Story

1957 saw the launch of the first object to enter the earth's orbit – Sputnik 1. There was a marked increase in UFO sightings, particularly around sensitive top-secret research institutions, around this time. This photograph of a UFO was taken in New Mexico, near Hollonan Air Force Base, on October 10, 1957 – although opinion is divided as to whether it is a lenticular cloud or a strange alien craft.

AN ALIEN WARNING

In the weeks between the Cook encounter (see page 32) and Villas Boas being seduced by an alien lover (see page 34), major events were unfolding in the world of astronautics. The USSR took America by total surprise and successfully launched Sputnik 1 – the first object to enter earth's orbit. As this tiny metal ball floated around the earth in October, 1957, its bleeping signal heralded the dawning of the space age and mankind's entry into the galactic club.

Although this first launch was important, it was the instant successor, Sputnik 2, that really proved to be the key. This carried the first lifeform from planet earth into space, in the shape of Laika the dog.

Any alien intelligence viewing or visiting the earth must have seen October and November 1957 as being of huge significance. It is interesting to note the way in which a series of cases seem to have slotted together at precisely this moment in time.

Not only did we have the encounters such as that of Villas Boas, but between late October and early November there was a wave of vehicle-interference cases throughout the American west. UFOs would hover over cars, stall their engines and cut out their lights in a display of superiority.

Dawn of the space age
Sputnik 1, the first man-made satellite, was launched in October 1957. Radio contact was maintained for 21 days; the satellite orbit decayed on January 4, 1958, after 1400 circuits of the earth.

This warning was to have its most dramatic effect on the night of November 2–3 in and around Levelland, Texas, when almost a dozen vehicles in the space of a couple of hours were buzzed by UFOs and independently stopped in this fashion. The local police were on full alert. One of their patrol vehicles, with the sheriff on board, was even involved in the sightings.

At 3am on that same morning, another object was seen descending into a top-security bunker in the White Sands missile grounds in New Mexico. This was a most important bunker – it was the one used for the world's first atomic detonation in July, 1945.

Simultaneously, allowing for time zones and as near as we can calculate the dates, yet another UFO was appearing in full view of startled RAF personnel then dismantling the remains of the world's most recent atomic explosion. The defiant UFO was hovering right over the blast site at Maralinga in the Australian outback.

That the intelligence behind these UFOs should show its teeth by demonstrating its ability to make our technology useless is intriguing. That it should at the same time appear at the sites of the world's first and most recent atomic blasts (and, for all we know, over the sites of other detonation points which secrecy has prevented us from hearing about) makes one think that some kind of plan might have been afoot. That all these incidents should occur as the secret countdown was under way in the USSR and the earth's first ever astronaut was climbing free of gravity and projecting the planet into a new era seems to hint at just what kind of message our alien friends had in mind.

Someone, somewhere knew what we were up to and was determined to inform us that our entry into space, with our cargo of deadly nuclear technology, came with a hefty price tag. If we were to join the intergalactic club then we had to accept that our progress would be very carefully monitored by alien lifeforms who had the best interests of the solar system at heart. It was possibly the clearest sign yet that our actions were being scrutinized.

telepathically that he was being invited into the alien craft, but to do so he would have to jump onto a rail that led up to the inside of the craft. The aliens had been unable to land in the wet weather because their machines used an electrical field; had Cook touched its surface and the wet earth at the same time he would have been electrocuted.

Once inside, Cook noted a feature that so many other UFO witnesses had observed without understanding its significance – lighting that oozed out of the walls in a soft manner unheard of during the 1950s. The same telepathic message told Cook to take off all of his clothes, which he did without hesitation. He was then asked to don a one-piece silver jumpsuit and transfer to a larger craft that had landed further up the hillside.

He was told that the small craft were only used for short hops and could not travel between the stars. These generated an electromagnetic field in flight. The larger craft utilized ion propulsion and rarely ventured into the earth's atmosphere as their motors could damage the environment. Odd as this aspect of the incident may sound, it has cropped up in other alien-contact stories .

Once aboard the larger ship, James Cook met the occupants – tall, fair and baby-faced, but otherwise human in appearance. They came from the planet Zomdic and were androgynous (neither male nor female). They had no hostile intentions for planet earth but were concerned about its future – a typical tale.

The aliens gave Cook a warning to pass onto the people of Earth. They feared that we were upsetting the planet's balance by persisting in using force instead of pursuing harmonious existence. Cook should tell the world as soon as possible. Quite reasonably, he argued that he was just an ordinary chap and that nobody would listen to him. The alien leader replied, 'Nor anyone else either', with an expression that almost amounted to a sigh.

Cook returned home but forgot the warning about not touching the ground as he leapt from the shuttle craft and burnt his hand on the rail as he put his foot on the soil. He was amazed to discover that it was now late on September 8. Somehow, 45 hours of time had passed, far more than Cook had anticipated. This case has many features that would be found in subsequent abductions where human entry into the UFO was rather less voluntary. In that respect, it can be seen as a very important transitional episode.

Space sirens

A month after James Cook met the men from Zomdic, a Brazilian cowhand called Antonio Villas Boas was about to have an encounter of the closest possible kind.

At 1am on October 16, Villas Boas was working on his tractor at Sao Francisco de Sales when its engine and lights both failed and he was physically accosted by four men of smaller than average stature. They dragged him into a strange craft that had landed in the field.

Once aboard, the startled young man was confronted by a peculiar-looking woman of similar size to the men, but with a mane of red hair and oriental features. Villas Boas was made to take off his clothes, just as Cook had been, but what happened next was rather different thanks to the involvement of the female alien. She effectively 'raped' the frightened victim after he was seemingly disinfected and anaesthetized by a gaseous vapour. She then rubbed her belly and pointed to the sky in a gesture that seemed to suggest, 'I am going to have your baby up there in space'.

Villas Boas made no attempt to cash in on this adventure and told hardly anyone about it until February, 1958, when he made a costly visit at his own expense to meet Dr Olavo Fontes in his Rio office. Fontes found what he took to be symptoms of mild radiation sickness in the farmhand and was impressed by the man's

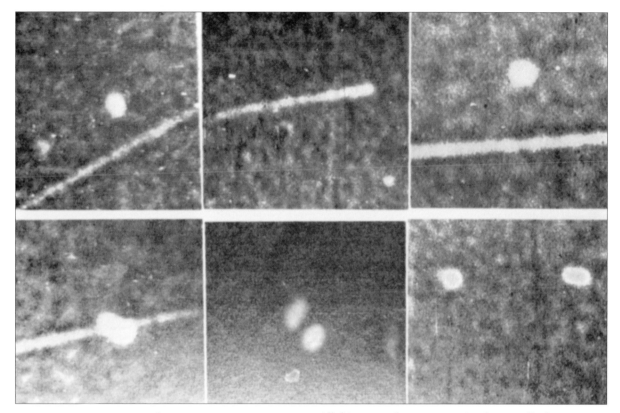

Rio's UFO carnival
Strange light phenomena filmed over Rio de Janeiro, Brazil, in December, 1957, during the wave which produced the Villas Boas abduction case.

trauma, sincerity and lack of motivation for publicity or money, despite his relative poverty.

Unsurprisingly, Fontes was utterly perplexed by the case. He had come across nothing like it before and its sexual fantasy overtones would probably do more harm than good to the credibility of the UFO movement. While there were isolated cases that seemed to form a pattern with this amazing case – such as the events in Cordoba or those only weeks earlier in Runcorn – these were virtually unknown even to people knowledgeable about UFOs. The number of books written on the subject, even in countries like the USA (let alone Brazil), could still be counted on the fingers of one hand and not even UFOlogists were taking alien-contact cases very seriously.

All this meant that Fontes sat on the case file for three years before it came to the attention of Brazilian UFOlogist, Dr Walter Buhler. Buhler sent a report to the leading UFO journal, *Flying Saucer Review*, which had been launched in Britain in 1955. The fact that *Flying Saucer Review* came to receive this report in 1961 would prove to be of great importance in the scheme of things. However, even the UFO magazine was unsure what to make of the story at first and did not publish it until 1964. It would be quite some time before the incident became known in its native land.

Sceptics are bound to charge that Villas Boas invented this tale, but the evidence does not back this up. His behaviour throughout the many years of study supports his sincerity and future cases that duplicated many of its features only add further weight. Villas Boas eventually became a lawyer and died in the late 1980s, still insisting that the case had really happened.

1958: ALIEN COLONISTS

Space baby

Within a few days of the launch of Sputnik 2, the alien masterplan, if such it was, took a step forward in the most unlikely of places – the suburb of Aston in Birmingham, England.

Cynthia Appleton was a 27-year-old mother of two. On the afternoon of November 18, 1957, a strange atmosphere descended on her living room accompanied by a whistling and flash of light. A tall, blond-haired entity materialized. The being was a classic example of the then dominant European entity type – the Nordic.

He explained that he came from a planet called Gharnasvarn and he could visit Cynthia because her brain was tuned to the right frequency. The stranger came back several times during the next 18 months. Once he even

brought a colleague and the two drove off in a dark car. They wore human clothing and could have been passed in the street without attracting much attention. There was no hint of a UFO at all apart from at the very first meeting.

The man from Gharnasvarn regaled Cynthia with various stories, some of which are found in other cases and others that are quite unusual. He raised fears about mankind entering space and showed her images of atomic explosions, adding that we were undertaking spaceflight in the wrong manner; to reach the stars we should not go 'straight up against gravity' but travel 'with a sideways attitude'. There was also much philosophy about how time was an invention, life was joined at an atomic

ISLAND MYSTERY

One of several photographs taken from the Brazilian naval survey vessel the Almirante Saldhana in January 1958. While it was moored off the uninhabited island of Trindade in the Atlantic Ocean. A team of scientists on board were setting up a meteorological station when the UFO appeared, caused the ship's electric winch to stop and circled the island.

SPACE DEMONS

The Birmingham space baby case is not well known in UFO circles but has a crucial role to play in the developing saga of alien contact. For it was another step along the route first set in motion by the Villas Boas encounter and would go through a number of fascinating twists and turns that, from today's perspective, seem a grand design. It is hard to see how they could come about by chance.

It is interesting to compare this subtle form of involvement in human affairs with the much more blatant version that science fiction had to offer. A Hollywood movie entitled *I Married a Monster from Outer Space* made its debut and, as the title suggests, was not about genetic engineering to create a human baby (a concept unheard of on earth in 1958). It was more akin to a horror story sit-com in which the evil aliens have monstrous intentions for the planet.

However, there was a glimmer of true sophistication on the horizon in the form of a BBC television serial written by Nigel Kneale. It was transformed into a Hammer Films big-screen movie a few years later with an almost identical storyline. The serial, however, remains superior.

In the story, *Quatermass and the Pit*, debris from a crashed spaceship is dug up from an underground station in London during renovation work. Psychic forces are unleashed in the process and goblin-like creatures are found buried in the wreckage. Kneale speculates that the ship has been hidden for millions of years and whenever stress has been placed on it, such as during building work, psychic forces have been triggered. This has led to the area gaining a reputation for being haunted, as witnesses suffer hallucinations of the 'horned demon' images released from their subconscious mind.

As the truth unravels, we find that the aliens in the UFO were visiting earth millions of years ago to help apemen to become an intelligent species. The visitors had engineered modern humanity by starting intelligent life on earth, making us alien colonists evolved from these creatures. The psychic link between them and us is still powerful within our subconscious mind, hence the hallucinations and the motif of the goblin-like aliens that mankind had constantly experienced throughout history.

Today we reach out into space ourselves and the force is stirring once again. Indeed, we might further speculate that the psychic overtones that were only gradually beginning to appear during alien-contact cases (with witnesses describing poltergeist attacks and aliens walking through walls) are a result of these forces being unleashed from the mind and triggering visions that date back from our alien past.

In many ways Kneale's extraordinary story is decades ahead of its time. It foresees numerous strands of modern research – such as the 'stone tapes' theory, arguing that psychic forces can be recorded and replayed across the centuries inside rock; the 'earthlights' concept of electromagnetic forces triggering subconscious hallucinations from the natural environment; the discovery of 'window areas', where a history of strange phenomena has turned a small area into a 'UFO-haunted zone'; Dr Carl Jung's suggestion, published in 1959, that UFOs might be an important symbol within the collective unconscious; and the 'ancient astronauts' school of thought, where visiting aliens actually kick-started *Homo sapiens*. It was far more sophisticated than any of these and was the first truly intelligent UFO fiction.

level and a molecular theory to cure cancer.

This astounding case became even more incredible in September, 1958, when the alien arrived to tell Cynthia she was about to give birth to a space baby! The father was her husband but the child would be 'of the race of Gharnasvarn'. No explanation as to how or why this would come about was ever offered, but precise details of the birth date, sex and weight were provided. Cynthia's pregnancy was confirmed by her doctor later that month.

A number of investigators visiting Cynthia, including a psychologist and a local church minister, were convinced of her sincerity. As a result, the space baby story saw print before the blessed event and the accuracy of the prediction was verified when the child was born in late May, 1959; the boy fitted the description provided by the man from Gharnasvarn exactly.

1959: HELLO EARTH

The missionary's position

Anglican priest Father William Gill became one of the most convincing witnesses so far to the alien-contact phenomenon when he and 37 of his flock had a remarkable experience on Papua New Guinea. Sightings of a strange light around Mount Pudi had been coming in during mid-1959 and another priest was already collecting reports from the villagers at Boianai when, on June 26, a light descended from the mountain and hovered above for several hours.

Gill was intrigued to see a number of human-like figures standing on a rail encircling a plate-shaped object with four legs coming from its base. The beings appeared to be working under the object. When the UFO returned next evening, Gill decided to try and establish friendly contact. He waved at them and one waved back. Gill was then joined by one of the villagers and when both waved, two of the occupants of the craft reciprocated. He then used a flashlight to send morse code signals and the UFO responded by swaying from side to side.

The entities eventually disappeared from the rim. Father Gill then did something which critics describe as incredible – he went inside to eat dinner. When he came back out, the UFO had risen higher and it eventually vanished altogether. The UFO did return briefly the next night, but there was no further contact with its occupants.

In all cases of this type that I have studied, the explanation tends to be a regularly occurring astronomical phenomenon, such as a bright planet. Here the planet Venus was bright in the New Guinea sky at the time and, coupled with alleged eyesight problems suffered by the priest and the lack of education of the natives, the case appears suspect.

However, all those who have met William Gill, including noted UFOlogist, Dr J. Allen Hynek, who in 1959 had already worked for the US Government as their official scientific UFO consultant for 11 years, dispute this. Father Gill says he was not regularly wearing spectacles at the time and the villagers, far from being uneducated, had spoken English from childhood. He also showed that he had observed Venus at the same time as the UFO and had written as much in his account penned in 1959.

As for his amazing decision to have dinner whilst aliens hovered overhead, Gill notes that the idea that the object was an alien craft only surfaced much later. He assumed it was a novel aircraft or hovercraft (a device only recently invented at the time) and the entities were simply its American or Australian crew. If they did not want to communicate further, he was not going to hang about waiting for them.

Alien telepathy

In late October, another UFO made a less controlled descent towards earth and a similar attempt at communication was made by one witness. This time it was not so successful.

One of the main witnesses was electrical engineer Gideon Johansson, who lived in Mariannelund, Sweden. He was first alerted to a problem when there was a power cut in his house. Rushing outside to look for the cause, he met his adult son pointing to the sky, where a white ball was plunging towards the house.

The falling object rocked to and fro and swerved to one side, missing the building but crashing through the top of a maple tree in the garden. It came to rest only a few feet above the ground. Gideon got to within 10 feet of it and could clearly see a bell-shaped craft with a large window in the front. From this came 'an unusual white light, very compact'.

The Earth's Roswell

The programme to explore space took its next few steps during 1959. NASA had been created in the USA in late 1958 as the world's first civilian space agency. In 1959 it picked the USA's first seven astronauts destined to take the nation into an epic decade.

This same year also saw Luna 2 launched by the USSR and impacting on the surface of the moon. There were no selenologists to see it fall, but one can imagine the consternation of a lunar equivalent of rancher Brazel if they had witnessed this hunk of metal crashing into the dust and rocks. The earth had created its own version of the Roswell case.

What this event finally established was that travel to another world was undeniably possible. We had done it. From that day on, all those cynics who claimed that the alien-contact cases were not the result of visitors coming to earth from another planet would face a much more difficult task.

Cape lift off
In 1959 NASA began operations from Cape Canaveral which, over the next few years, saw the launch of several military satellites. It is still operational.

Also in the dome were two small figures, evidently the pilots. They had dome-shaped heads with pointed chins and large, beautiful eyes. These penetrated the witness and, he feels, transferred telepathic visions into his mind. He could 'see' one of the figures working on a cone-shaped object under the window, as if the scene were projected into his head.

Johansson tried to communicate by waving a friendly greeting, but the occupants ignored him. Then suddenly the object shot away to one side and stopped about 25 feet away, its light going out. There was a flash and it disappeared. It had gone, as the witness put it, 'like a ghost in the night.'

The engineer was ill for several days, suffering from nausea, tiredness, prickling sensations and pains and swellings in his glands and testicles. His doctor was baffled, but similar symptoms were reported by Antonio Villas Boas; after careful study he was said to have been suffering from mild radiation sickness. Thankfully, Johansson soon recovered.

Although damage was found to the overhead power lines about a mile from the encounter, the power failure was never resolved. Strange silvery powder was also discovered on the lines. Gideon concluded that the UFO must have crashed into the power cables, then landed on his property to repair the damage.

1960: CLOSE ENCOUNTERS

Surprise arrivals

While this was not a busy year for alien contact reports, there were a number of unusual close encounters. Brazil was experiencing a wave of sightings and on May 14 strange lights were seen over a wide area throughout the night. Farmer Raimundo Santos had one of the most intriguing close-up meetings with these craft when he saw two of them land on the beach at Paracura in the north-east of the country. Standing beside the machines were several aliens, rooting about in the sand as if inspecting the beach for a likely spot to plot up. They were small in stature and pale, but not much else was noticed about them in the dark except that they were humanoid in appearance.

About three weeks later, a family driving across the desert to holiday in California had a frightening midnight encounter near Globe, Arizona. The wife was driving and had just rounded a bend miles away from anywhere when she ran straight into a figure standing on the road. She knew immediately that it was not an animal, but an erect humanoid being. It stared at her, illuminated by the headlights. She instinctively screeched the Cadillac to a halt and turned back to see the figure once more. It had been dazed by the collision, but was seemingly unhurt and was now rushing off to the side of the road and disappearing into the scrub. The entity was only about 3 feet tall, with a head shaped like a pumpkin and two large rounded eyes that glowed yellowish orange. It seemed to have a fuzzy coating to its skin.

There are some clear similarities between this isolated being and the terrifying goblin-like creatures that laid seige to a farm in Hopkinsville, Kentucky, on August 22, 1955, after a UFO had landed near by. The Sutton family had then reported how several such beings climbed trees and fences and, while not overtly hostile, were highly unwelcome guests on their property. Frank Sutton blasted one of them with a shotgun and it staggered away, dazed but apparently not seriously hurt despite taking the full brunt of the explosion in the chest.

Such monstrous aliens were the exception rather than the rule by 1960 and have become even less common since that time.

No bluff at Red Bluff

At midnight on August 13–14, 1960, one of the best documented cases of all time occurred. No fewer than 14 police officers, two deputy sheriffs, a town jailor and numerous prisoners were witness. The latter had been marched onto Tehama County jail roof to watch the spectacle in the skies above Red Bluff, California.

The first sighting was made by two patrolmen, Charles Carson and Stanley Scott, who broke off the hunt for a speeding motorbike to observe a large oval-shaped craft immersed in a white glow that plunged out of clouds and performed extraordinary manoeuvres in mid-air. A red beam emerged from the UFO and swept the ground as if searching for something. Every time the police officers tried to close in on the object, it backed away. As they approached, their radio communications became filled with static.

Radar operators at the nearby air base confirmed to the sheriff's office that they were tracking an unknown object in the Red Bluff area at the same time and that all attempts to identify it had failed. However, the US Air Force later claimed the sighting was nothing more than a mirage caused by stars and freak weather conditions. This did not convince the police witnesses, who said that the object reacted to their presence as if under intelligent control.

ANYONE OUT THERE?

Late the previous year an important paper had appeared in *Nature* magazine written by astronomers Philip Morrison and Giusepio Cocconi. They had suggested that it might be possible to contact other civilizations in space by using radio signals. But what frequency would be used for communication? There were billions of possibilities and it would take centuries to search them all. So the researchers proposed the natural frequency at which electrons in hydrogen reverse their spin – a universal standard within the most common element found in all solar systems.

There is no basis other than guesswork for supposing that this frequency is a focus for interstellar contact. Indeed, there is no reason to suppose that radio, limited as it is to the speed of light, would be used at any frequency. Say hello to the nearest possible inhabitants and you must wait ten years for a reply. Most round trip times are measured in decades.

Nevertheless, radio communication was the only option we had in 1960 and Dr Frank Drake at the National Radio Astronomy Observatory in Green Bank, West Virginia, launched Project Ozma to listen in. He tuned in to the suggested frequency and pointed his instruments at Epsilon Eridani and Tau Ceti – the two stars nearest the earth with a good chance of having habitable planets near by. He heard only silence in the short time available, but the search for alien contact by earth's scientists had begun.

THREE IN ONE

By 1960 UFOs flying in formation were rare, although they had once been quite common. This photograph taken over Italy on September 26 led to much speculation. Was it a flock of birds or aerobatic aircraft? Or could it be a most unusual trio of UFOs?

1961: ABDUCTION

Alien cookery

One of the most delightful stories of alien contact befell a 60-year-old chicken farmer called Joe Simonton on April 18 when a UFO landed on his property at Eagle River, Wisconsin. Like a scene from the quirky TV series, *Picket Fences*, which was also set in this agricultural state, it was rich in Americana and modern folklore. Indeed, it was perhaps the last great case of the old style of alien encounter before the new breed took off – both figuratively and literally!

Simonton heard a strange noise over his farmhouse and rushed outside to see a silvery oval craft descend onto his land. As he walked towards it, a hatch opened and several small men wearing blue one-piece suits emerged. One held what looked like a pitcher and motioned as if to drink. The utterly unphased farmer understood immediately, took the jug away and filled it with water.

On his return to the UFO, he popped his head inside and saw one of the aliens cooking what looked like cookies or small pancakes on a hot plate. Simonton gestured that he would like one, the alien handed four of them to him and the hatch began to close. The UFO then took off, bending over the trees in its path, and Joe was left with some extraterrestrial cooking as proof of his encounter.

Nobody has ever accused Simonton of a hoax, but even most UFOlogists at the time had a hard time accepting that the case had really happened. Although the local sheriff believed the farmer and a county judge acted as his go-between, passing on a pancake each to UFO group NICAP and the US Air Force, the case lacked the kind of investigation it deserved. Only Dr Jacques Vallee, a young scientist from France (who went to live and work in the USA with USAF consultant Dr J Allen Hynek) recognized the way in which this apocryphal tale had many elements of fairy folklore about it; fairies often handed over 'bread' in exchange for kindness from human beings.

Simonton ate one of the pancakes and said it tasted like cardboard. The analysis of the others found them to have no discernible exotic features and to consist of fairly typical, if not especially appetizing, earthly ingredients.

To some, the absurdity of the case and the feeble nature of the alien evidence is proof that the case has to be a fantasy. However, it is reflective of a whole series of encounters in which gifts from the UFOnauts turn out to be less substantial than they appear.

In a case from the late 1960s, a scientist in an isolated cottage in Sussex, England, met several aliens who indicated that they wanted to abduct his dog. He eventually persuaded them to take a china ornament instead of his pet. They gave him some 'diamonds' in return, but when UFOlogists had these analysed by a leading diamond assessor, they turned out to be worthless quartz crystals. The witness was stunned, not at losing out on any money, but at the duplicity of his alien friends.

As recently as 1992 an alien-contact case in Somerset, England, involved an 'alien rock' dropped by the UFO. Study by the geological museum in London quickly established what the UFO investigators had suspected – it was proof of nothing and was made from plastic used to create fish tank scenery!

The journey home

By the autumn of 1961, amidst various reports of voluntary trips in UFOs, there had been just one or two cases of possible forced abduction.

Notably, there was the strange affair reported in Brazil by Antonio Villas Boas. While this incident had occurred nearly four years before, it had still not been published and almost no UFOlogists had heard about it.

It seemed scarcely possible that anything like this amazing case could occur elsewhere, but that is exactly what happened when Betty and Barney Hill were returning from a short vacation in Canada on September 19.

They were driving through the White Mountains towards their home in Portsmouth, New Hampshire, where Barney (a negro) was a postal operative and Betty (Caucasian) served as a social worker. On the way, they saw an unusual light and followed it in their car. At one point they stopped and Barney got out and walked towards the glow. It was now hovering nearby and looked like a banana with windows in the front. Through binoculars he could see small humanoid beings staring out and, when the craft began to descend, Barney developed a terrible fear that they were trying to capture him and fled back to the car. The couple drove off as quickly as they could, heard a strange 'beeping' noise and then proceeded to drive home as if all was normal.

However, things were far from normal when they got back home in the middle of the night: the journey had taken two hours longer than it should have done and there were strange spots on the car's metal body. Betty behaved irrationally, bundling up her clothing and discarding it in the back of her wardrobe, then went and took a bath as if trying to rid herself of an irrational sense of being dirty. In retrospect, there were clear signs of the kind of behaviour exhibited by rape victims. Yet Betty Hill had not been raped.

The UFO sighting was reported within days of its occurrence. I have seen the original letter and proof of its dating on the files of the Center for UFO Studies in Chicago. But as weeks and months passed by, both witnesses began to develop fears, neuroses and had severe nightmares – which included seeing cat-like eyes in the night.

After visiting a succession of doctors, they were finally led to Dr. Benjamin Simon, an eminent neurosurgeon in Boston. The Hills paid out a substantial amount of money to have years of treatment with no motive to do so, except that they wanted to get better. They were certainly not attempting to tell the world about their close encounter.

However, Dr. Simon had a method that he sometimes used on patients. He liked to get his patients to relive a trauma by experiencing it once more under regression hypnosis. In this way they could confront their fears and try to overcome them.

When he uncorked the bottle in Barney and Betty Hill's subconscious minds, Dr. Simon had absolutely no idea of the powerful genie he was about to unleash.

Taken away

Over a period of some months between December 1963 and June 1964, the Hills had numerous sessions at Dr. Simon's office and a truly incredible story emerged. It told of how the UFO had landed and the Hills had been physically abducted aboard, although with no real violence. It was as if they were being mentally controlled by their alien captors.

Their captors were small men with cat-like eyes and an Oriental appearance. There was also a taller figure, which Betty called 'the leader'. He controlled the others, but she had a major mental block and could not, or would not, describe him, other than to note that he was 'different'.

This was the first case to really offer a clue that there were two types of entities – the tall ones and the small ones – and they could work together inside the same UFO. This feature remains a little-understood aspect of alien-contact history but is extremely consistent. In

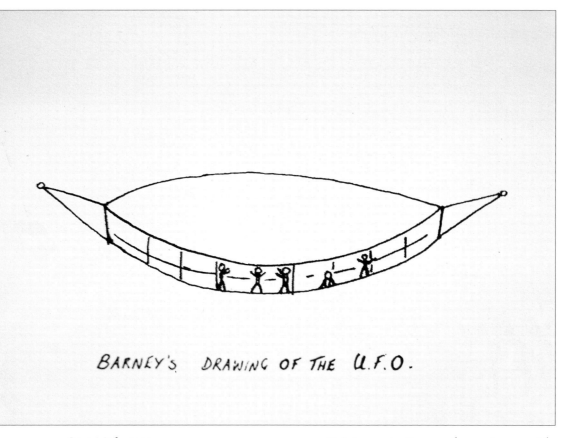

BARNEY'S DRAWING OF THE U.F.O.

Barney's banana
The sketch of the banana-shaped UFO and its aliens made by Barney Hill after his September 1961 encounter in the White Mountains and before his abduction memory was retrieved by hypnosis.

every case that I can recall, the tall ones rule the roost while the smaller beings act like trained menials or robots.

Inside the UFO the witnesses say there was a table or bed used for examinations and this was evidently not designed for anybody as tall as Barney Hill. His legs kept dangling over the end when he was placed onto it.

The strange aliens separated the witnesses and conducted medical tests on them both. They were clearly intrigued by the physical and skin colour differences between the couple and pored over false teeth with fascination. Samples of nail and skin were taken with little heed to the resulting pain to the couple.

Betty's examination was the most severe. A long, thin needle was used to puncture her abdomen and take out a 'fluid' sample. This was a painful procedure but Betty was informed that it was a type of pregnancy test. But Betty was not pregnant. Nor was it like any kind of test she had been familiar with before. However, when human science evolved over the coming years and a test of an embryo by drawing amniotic fluid was perfected, the similarities became all too apparent to those familiar with this case.

According to their 'hypnotic memory', the Hills were released after the tests without any clear understanding of what the aliens were up to. The memory had been blocked from their mind, partly by the aliens' crew and partly through their own trauma. There was little doubt that the Hills felt they finally had an answer to their nightmares and cooperated fully with all future investigations.

REACH FOR THE STARS

A human being finally made it into space when the Soviet astronaut Yuri Gagarin blasted into orbit. America was not far behind, but its first astronaut, Alan Shephard, could only make a sub-orbital flight in 1961.

The space race was well and truly ignited when the newly elected US President, John F. Kennedy, announced a massive investment of money and expertise into NASA with the intention of landing a man on the moon before 1970. The battle between Communism and Capitalism was putting the planet on the brink of nuclear destruction, but it would also propel mankind into space much further and faster than would ever have been the case had this been a purely scientific quest.

As Dr. Drake had failed to detect radio signals during his search of nearby suns, heartening news came in the discovery that some stars seemed to rotate more slowly than expected. It was believed that the 'drag' was as a result of as yet unseen planets circling around them – planets upon which aliens just might live. All we had to do now was find them.

Dr. Simon was not so sure. He spoke of shared hallucinations and, while he agreed that the Hills were not inventing the story, he was not convinced it had any reality outside the minds of the witnesses. But at least the doctor's sole objective – which was to help the Hills overcome the memories of that terrible night – had been achieved.

The magic wand

Unfortunately, despite Dr. Simon's warning that hypnosis was not a magic wand to reveal hidden memories or truths, UFOlogists were thrilled with this potentially useful new tool. How often did innocent cases hide alien abductions, they wondered? Could hypnotic regression unlock the door to these secret parts of the mind? This question would dominate the UFO world from that day on, and over 30 years later it is still the central hub of much UFO research.

It is worth recalling that when the Hills were piecing together this memory (or fantasy) in Dr. Simon's surgery, only a handful of people knew about the Villas Boas case. An account had been placed with the British UFO journal, *Flying Saucer Review*, and would be published soon after the Hills case was documented by their doctor, but before it was yet on public record. Therefore, these two cases are undeniably independent of one another. Both feature alien kidnaps and both of those different versions of the same motif – medical tests and attempts by the aliens to create 'babies' – one in an alien woman, another in a human woman who was not (and, as far as we know, did not become) pregnant.

Only then can we see the curious way in which the Cynthia Appleton case also weaves into the same mixture. Soon after Villas Boas had his encounter, Appleton was visited by aliens and told she was having a baby which is somehow her own and fathered by her husband, yet different in a way that is never explained – a child of the alien world.

It is difficult to imagine that these things are simply a series of coincidences, but what did they represent? Was there really some kind of alien genetic experiment taking place? If so, it was well beyond the earth science of 1961 (although by 1997 such an experiment is becoming more of a reality for doctors). Was the purpose of the abductions to test our biological make-up – and to create a being that would not be entirely human? It is difficult to accept the truth of these independent stories and interpret them in some other way. Of course, if they are true, what of Cynthia Appleton's 'space baby' – who is presumably out there somewhere?

1962: Under Wraps

Since the Roswell crash, there had been persistent stories that the recovered wreckage and alien bodies were located at Wright Patterson Air Force base. There is no doubt that this is where the Roswell debris (whatever it proved to be) was taken, as we have government records confirming the fact.

If all this is true, it puts a new perspective on things. It means that the US Government knew that alien contact was happening from the very start of the UFO mystery and has therefore lied to the world for 50 years. Is this credible? Surely the truth would have been exposed by someone, somewhere, in a position to do so regardless of the risks or the consequences?

Researchers argue that this is precisely what has happened. We know what we know about the recovered bodies as a result of these leaks and death-bed confessions. The stories are remarkably consistent. This either means that they reflect the truth or that each tale builds on the last one, becoming a form of space-age folklore.

There are claims that President Eisenhower was shown the bodies, preserved in ice, on February 20, 1954. Officially that day he was 'missing' for several hours to have dental treatment, but there are accounts that suggest he may have been otherwise engaged. Entertainer Jackie Gleason, a good friend of Eisenhower, told his wife just before his death that it was true. The alien bodies, he said, were real and it was the greatest secret in the world.

Len Stringfield, one of the most prominent researchers into crashed UFO stories, also interviewed a US Navy test pilot who claims he

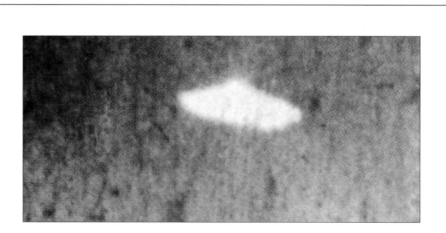

UFO Reality

In 1960 the typical UFO shape was not the 'flying saucer' or the 'flying disk',
as indeed it never had been. Instead it was the oval as seen in this photograph
from that year whose identity was otherwise shrouded in confusion.

INTO ORBIT

As these dramas unfolded well out of the pubic eye, NASA continued its exploration of space. John Glenn emulated Yuri Gagarin and became the first US astronaut to reach orbit. From then onwards, space flights became more and more frequent and their success rate was staggering. The space programme induced a sense of euphoria bordering on omnipotence, a belief that nothing could go wrong.

Mariner 2 also set off for Venus and sent back the first information about the earth's nearest planetary neighbour. Science-fiction stories (and alien contactees) had, during the 1950s, told of how this world was very much like our own and (the contactees alleged) the home of the tall, blond aliens that had been frequently reported. Unfortunately, Mariner 2 (and a series of space missions that followed) showed Venus to be a 'hellish' world, with enormous temperatures and poisonous gases – the result of the greenhouse effect gone mad. There was no possibility that humanoid aliens could exist there. Indeed, the prospects for any type of life there were considered very slim. Science had shattered the illusions of both the fiction writers and the contactees, whose influence was starting to wane very rapidly.

Meanwhile, the early attempts to use radio telescopes to detect messages from distant solar systems drew to a close and top astronomer Professor Zdnek Kopal warned: 'If we should hear that space phone ringing, then do not answer.' His reasoning was simple. Any race more advanced than ours would instantly see the threat that we posed to them and would probably decide to eradicate us, similar to a plague of vermin being killed before they take over your house. We were better off remaining isolated and invisible.

But as humankind moved inch by inch deeper into the solar system, all hope of isolation was gone. Like it or not, we had clearly announced our presence to anyone out there who had the technology to listen. Indeed, our television signals were already ten light years from earth on a non-stop journey to the outer reaches of the solar system. It was highly probable that sooner or later someone, somewhere, would intercept them!

was leading a group of men running through Wright Patterson in April 1962 when they stumbled upon an intact UFO inside a secured hangar. Despite the pilot's top-security clearance, they were ordered to leave, and it was later intimated that they should keep the matter to themselves. What the pilot had stumbled across was the greatest secret in the US Government.

There were also stories from a higher ranking officer (a Colonel) that a retrieval occurred in the New Mexico desert in 1962. The craft contained two small humanoid beings dressed in silver and this time they were taken to the more local Holloman Air Force base, from where they reached Los Alamos and were studied by security-cleared scientists.

One of the scientists who was, he claims, invited to participate in the study of the recovery of these craft and bodies was Dr Robert Sarbacher. Sarbacher told several UFOlogists just before his death that the subject was classified 'two points higher' than the atomic bomb and was the biggest secret in the USA. In addition to this, he said that the scientific team had not been able to duplicate or even understand the UFO technology (possibly the reason for the continued cover-up) and that the craft were made of extraordinarily light material. Furthermore, he reported that the small alien pilots had bodies constructed rather like certain insects on earth, with low mass and an ability to withstand the enormous inertia forces incurred during the phenomenal accelerations produced by the UFOs in flight.

All these people could, of course, be lying – but why would so many of them tell such inter-locking stories in the last few years of their lives? Could it possibly be due to the fact that they felt free to do so because their deaths would mean that they would soon be out of the reach of the government's policy of silence?

1963: IT'S OUT THERE

Land of the giants

As scientists sought to find traces of life elsewhere in the universe, the diversity of life reaching earth via the alleged alien-contact cases was continuing.

On August 28 at Sagrada Familia, a suburb of Belo Horizonte in Brazil, the Eustagio family and their neighbour had a fright when a round object appeared above their well that evening. They could see faces behind windows inside the craft and then two beams of light emerged and struck the ground near by.

Suddenly, one of the beings got out of the UFO and slid down the light beams, seeming to hover in mid-air as it did so. This alien was a giant, perhaps 7 feet tall – an unusual size for South American encounters. It had one central eye like a cyclops and wore boots with a spike on them. The spikes left an indent in the ground that was still visible days later.

The creature wandered around the garden, teetering as if struggling to adjust to the earth's gravity, and then sat down on a rock. After catching sight of the two boys near by, the entity lunged towards one of them as if trying to grab hold of him. Fernando Eustagio picked up a brick to defend himself but, in the act of trying

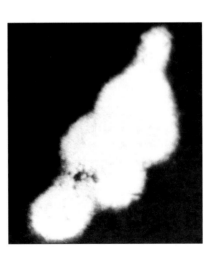

BOLDLY GOING

In 1963, space travel was at last becoming a reality and the first curious photographs were being taken by astronauts in orbit. Some looked surprisingly like UFOs, but the official verdict is that they result from the crew's own waste matter, ejected from the tiny capsules and reflecting the strong sunlight as they drifted away. A true case of the men from NASA boldly going where no one had gone before!

TERRIFYING TRIFFIDS

In 1963 the most successful science-fiction movie was *The Day of the Triffids*, based on the novel by John Wyndham. In this story, walking plant-like monsters take over the earth. In the same month that the Saltwood sighting occurred (see below), BBC television launched its hugely popular science-fiction series, *Dr Who*. For 30 years it terrified the youth of Britain.

Perhaps none of these fictional representations was quite as scary as the monster that was allegedly seen in Saltwood. But it is difficult to say whether the plethora of real-life monster cases that occurred during 1963 was in any way connected with the fact that monsters were such a prominent – and popular – theme of science-fiction movies and writings at the time.

to throw the brick at the giant, was frozen to the spot by a beam of light fired from the being's chest. He felt completely paralysed.

However, the alien had abandoned its abduction plan and returned to the light beams, riding them back up into his UFO. The witnesses said they felt that the beings had not intended to hurt them and were there just as explorers. They also felt sure that they would return one day. This same feeling has been shared by countless alien contact-witnesses.

Further huge beings, thought to be robots by the truck driver who encountered them, were seen during the wave on October 12 near Monte Maiz in Argentina. A brilliant white light and sensation of heat projected from the UFO and forced driver Eugenio Douglas into a ditch. He got out and fired his revolver at the beings, who were now standing in the road, but they simply returned to their craft unharmed and attacked his truck once more. The beams heated up the inside like an oven before the UFO departed. When police arrived to conduct an investigation, they found all the electrical wiring in the truck burnt out and strange footprints about one and a half feet long in the mud.

Monster madness

During this wave, a highly unusual encounter took place in Britain. Like many of the South American monster sightings, the prime witnesses were teenagers — four youths aged 17 and 18. The encounter occurred at Sandling Park in

Saltwood, Kent, on November 16. It began when a star seemed to fall from the sky behind some bushes. The witnesses then realized that the star was following them. It appeared to be golden in colour and oval-shaped.

The young men fled from the park pursued by a dark, monstrous form heading straight for them across the fields. The form was totally black and had no obvious head. Instead it was dominated by giant bat-like wings.

Subsequent investigations in the woods revealed a number of sightings of strange pulsating lights. There was also an area of crushed bracken close to the spot where the monster had appeared and footprints that were far larger than those of a normal human being. These were some two feet long and made inch-deep impressions into the ground, suggesting that something very heavy had created them.

Within two years, giant winged creatures were again to appear in parts of Ohio and West Virginia in the USA, where the name 'Mothman' was to be adopted for such sightings. The American public took these apparitions far more seriously than the Saltwood monster and New York journalist John Keel undertook a career chasing what he termed 'creatures out of time and space'. Ultimately, he came to regard the entities seen in Kent and Virginia as being more paraphysical than extraterrestrial and came up with the notion that there were inter-dimensional 'windows' through which such strange forms could slip.

1964: Time Bandits

Time cycles

That aliens travel to the earth through space is usually taken for granted. However, travel between stars involves speeds far in excess of a NASA rocket and at such velocities that the physics of relativity come into force. When Albert Einstein revealed the intricacies of relativity, it was clear that time and space are inextricably woven together in a way that we still do not really understand. Aliens travelling at such rapid speeds would, by definition, move through time as well as through space. Or, indeed, they might literally be coming through time alone. They may not be arriving from another planet at all but from another time zone.

The possibility that these mysterious visitors are coming back from our own future is illustrated by a batch of cases that occurred in 1964. Two occurred on one remarkable day, April 24, and began with the bizarre adventure of farmer Gary Wilcox of Tioga City, New York State. Inspecting a field on his dairy farm, he came upon a shiny aluminium egg-shaped object on the ground. Reluctant to consider that it was a UFO, Wilcox contemplated various other options instead – that it was a discarded fridge or part of an aircraft wing that had fallen off. Only when he got closer to the structure did he realize that both ideas were impossible. It was then that the little men appeared.

They were 4 feet tall and dressed in a cover-all uniform. They spoke good English, and told the farmer they were from Mars. Each carried a tray of soil that they had evidently removed from his field. A discussion followed about alien methods of agriculture and the Martians asked for a bag of fertilizer to take home. Gary obligingly went off to get one and when he returned the UFO had vanished. He left the fertilizer in the field and by the next day it had disappeared.

As usual, the aliens had a good deal to say about mankind's folly in attempting to conquer space. In many other cases they had appeared scornful of our 'primitive' methods and unconvinced that we would get very far. They also posed a curious question to the farmer: what is your time cycle? Indeed, they appeared remarkably unaware of the way in which we judge time.

This was not the first time that such matters had been raised by the aliens. In the Cynthia Appleton encounter in Birmingham during 1958 (see page 36), our problems with space flight were coupled with a discussion about the nature of time. The alien alleged that we had invented this concept and that time does not actually exist in the sense that we imagine. The nature of time was set to become another recurring feature in many cases that followed.

The perfect case

Until April 1964, many UFOlogists were reluctant to believe in alien contact. The wild contactee tales from the 1950s dented the credibility of the subject in the eyes of many people. Even when witnesses were trustworthy, their stories were still often absurd – swapping water for alien pancakes, for instance. It all seemed counter-productive to investigators struggling to convince a disbelieving world that UFOs were real.

However, a few hours after Gary Wilcox met his time-travelling Martians, an incident took place that would convince many doubters. Even the US Government were so baffled by the incident that they spent months trying to find a rational answer – and failed miserably. Their scientific advisor, Dr J Allen Hynek, was now convinced that alien-contact cases were real. He flew to the landing site within hours and conducted one of his most thorough investigations.

The incident happened at Socorro, New Mexico in the late afternoon of April 24. A highly respected police officer and trusted member of the local church community was the key witness, with his sergeant another witness.

Officer Lonnie Zamora was chasing a speeding motorist when he saw flames in a desert gully outside the town. The flames came from a dynamite-filled shack and he broke off his pursuit to investigate. When he arrived, the shack seemed intact and the blue flames had gone.

As he edged towards a little bowl in the scrub, the policeman saw what at first looked like an overturned car glinting in the sun with some teenage joyriders near by. Only as he walked towards it did he realize that the object was a white metal egg with a curious symbol etched on its side. The youths were, in fact, two small men, normal in appearance and wearing white coverall uniforms. The similarities with the Gary Wilcox sighting thousands of miles away and just a few hours earlier are obvious.

By the time Zamora reached the top of the gully, the men – who had seen him and reacted with surprise – had apparently returned to the craft. It was emitting a high-pitched whine that rose to a deafening roar. As it took off, the policeman feared its flames would detonate the dynamite in the nearby shack and ran to place his patrol car between himself and the explosion that never came. He radioed for help, but the object rose and flew away across the desert.

Zamora's boss, Sergeant Chavez, arrived moments after the UFO's departure, but in time to see the scrub burning. While inspecting the damage, a number of heavy landing imprints were found by the two men. The FBI were called in, followed by the USAF and scientists such as Hynek. The government recognized immediately the similarity between the UFO and secret research being undertaken elsewhere in the same state into a lunar lander vehicle that would be used by Apollo on the moon five years later. It was assumed an early test was under way, but why so close to a major town?

They soon established that there was no test and that the lander could not have flown to Socorro. The sighting was like a scene from 1969 transported back through time, or as if someone was deliberately mimicking our own future technology – perhaps trying to show us how 'primitive' it was!

The man who wasn't there

Exactly a month after these two dramatic cases in the USA, a further amazing episode unfolded on the other side of the Atlantic .

On Sunday May 24, Carlisle fireman Jim Templeton took his new camera onto Burgh Marshes, some five miles from home on the banks of the Solway Firth. With him were his wife and their two daughters. It was a lovely summer's day and he took some photographs of his youngest daughter Elizabeth posing in her

Solway spaceman
Elizabeth Templeton in May 1964. Note the strange helmeted figure in the background.

new dress holding a bunch of flowers. Nothing odd was seen and the marsh was almost deserted. But the local cows were behaving oddly and there was a strange 'electric' atmosphere as if a storm was about to break. However, the weather remained fine all day.

When the prints were developed a week later, the storekeeper remarked that it was a pity that the best shot was spoiled by the man in the background. Yet there had been no man at the time. But sure enough, there was a figure behind Elizabeth's head. It looked like a tall humanoid in a white astronaut's suit.

The police were called in to try to resolve the mystery, as indeed were the Kodak laboratories. The latter assumed at first it was a double exposure; perhaps an earlier photograph of a colleague in a fireman's suit had been accidentally superimposed during photographic development. Investigation soon ruled this out. This was a single exposure of something apparently in the field of view of the camera lens when the shutter was briefly open. Kodak eventually offered free film for life to anyone who could crack the riddle as it had beaten all their experts. The police also wrote the matter off as 'some kind of freak picture' and left it at that.

Only it was far from the end of the matter. The Templetons got a call soon after asking if they would answer some questions. Two men arrived in a car, wearing dark suits and flashing identification that suggested they were government intelligence agents. They referred to one another only by numbers and got quite irate when they drove Jim to the site and he refused to accept their claim that it was just an ordinary passer-by that he had photographed. They asked him various questions about the weather and if the birds had stopped singing. Then they stormed off and left him to walk the five miles home.

This is one of the earliest appearances of the 'Men in Black' legend in British UFOlogy, but the words meant nothing to Jim Templeton. He has no interest in UFOs and had never heard of Men in Black. As far as he is still concerned he is just disgusted at how the British government treated him that day.

Launch surprises

A year after his encounter, Jim Templeton went back to the site to take some slides so that he could give a talk on the case to his fellow firemen. However, these shots were taken away from the processed film before the rest of the slides were returned to him. The police were brought onto the case of his 'stolen slides' and they could only establish that the Ministry of Defence were interested in his photographs because they had been taken near a site on the marshes where missiles were being built.

However, it turned out that there was a lot more to it than that, for there had been a whole spate of incidents at the launch site of these same Blue Streak missiles – which was at Woomera in the Australian desert. UFOs had often been seen above the range.

Group Captain Tom Dalton-Morgan was in charge of the Woomera facility between 1959 and 1963 and he told of one sighting to which he personally was a witness. It was prior to the firing of an earlier rocket, the Black Night. One of the observers about 100 miles down range called to say that a light was heading towards the site at incredible speed. Dalton-Morgan and several scientists watched as the light circled the facility and then shot away into the sky. After his retirement, the Group Captain said of this event: 'I am unable to conceive of any object, plane or missile during my posting to Woomera that was able to perform the manoeuvres seen by my team.'

This area was, of course, restricted air space and no aircraft were cleared to fly there. However, according to what Jim Templeton was told after police enquiries, the British government's interest in his photograph stemmed from another incident during the same week in May, 1964. They had aborted the launch of a Blue Streak test at Woomera when a similar 'white being' was seen on the automatic cameras.

DISTANT WORLDS

1964 was another exciting year for space flight. The first three-man mission was launched by the Russians, a prelude to their planned moon flights with multiple astronauts. Meanwhile, NASA had sent Ranger 7 to the moon and it had returned the first close-up photographs of the rugged, cratered nature of the terrain that would face future visitors.

A phenomenon had also been picked up by radio telescopes that at first suggested it was that elusive signal from an alien civilization. Regular bursts of fantastic energy were picked up coming from vast distances way across the galaxy. They were so powerful that they resembled stars, but they seemed to be artificial in nature. The term 'quasar' (standing for quasi-stellar source) was adopted. However, it was soon shown to be a natural phenomenon and not in any way a type of intelligent communication.

Lunar landscape
Moon views captured by NASA and Russian spacecraft gave greater insight into the planet's geography. Features such as scarps (cliffs) and rilles, or valleys, were identified for the first time.

My search through Public Record Office files found no evidence, although there are several references to 'the Cumberland Spaceman photograph'. The BBC helped me search for film of the relevant missile launches and although there is countless footage of almost every Blue Streak flight, the key one from this period is missing.

There is nonetheless some reference to film taken during a launch. My investigation found that it was taken at 9.14am on June 5 (less than two weeks after Jim Templeton's Burgh Marsh photograph was taken) and it is possible that this is the source of Jim's story. On the official film taken that morning, a white disc-like patch of light is visible adjacent to the Blue Streak rocket. The Ministry of Defence suggests that this is the low sun reflecting in the lens and causing what is known as 'lens flare'. However, the photographers at Woomera say that the camera had a lens hood on it to prevent just such an effect.

The white patch on this film does not look like a 'spaceman' or even closely similar to the object photographed by Jim Templeton. But the fact that two weird images were captured so soon after one another at rocket construction and test sites thousands of miles apart must have intrigued the Ministry of Defence. Was it further proof that 'they' – whoever 'they' were – could intrude into our technology as and when they chose?

1965: ALIENS IN ORBIT

Return of the little men

On July 1 Maurice Masse was about to start work in his lavender field at Valensole in the south of France when he heard a whistling sound. When he looked around, a white egg-shaped craft about the size of a car had landed near by. Two 'youths' had got out and were inspecting his crop; the farmer assumed they were stealing it and so he went to confront them. He then saw that they were not human. They were less than 4 feet tall, with large heads and slitty mouths. Their skin was white and they wore blue-green one-piece suits.

One of the entities picked up a tube from a belt on its side and pointed it at the farmer. He was instantly rooted to the spot, although he remained conscious. He claims that he saw the beings return to their craft – complete with plant samples – and take off skywards.

For years afterwards the lavender did not grow properly in the area where the UFO had landed. Masse himself implied that he had not told the whole story because nobody would have believed it. The original investigator, Aime Michel, did eventually get the truth from Masse and he hinted to me in a letter that this included an on-board 'abduction' after the farmer was paralysed on the spot.

Soon after Maurice Masse told his story, the first news broke about the Betty and Barney Hill 'abduction' in the USA. This had occurred in 1961 but had taken four years to become public knowledge after the long period of regression therapy undertaken by the witnesses.

The new wave

Immediately after Valensole case, the focus switched to South America, where a massive wave of alien-contact cases took place. Throughout Uruguay, Peru and Mexico, a wide range of beings – from the little men to the tall, blond ones – was sighted, usually engaged in simple surveillance operations.

In fact, there was a near duplication of the Valensole case on September 10 in Sao Joao, Pernambuco, Brazil. Just after dawn a farmer was working in his maize field when he heard a

The farmer's plight
Reconstruction by artist and UFOlogist Roy Sandbach of the landing and alien contact experienced by Maurice Masse at Valensole in France.

THE ASTRONAUT'S TALE

As preparations for the Apollo missions to the moon began, the first UFO contact in space was recorded by a NASA astronaut. Gemini 4 was in orbit over Hawaii on June 4, 1965, when Brigadier General James McDivitt saw something strange. His fellow astronaut was asleep, but McDivitt used two different cameras to try and film an object that looked like a 'beer can' before the rolling spacecraft took them into the glare of the sun and the UFO was lost to view.

On landing, NASA released photographs of the 'UFO' to placate the media as McDivitt refused to hide his sighting. The astronaut says both he and NASA knew that these pictures were certainly not of the UFO – he believes they show sunlight shining on window bolts. As for the real photographs, he had searched through the thousands of mission shots and failed to find them. His best guess is that they were spoilt by the sunlight and did not develop properly.

However, despite attempts to argue that he mistook his own booster rocket (which McDivitt has easily disproven), this remains one of the best UFO encounters from space. McDivitt has always insisted, 'we were never able to identify what it could have been'. A scientific study of the case for the US government called it a 'challenge to the analyst' and the whole episode persuaded the astronaut to take UFOs seriously. He says of them: 'They are there without a doubt, but what they are is anybody's guess.'

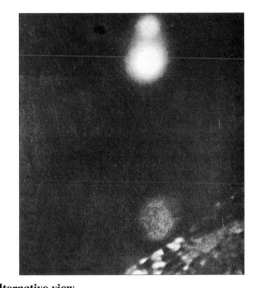

Alternative view
James McDivitt suspects that this photograph, released by NASA, shows window bolts reflecting bright sunlight. He has never been able to find the real photographs of the UFO he claims he saw.

whistling hum and saw a small disc from which two smooth-skinned creatures dressed in one-piece suits emerged. The beings' unintelligible chatter as they examined some tomato plants was also a feature of Maurice Masse's story.

The truth about abductions?

Possibly the most important case of this wave befell three men on 7 August at San Pedro de los Altos in Venezuela. It was late afternoon when, after a flash of light, they saw an egg-shaped object descending to the ground. A soft humming sound filled the men's heads and on a beam of light that projected from the object were two beings.

The entities were of the classic Nordic type, and, after a telepathic voice was heard, one of the men took the opportunity to ask some questions of the entities. The aliens said that they were from Orion and were coming to earth 'to study the psyches of humans ... and the possibility of inter-breeding'. They insisted that they were friendly but warned that another race of aliens – the 'grays' – was also visiting the earth and that these aliens were more ruthless

This story is extraordinary, for it suddenly makes sense of many things. The friendly nature of the Nordics and their 'psychic' powers are well attested, as is the lack of concern for our well-being displayed by the 'grays'. That a description of both types as well as a plan to interbreed with humans should be spelt out so clearly in this case is fascinating. Was it deliberately intended?

1966: Star Trekking

Window wonderland

By 1966, journalist John Keel was beginning to formulate the idea that certain locations were 'window areas' which allowed the alien phenomena from another dimension to 'pop through'.

A window area that was very much in action during this year was located at Aveyron in France. A farming family in this rural area were plagued by sightings of balls of light that would float across their land, climb trees and walls and seem to emerge from, and then disappear into, a large cylinder of light that appeared in one of their fields.

This wave of sightings began in June and lasted many weeks. In the winter of 1966 there occurred a dramatic episode when the farmer's son decided to give chase. He pursued one of the light balls to the field, where it and several others were blending into the cylinder of light like soap bubbles being blown in reverse. However, one of the bubbles floated above the road ahead of him, and as the man got to within a few feet of the light, all power drained away from his car.

The young man then noticed a small craft drifting towards him from across the fields. It was about the size of a car with two transparent bubbles on top. In each of these bubbles was a small humanoid figure surrounded by a greenish haze. The entities came close to the witness, as if they were inspecting him, and then shot off at great speed accompanied by a stifling wave of heat that filled the inside of the car. A metal road sign also began to vibrate as if it was resonating to some high-frequency energy.

A decade later, when Steven Spielberg made his classic UFO movie *Close Encounters of the Third Kind*, this incident, complete with vibrating road sign, was recreated in a fictional American setting. This was no coincidence, since Spielberg based much of the film on actual alien-contact stories.

Devil places

As a result of cases such as this, French researcher Fernand Lagarde began to develop the 'window area' theory into a scientific framework. He noted how the Aveyron lightballs seemed to drift along set routes close to the ground and when he plotted these paths in conjunction with local fault lines under the surface and lines of magnetic energy, he found a strong connection.

This was the first step in a theory which claims that many UFOs are natural physical energies generated by the earth itself. In Britain, Paul Devereux invented the word 'earthlights' to describe these phenomena. In his view, the balls of energy are triggered by stresses and strains in fault lines during quarrying work, or when there is great water pressure on the rocks.

To earthlights researchers these energies are completely natural. They have even successfully duplicated them in laboratories, putting rock samples under pressure and filming the results. Mini UFOs are indeed generated, but they are tiny sparks and very short lived. People claiming to have seen spacecraft have, earthlights theorists contend, merely experienced hallucinations resulting from this physical energy scrambling their brainwaves. In a Canadian experiment, volunteers were placed inside intense electrical fields similar to those that, in theory, exist in connection with large-scale earthlights and the subjects did indeed experience altered states of consciousness.

The question is whether the 'out-of-body sensations' result from the intervention of aliens or

TELL THE TRUTH

The first ever soft landing on another planet occurred in 1966 when Surveyor 1 touched down on the moon. Now human science was duplicating the alien-contact sightings.

As a result of a wave of reports in Michigan, the then Senator and future US President Gerald Ford demanded an official enquiry into UFOs and said that the public 'are entitled to a more thorough explanation than has been given them by the Air Force to date.' A commission was set up under the directorship of optical physicist, Dr Brian O'Brien. One of its members was a young cosmologist called Dr Carl Sagan, a future writer and broadcaster who would go on to become a household name. The commission strongly recommended a scientific study of UFOs, declassifying Air Force files and establishing centres at various universities to investigate landing cases. It was to prove a turning point in research into alien contacts.

Ground control
Rocket technology on view at the Kennedy Space Centre.

whether natural earth energies could really account for such events. Window areas certainly exist and this supports the earthlight theorists, for many UFO regions are teeming with faulted rocks. Perhaps more important is evidence that these windows existed long before the alien-contact stories. Tales of UFOs may just be modern interpretations of events that, in past centuries in the same locations, would have involved dragons, fairies and other mythical and mysterious entities.

American researcher Loren Coleman noted that many of these places have what he calls 'devil names', given to them by locals because of supernatural phenomena reported there. In the vicinity of the key French window area, for instance, there is a town called Draguinan (a name for dragons) and a peak called La Malmont ('the evil mountain'). In Britain, hotspot encounters in the Pennines have been concentrated around places such as the Devil's Elbow and Hob Tor, hob being an old name for demons.

The *Quatermass and the Pit* television series included all these elements years before they were recognized by researchers, and portrayed contact hallucinations as being the result of a centuries-old memory of real aliens buried deep in our subconscious. Perhaps there is truth in that too!

1967: Science and Aliens

Visitors from UMMO

One of Europe's most extraordinary alien contact incidents took place in 1967 with the so-called 'UMMO Mystery'.

For some months UFOlogists in Spain had been receiving letters and telephone calls purporting to be from aliens living on earth. A complex web of data was built up and eventually 'UMMO files' were received in other parts of Europe such as France and Austria. According to the hundreds of pages of documents and phone messages over many years, the planet UMMO is supposedly found around the distant star, Wolf 424. It is populated by an ancient race of tall human-like beings that may well be the Nordic type commonly reported in Europe.

The Ummites could pass for earth people but few could speak to us; their form of communication was telepathy. A very sophisticated account was built up of the society on UMMO, from its politics to its science and religion. Yet no individual who received UMMO messages had the complete story.

Then, on June 1, 1967, an encounter took place that turned the UMMO affair on its head. At San Jose de Valderas, a suburb of Madrid in Spain, a UFO floated over a park for several minutes and was seen by numerous witnesses. It flew off along the Extremadura Highway, where many others saw it, before briefly landing near a café in Santa Monica. Here, landing traces were found, the grass was burnt and several small metal tubes were recovered. One of these was broken open by a young boy who was first on the scene. He said that a liquid poured out which evaporated. Inside the tubes were small green plastic strips which bore a symbol. This symbol was almost identical to the astrological glyph for the planet Uranus and it had also been seen on the underside of the UFO that had just taken off.

Moreover, it was the mark of UMMO and had appeared on the many documents received by UFOlogists in the preceding months.

There seems little doubt that this sighting actually happened and the tubes and green plastic were very real. Samples were sent off for analysis by INTA, the Spanish Institute for Space Research. Meanwhile, two sets of photographs mysteriously turned up, one of which was left for a newspaper to collect. The other was supplied by an anonymous witness who refused to be interviewed. Both claimed to show the Madrid UFO and did indeed depict the craft.

Computer study of the photographs in the USA quickly revealed them to be a hoax; the string holding up a model was uncovered using techniques developed from deep-space photography. However, the plastic strips were a bigger mystery. They were made out of polyvinyl fluoride, a substance not commercially available and in 1967 made by only one known source – an American company manufacturing the material for NASA spacecraft!

UFO from 'UMMO'
A photograph of the craft with the 'UMMO' symbol in 1967.

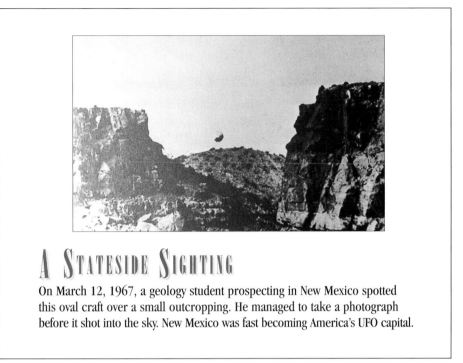

A Stateside Sighting

On March 12, 1967, a geology student prospecting in New Mexico spotted this oval craft over a small outcropping. He managed to take a photograph before it shot into the sky. New Mexico was fast becoming America's UFO capital.

A patrolman's tale

Another important case occurred on December 3, 1967, and is significant in that it was the first ever abduction to be investigated more or less immediately after it had happened. The location was the rural farming town of Ashland, Nebraska, and the key witness was a state police trooper called Herb Schirmer.

At 2.30am Schirmer went to investigate some cows that had been causing a disturbance. He came upon some lights by the road and initially thought it was a broken-down truck. Instead he saw a strange oval object that seemed to be drawing power from the overhead electricity lines. Suddenly there was a screeching noise and the object took off. Schirmer drove back into town and filed a report saying: 'Saw a flying saucer at junction of highways 6 and 63. Believe it or not.'

However, the patrolman felt tired and unwell and went home to 'sleep it off'. He also could not understand why it was 3am when he arrived back at the station house – he estimates that 20 minutes of his journey were unaccounted for. A subsequent investigation used regression hypnosis to try and solve the mystery.

Schirmer recalled how his car was drained of power as it approached the UFO and was then 'towed' up a hill by an invisible force. Two small men with grayish skins and cat-like eyes got out. They engulfed the car in a green light fired from a box on one entity's chest. This seems to have put the police officer into a sort of trance, during which he was asked telepathically, 'Are you the watchman of this town?'

The beings then led him aboard and Schirmer was fed detailed information about the alien mission, as if his position of authority would make him a good representative for such a message. He was shown a circle of spinning drums that gave off rainbow colours, and told it was their propulsion system that adopted 'reversible electrical-magnetism'. They added that it was a danger to the environment through its ionization field, another little-known yet recurrent theme in alien-contact stories.

A holographic image was also shown to Schirmer, though in 1967 he had never seen a hologram so he had no idea what he was describing. It was a map of a sun and six planets and was the alien home 'in a nearby galaxy'. Schirmer was told that the aliens would return twice and that they were peaceful. They were taking animal and plant samples and had a human 'breeding analysis' study under way. Yet again, these aspects make remarkable sense in the light of other cases we have come across – cases that Herb Schirmer could not have been aware of when he told his story.

Most fascinating of all was the reason given to Schirmer as to why the aliens would block out part of his memory. They said that the military were hostile towards them, had chased them in planes and even fired guns and rockets at them. They did not wish the government to know what was going on, so they acted randomly and prevented witnesses from remembering the actual contact phase of their ordeals.

The Condon con

In the aftermath of the 1966 O'Brien commission, the US Government allocated hundreds of thousands of dollars to allow an institute to mount a full-scale study into UFOs. Unfortunately, the US Air Force had done such a good job of debunking the reports that nobody was interested. NASA turned it down, as did prestigious universities such as MIT. The University of Colorado eventually agreed to take it on, under the direction of atomic physicist Dr Edward Condon. Classified papers leaked to the press subsequently revealed that the university had taken on the project as a scam – they would convince the public that they were being objective whilst knowing that the project was a waste of time.

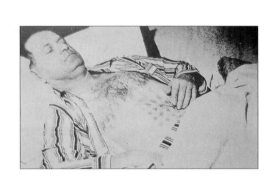

Painful Proof

At Falcon Lake on the Ontario border, Canadian prospector Steve Michalak was searching for minerals when he came upon a landed object. Walking up to it, convinced it was a secret American aircraft, he looked inside to find it empty apart from strange flashing equipment. Suddenly the door began to close and a jet of steam escaped from a vent and set his shirt alight. Staggering back to civilization, Michalak checked into hospital suffering from nausea and burns. This chequer pattern on his skin was said to match the grill structure on the UFO vent.

THE PRICE OF PROGRESS

This was a tragic year in the space race. For the first time, humanity learnt the price we would have to pay to conquer the solar system. NASA astronauts Chaffee, Grissom and White were killed on the ground practicing for the forth-coming moon landings when a fire trapped them in their tiny capsule. Russian cosmonaut Vladimir Komarov also died, becoming the first victim of an actual flight (rumours of previous hidden disasters apart) when he died during the landing of Soyuz 1.

Regular pulsating signals were also picked up from deep space by British astronomers Jocelyn Bell and Anthony Hewish. So artificial did they seem that it was believed that they had to come from an alien intelligence – they were a message transmitted to the earth. Science was agog with the news for a short while until the sad truth dawned – like the quasars before them, these newly named 'pulsars' were also natural bursts of energy that resulted from rapidly rotating stellar sources in deep space.

Partly as a result of the embarrassment of this latest false alarm, scientists have, since 1967, been much more wary about announcing findings to do with anomalous signals from space. There are now protocols in operation which require checks and double checks and long delays. If a real message is picked up, it is unlikely that we will hear about it on the television news that same day.

This inauspicious start would haunt the Condon Report. In fact, in 1968 it received more funds whilst firing scientists indirectly responsible for leaking the so-called 'trick memorandum'. The fired scientists went on to complete their own study and the end result was two separate reports – the official one, heavily touted by the government and openly dismissive of there being anything of interest in the UFO subject, and one entitled 'UFOs? Yes!' written by the other half of the project staff. They studied the same cases but reached almost entirely opposite conclusions!

During the 18 months of the Condon Report only about 60 cases were studied. Of these, about one-third defied explanation even in the view of the sceptical report. This 1000-page document, whilst concluding that UFOs were nonsense, stated that in some cases, 'genuine UFOs' were involved, that 'unknown' objects were being seen and that phenomena 'so rare they had never been reported before or since' were responsible for sightings.

One of the few alien-contact cases to figure in the 60 investigations was the Herb Schirmer abduction. The Condon team conducted psychological tests on the trooper, using Dr Leo Sprinkle from the University of Wyoming to carry out the hypnosis. The story linked neatly with other alien-contact cases, of which Condon was probably unaware.

Yet the official report devotes only two pages to the Schirmer case. It tells only of his conscious memory and of Sprinkle's regression says simply that 'new information was added to the trooper's account'. Not a word was said about the content of that new information.

Condon concluded, without evidence, that there were no grounds to presume that the Ashland encounter was real, yet added that Schirmer had voluntarily requested a lie detector test and this had revealed nothing inconsistent with his claim.

Then there was Dr Sprinkle ,who added that, in his judgement, the trooper was telling the truth. Sprinkle went on to devote the rest of his life to studying further alien encounters, having been so intrigued by Schirmer's story.

Thankfully, a number of people ignored Condon's conclusions and came to appreciate that, try as he might to dismiss the phenomenon, Condon had produced the best scientific evidence yet that something very strange was taking place.

1968: THE INVADERS

To see if we can

The 'breeding analysis' programme which trooper Schirmer was told about took its next step five months later.

At 4am on May 3, 1968, 19-year-old nurse's aide Shane Kurz saw a strange light outside her home in Westmoreland, New York State. The next thing she recalled was 'coming to' in her bed with her mother by her side. Muddy footsteps led to her room from outside. Her mother had arrived after hearing noises, which appears to have been Shane returning from her 'sleepwalk' outside. The young woman had no memory of going outdoors but was to suffer an intense period of physical after-effects. These included migraines, traumatic nightmares about being 'captured' and peculiar red rings that surfaced on her abdomen. She also stopped menstruating.

Concerned by her condition, she went to see her doctor who referred her to a gynaecologist. Apart from the possibility that the loss of her periods was stress related, no physical cause was found. The trouble continued for almost five years before Shane began to regain her physical well-being. She was still troubled by nightmares.

Eventually the woman, now 25 years old, went to see a psychologist in New York and he decided to regress her to that night in 1968. A classic alien-abduction memory was revealed.

The beings were small and hairless with off-white skins and large probing eyes. They communicated by telepathy and, most worryingly, seemed to be aware of who Shane was.

Under some form of invisible control, she was taken outside to the landed UFO, but does

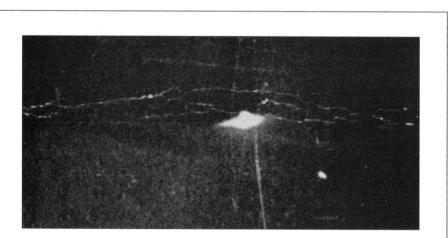

OBSERVATORY OBSERVATION

Astronomers look at the sky every night and contrary to popular sceptical belief they do see UFOs from time to time. In 1968 scientists at the El Infurmilla observatory in Chile succeeded in photographing this object detected by their telescopes.

CHRISTMAS ANGELS

The Apollo programme got into full swing in 1968 and peaked just before Christmas in a carefully planned PR campaign. As the holiday approached, the crew of Apollo 8 flew all the way from the earth to the moon, circled this barren world, but did not land. Their Christmas message looking back across the void at the blue planet earth floating lonely in the blackness of space was a moment of almost divine inspiration for millions of people.

This vision illustrated the fragility of life on earth. For the first time we saw just how enormous the universe was and how tiny earth was. In many ways Apollo 8 was the high point of the space programme and had a deeper philosophical and psychological effect on the population of planet earth than any of the programmes that would follow in the next few years.

Possibly capturing this mood, Swiss researcher Eric von Daniken hit the world with a series of best-selling books with the theme 'Was God an astronaut?' The 'ancient astronauts' theory had not actually been invented by him; British writer Raymond Drake had already published several books with far more limited success. However, timing is of the essence in these matters, and it made von Daniken a star, especially in German-speaking nations.

The theory argued that a number of puzzling anomalies about the ancient world – from the engineering brilliance of the pyramids to a mysterious stone battery and cave paintings around the world that seem to depict UFOs – point towards alien contact on earth tens of thousands of years ago. Perhaps human civilization was actually developed by such visitors

providing us with technology and therefore acting, in a sense, like God.

That Christmas, the movie *2001: A Space Odyssey* entranced the world. Stanley Kubrick and sci-fi writer Arthur C. Clarke pefectly captured the mood of the day. With stunning special effects showing spacecraft of the future, the movie featured earth's first encounter with an alien race. They had left black monoliths in the solar system to prove that they had come here millions of years ago and, as von Daniken was suggesting, set us on our way to becoming an intelligent ciliization.

Earthrise
Earthrise from the moon.
This photograph was taken during the
Apollo 8 mission of December 21–27, 1968.

not have full memory of the process. Shane recalls being inside a room with a table or bed and being told to get onto this. She found herself unable to resist. A long tube was inserted into her navel and fluid was drawn out.

Shane Kurz claims that the aliens told her they were extracting ova samples. She had been chosen to provide them with a baby so that they could carry out genetic experiments upon the child. 'We are studying. We want to see if we can,' they insisted.

Here is another case which seems independent of all the others but which fits in remarkably with the ongoing theme of an alien experiment to try to 'grow' a baby using biological samples from human abductees. While alien genetic experiments with babies are seen in various modern UFO books, none of them were in print before 1987. The cases that we come across before that time do not result from contemporary interest in the subject. They stand very much alone.

1969: ALIEN END GAME

A quiet year

In 1969 aliens were more notable by their absence than their presence. What few encounters there were took place in the southern hemisphere.

On April 25, a woman and her daughter were travelling by taxi past Roberts Park in Greenacre, Sydney, Australia, when they spotted an object over the fields that looked like a Chinese lantern. Asking the taxi driver to slow down, they wound down the window and took a closer look. A transparent dome on the front of the object had a blue glow which allowed the interior of the craft to be seen.

Inside the dome were three figures. They were of normal height and dressed in dark coveralls. One was working at the controls and another was pointing excitedly at the witnesses. The taxi driver was clearly upset and drove off at speed, insisting that they were only seeing the floodlights from the park's football field.

Then, on June 10, the action moved to the Philippines in Rizal, east of Manila, at the site of the nation's satellite ground-tracking station.

The witnesses were local farmers and an engineer from a nearby site. They describe a white egg-shaped craft that landed briefly. It was

EPIC MOMENT

In the summer of 1969 NASA fulfiled John Kennedy's promise and successfully sent Apollo 11 to the moon. When Neil Armstrong and Buzz Aldrin became the first humans to set foot on an alien world on that July day, an amazing scientific project had gone from nowhere to the surface of the moon in an incredibly short time. The earth had finally become a race of fully-fledged space travellers.

ADVANCING SCIENCE

In January, the Condon Report was finally published, with its damning conclusions on UFOs. Within weeks, the US Government convened secret meetings and decided to close down Project Blue Book – the USAF investigation project that had been in operation since 1948. Dr. J. Allen Hynek, the astronomer contracted as scientific consultant from the beginning, was notified of this decision soon afterwards but told to keep the news quiet. The US authorities were awaiting the right moment to tell the public.

When Colonel Patterson investigated the Philippines encounters in June, he was evidently aware of these behind-the-scenes moves and it is curious that it was felt worthwhile sending him to the site at all. His press comments almost seem like a public relations exercise to shoot down UFOs.

However, in the wake of the disenchantment over Condon, other moves were afoot, including plans to get the AAAS (American Association for the Advancement of Science) to debate UFOs. Such a prestigious organization could lend huge credibility to the field and seriously undermine the negative tactics of Condon and the unannounced closure of official US Government investigations.

The instigator of the idea was rocket scientist Dr Thornton Page, who in 1953 had been a member of the CIA panel that had set up the protocol to debunk UFOs out of existence. Page was now persuaded that something important was going on. He enlisted the AAAS and Dr Carl Sagan, the cosmologist who had sat on the O'Brien government enquiry into UFOs in 1966. Sagan agreed to work with Page on the event, scheduled for Boston in late December.

Determined to be open minded in this two-day event, scientists such as Allen Hynek and atmospheric physicist Dr James McDonald were invited and came to present the scientific evidence in favour of UFOs. But sceptics were invited too. Some came, such as Dr Donald Menzel, who believed UFOs were often optical illusions, but Edward Condon flatly declined.

In fact, Condon went much further and fought hard to try to stop the AAAS from staging the symposium. He even tried to use his friendship with vice-president Spiro Agnew to stop it from going ahead. He failed and was reportedly furious. Page writes that some time later he spoke to Condon whilst writing an encyclopedia entry on UFOs and the physicist allegedly smashed the phone in a rage!

The AAAS symposium was a great success and Page and Sagan edited the papers to create the first truly comprehensive scientific book on the subject, which was due to be released in 1972. Meanwhile, in an obvious attempt to scupper any positive publicity from the conference, the Pentagon chose the very week of the AAAS event to announce its closure of Project Blue Book (a decision made nearly a year earlier). They emphasized their conclusion that there was no such thing as UFOs. However, secret memos not released until 1977 show that they kept UFO reporting channels open. It stands to reason that they did not tell the press that they were doing so!

so close to the witnesses that they had a clear view of the two pilots inside. These beings were 6 feet tall and quite human in appearance, if pale in complexion. They wore white 'flying suits' with plastic headgear.

The engineer describes how he saw a huge yellow ball of fire shoot away across the complex. He himself had an interesting name in view of events that were going on in NASA during that same month. His name was Leonardo de Luna.

The US Government sent USAF Colonel Alfred Patterson to the satellite station to investigate this bizarre sequence of events. Patterson was the air attache to the American embassy in Manila and after looking into the stories he announced to the press his scepticism that anything of significance had happened in the region. He said that the US Government had decided that 'there ain't no such thing' when it came to UFOs. However, Patterson did add that 'the US Air Force have an interest in this type of thing' and that was why he had personally investigated the matter; it was not just to satisfy his own curiosity.

Put in context of the measures that the US Government were then taking with regard to the study of UFOs, the investigation is intriguing.

1970: THE ALIENS RETURN

Snowbound terror

Within days of the AAAS symposium, the aliens were back in business with a vengance. The scene was a forest outside the village of Imjarvi in southern Finland on January 7. For those who have argued that alien contacts are simply hallucinations brought on during a state of semi-sleep, the circumstances of this encounter are vital. Forester Aarno Heinonen and farmer Esko Viljo were skiing at the time the events unfolded, a situation during which any lack of concentration could have proved disastrous for them.

With the temperature many degrees below freezing, they reached a clearing and heard a peculiar buzzing sound. They then observed a strange misty cloud circling the light and giving off a reddish glow. The buzzing sound emerged from here as it descended towards ground level.

As it reached tree-top height, it became evident that a plate-like object was inside the mist. This had three hemispheres on the base around a central tube. The buzzing increased in level until it was about 10 feet from the ground. The mist then cleared and silence descended on the woods.

As the men stood close enough to the object to reach out and touch it with their ski poles, a beam of light poured from

Ski attack
Cover illustration from the magazine *Flying Saucer Review*, depicting the attack on two Finnish skiers.

the tube and formed a circle in the snow. Then the same reddish mist spread out and filled the area surrounding the object, including the men.

Heinonen reports that he felt himself being pulled and thrust backwards. As this sensation overcame him, the two men spotted a frightening creature about 3 feet tall standing inside the circle of light as if it were floating there. It looked like a goblin or troll, with a waxy face and green clothes. In its hands was a box from which a pulsing yellow light was being emitted. The being turned and pointed this directly at Heinonen, who says it blinded him.

Multi-coloured sparks were now descending from the object and covered the men, but they felt nothing. The mist was also so thick that they could not see one another even though they were only a few feet apart. Then the light beam was sucked upwards into the tube and there was a silent explosion 'as if the mist was just blown apart'. The forest was left still and empty.

Immediately after the object had gone, Heinonen began to feel ill. The side that had faced the light and mist became paralysed and he could not walk properly. Abandoning his expensive ski equipment, he was helped back to the village by Viljo. It took them an hour to travel the one mile home. By then Heinonen was vomiting, had a pounding headache and was passing discoloured urine. His blood pressure was low and his limbs ached. These symptoms persisted for weeks. Viljo was less severely affected, suffering swollen eyes and reddened skin. The doctor who treated them both had no facilities with him to check for radiation exposure but said this is what their symptoms sounded like to him.

Although this account of a UFO landing is unusual, it is not unique. 10 years later a very

DISASTER LOOMS

In April, the third Apollo flight to the moon was struck by disaster when an oxygen tank exploded in the darkness thousands of miles from earth. For a time it looked as if the crew would be lost as there was no obvious way to get them back home before their air ran out.

However, in a remarkable twist of fate, NASA borrowed a trick out of a science-fiction novel published exactly 100 years earlier by Jules Verne in which he envisaged a space-ship called 'Columbiad' launched from a Florida site very near Cape Canaveral. They flew round the moon, using its gravity like a slingshot to accurately propel the mission back to earth. Verne's fictional crew got home. So, in real life, did Apollo 13. Its capsule was, by extraordinary coincidence, named 'Columbia'.

similar phenomenon was witnessed – again in a forest – this time near Ipswich in England. Dozens of US Air Force personnel were witness to the events that night.

An arable alien

On August 16, a 22-year-old maid looking after a farmhouse in Spain had a big surprise. The location was the village of Puente de Herrera near the town of Valladolid and she was engrossed in watching a late-night TV soap opera called *Medical Centre* when a whistling noise was heard above the television. The picture began to break up, with lines of interference spreading across the screen. The woman struggled to re-adjust the set, but to no avail.

By now the whistling sound had decreased but she went to the door to see what was responsible for ruining her programme. She was stunned by what she saw: A strange object had landed half on the approach road and half on the field opposite the farmhouse. It was the size of a small car, sat on legs and had a dome-like transparent canopy on top with a pulsating blue light on top.

Standing beside the machine was a man of about normal height, dressed in a dark one-piece suit and carrying luminous bands on both his ankles and wrists. He was staring fixedly at the farm's alfalfa crop, evidently interested in taking samples of it. Of course, we have seen this feature recur again and again in cases where aliens land in agricultural regions.

Down South
South America was struck by a major wave of UFO sightings in 1970. On September 14 this disc-like object was filmed over La Roja, Argentina.

The maid was terrified by her experience and quickly ducked back indoors. Soon afterwards the whistling noise increased in volume and when she dared to look outside again, the object and its occupant had disappeared.

Next day boot prints were found on the approach road. These were not unusual except that at night they glowed as if covered by luminous paint. Many people saw them over the next few days until they faded from view.

This witness was described as being practically illiterate and seemed utterly unaware of other alien-contact stories from elsewhere around the world. She was considered to be very trustworthy and had been deeply shocked by her encounter.

1971: UNDER THE SKIN

Through the square window

The town of Kempsey in New South Wales, Australia, had been having UFO sightings for many years. Its residents were well aware that it was in what was known as a 'window area'. However, for one stunned aboriginal man living in the small community a very different window experience was to befall him on April 2.

A pink light had been seen drifting above the Macleay River that evening towards Greenhill, the aboriginal settlement in the area. In the middle of these sightings at about 10pm, a man who was totally unaware of the lights in the sky went into the kitchen to get a glass of water and was astonished to see a small round face, pale in colour and with no sign of body hair, staring at him. The face was pressed up against the kitchen window. Suddenly the man felt a tugging sensation and he was sucked towards the window and up above the sink that was piled high with dirty dishes at the time.

Back in the living room the man's wife heard a gasp followed by the smashing of glass. She hurried into the kitchen and was just in time to see her husband's legs disappearing through the window! He was being pulled right through in a horizontal position, but she could not see who or what was responsible for this.

Rushing outside, she found her husband back on his feet, apparently none the worse after a seven-feet fall onto his back. He ran off in the direction of where the light had appeared, screaming and shaking. It was some time before he regained enough composure to describe what had taken place.

Many further sightings followed over the coming weeks, including an object that passed over Mount Sebastopol at the community of Willi Willi. It turned the sky pink as it flew overhead and local dogs and horses went into a frenzy.

Alien implants

One of the most intriguing new developments in the abduction phenomenon began slowly this year when a 10-year-old girl called Caroline started to have a number of visitations in her bedroom at her home in Adelaide, South Australia. Her remarkable story has been followed by care worker and UFO expert Keith Basterfield as it broke new ground in the whole history of alien contact.

Her numerous encounters involved two different types of aliens. There was a single, tall, blond haired figure which was 'the controller'. He appeared to have psychic powers and was always kind and helpful. He possibly assisted Caroline to develop her own abilities as a form of disassociation from severe family problems. During adolescence and early adulthood she had a whole series of paranormal encounters,

Southern sighting
A UFO over the Kempsey window area in Australia.

MARS HERE WE COME

As our infatuation with space travel drew to a close, the Apollo missions to the moon continued. Apollo 15 carried with it a vehicle that could move across the surface of the moon with astronauts as passengers. The moon itself was found to be dead and barren.

There was further tragedy when three Soviet cosmonauts died during Soyuz/Salyut missions. The romance with space exploration was definitely in decline.

This year also saw a NASA probe to Mars which produced the first close-up evidence of what the planet was like. After the bitter disappointments over Venus, Mars remained a possibility and scientists and science-fiction writers alike clung to the prospect of some kind of life being found. However, the new probe showed that the planet was very cold, had very little atmosphere, was bombarded by radiation and lacked any trace of water. Nobody from earth could survive on the surface unaided. The last real hope for life in the solar system had disappeared.

After a decade of failure to detect any sort of radio signal from distant stars, these negative findings from Venus and Mars about our own solar system were quite significant blows to morale. Science began to seriously question for the first time whether any alien life existed anywhere at all. Scientists started to wonder if, after all, the earth might actually be alone.

UFO or not?
One of several photographs taken during the moon landings which some say show UFOs 'spying' on the missions. Or are they simply light reflections?

that included encountering a poltergeist in her home and flashes of ESP.

However, there were also other beings who visited her room and took her away to a UFO for study. These were typical of the American style 'grays', under 4 feet tall, with hairless pale faces and large eyes. They worked tirelessly, clearly under the tutelage of the larger being. It was these smaller entities who performed a series of medical tests on Caroline at various stages during her life. These were explained to her as being 'check-ups' to monitor her progress, although it was never explained what progress was implied or what the aliens were actually up to.

The beings then told her that she would have an object implanted into her face. This would serve as a monitoring device to help them watch her development. Caroline does not recall the process of implantation, but a soreness on awakening told her that it was there.

During a routine dental appointment shortly afterwards, an X-ray was taken of her face. On the resulting images, a strange object appeared in her cheek region. The dentist was puzzled but assumed it was just a shadow on the plate – something that did occasionally happen. Caroline, of course, thought differently.

Arrangements were made for a more thorough examination. However, on these detailed X-rays there was no object visible. Caroline explained that in between the sessions she had been abducted once again and that the aliens had removed the implant!

Sceptics will no doubt argue that this is very convenient. But the abductions and implant were reported before the 'shadow' was found and I have seen that X-ray. There is no doubt that something does appear to be present in Caroline's face.

This was by no means the last time that 'alien implants' would feature in the abduction story. And the evidence that they could be real would continue to mount.

1972: Fading Vision

The man who wasn't there

As scientists started to have their first real doubts about the existence of aliens, an extraordinary case from Australia dealt a serious blow to the UFO fraternity.

The story began near Rye in Victoria on July 3, 1972, while Maureen Puddy was visiting her young son who had been hospitalized with a leg injury. He had been taken by air ambulance and when a blue light followed her car on the Mooraduc Road near Frankston she stopped to watch what she assumed was another helicopter. But this turned out to be an oval object that emitted blue light and hummed softly. After tailing her for eight miles, the UFO vanished and she drove to the police to report the matter.

Three weeks later, driving home from the hospital on the same route, the blue glow returned. All power was drained from her car and it ran onto a grass verge. As the object hovered overhead the young mother felt a vacuum surrounding her and a curious detached state of consciousness. A voice was heard inside her head stating, 'All your tests will be negative' (a phrase she has never understood) and 'Tell the media. Do not panic – we mean no harm.' Again she went to the police and, afraid that 'they' might return, she also called the media. Nobody took much notice.

Seven months passed and on February 22, 1973, Mrs Puddy heard the voice in her head again telling her to go to 'the meeting place'. She tried to resist by going out shopping, but it kept insisting. So she called investigators Judith Magee and Paul Norman, who had followed up her earlier sightings, and they agreed to meet her on the Mooraduc Road.

Mrs Puddy claimed that during the journey a figure materialized in the car beside her. She described him as being of human appearance with long, blond hair and dressed in a light one-piece suit. The two investigators met her at the site of her earlier encounters and sat in the car listening to this new story. Suddenly Maureen Puddy called out, 'There he is! Can't you see him?' Alleging that the being was now outside the car, she pointed in obvious distress. The investigators could see nothing.

Paul Norman got out and walked right through the spot (by the left headlight) where Mrs Puddy said the alien stood. She reported that it stepped back to let him pass. Then she fell into a catatonic state, mumbling that she was 'inside' a UFO and could not escape. She described a large console shaped like a mushroom inside the room. Eventually she reported that the experience had now ended and she was 'back in the car'. The investigators gave her something to drink from a thermos and then drove her home. Despite the evidence of their own eyes, they had no doubt she truly believed that she had been 'taken away'.

Both Magee and Norman know that the woman never really left the car in any physical sense – but they also insist that she was not making things up. Magee reported that during the spacenapping, 'I put my arm around her shoulder to try and calm her and could feel tears on my hand. She was really upset.'

The truth was disturbing to the investigators. How could they equate what their own eyes saw (or rather did not see) with the sincerity of this abductee's story? Moreover, on how many other occasions when no independent witness had been present had abductees insisted they had been spacenapped, when in reality they had not?

Since 1972, other cases have surfaced. Does this suggest that spacenapping occurs while the victim is in an altered states of consciousness?

NEW-AGE ALIENS

Even the movie industry showed its own disenchantment with space as a theme. Films in 1972 ignored this once staple diet for producers and writers and took off in a new direction, concentrating on the first hint of public fear about the environment that would blossom a decade later.

As a result, movies such as ZPG *(Zero Population Growth)* predicted a nightmarish future when the world had to be controlled to avoid over-population and environmental catastrophe and *Doomwatch*, a big-screen version of the BBC television series about scientists fighting the dangers wrought on the planet by the increase in technology and scientific progress.

Interestingly, around about the same time, the messages conveyed by aliens during their contacts began to adapt to the new mood of public concern. From previous preoccupations with space flight and atom bombs, aliens began to expound about the destruction being wrought on the earth by our own misdeeds. Before long the new-age community, which was the first place in which environmental concerns really flourished, would begin to move closer towards the alien contact field. Indeed, it would not be long before the two became almost indistinguishable, with mystical alien messages emerging alongside the more obvious traditional examples of alien contact.

The question this posed was whether the format of the alien contact responded to public concerns or whether these changes in our attitudes were brought about by the aliens themselves alongside their other, more direct, contacts. Were the visitors from outer space somehow responsible for social change?

CUFOS

With no official government study into UFOs in the USA, the USAF scientific advisor Dr J Allen Hynek liaised with a group of like-minded scientists. They had seen the positive side of the Condon report and the AAAS symposium. As a consequence, Hynek began work on his 'definitive' book about the science behind the UFO mystery (to be released as *The UFO Experience)* and launched the first science-based UFO organization – CUFOS (the Center for UFO Studies). CUFOS still operates today, but was renamed as the Dr J Allen Hynek Center for UFO Studies after Hynek's death in 1986.

The Ministry takes an interest

In Britain, there were widespread sightings. An ATV camera crew filming a farming programme near Enstone in the South Midlands captured footage of a UFO's vapour trail as it flew overhead. While that may have been a jet dumping fuel, other cases were more baffling.

During August, a convoy of cars, including a police patrol vehicle, came upon a landed UFO on the North Yorkshire moors. This was near the top-secret intelligence communications centre at Menwith Mill, operated by the NSA – America's satellite surveillance and electronic monitoring agency. The door in the side of the brilliant melon-coloured UFO opened in a mysterious fashion which baffled the witnesses.

Finally the year of activity ended in October on Beachy Head in Sussex when a hotel worker encountered a UFO that landed on a golf course as he walked through thick fog. An alien voice 'spoke' to him and he was 'repositioned' some distance away, having 'lost' several hours.

In these cases the British Defence Ministry launched a series of surprise initiatives. They interrogated witnesses, warned them not to speak in public, controlled press coverage or launched covert enquiries. At the same time they approached UFO group Contact UK to ask if they would cooperate with them!

Contact UK was founded by the Earl of Clancarty. Their task was to submit 500 current cases and modify their report procedures to better match those of the Ministry. The liaison did not proceed, although Contact UK were 'investigated' by intelligence services.

1973: MARK OF THE ALIENS

The month of October 1973 must rank as one of the most extraordinary in the 50-year history of alien contact. It generated so many sightings of alien entities that it earned 1973 the label 'year of the humanoids'.

Just after 10pm on October 17, Jeff Greenshaw, the police chief of the small town of Falkville, Alabama, responded to an anonymous call reporting a sighting of a UFO. This directed him to the outskirts of the town, where he was confronted by a figure about the size of a human being, but slightly under average weight and dressed from head to toe in a reflective suit.

Greenshaw had a camera in the patrol car to photograph scenes of accidents and was able to film the entity as he leapt to confront this strange intruder. He also switched on the vehicle's flashing red light, at which point the being ran off down a gravel track. The police chief got back in the car and pursued the figure down the track but lost it in the dark.

Within a month, Greenshaw was forced out of his job and had to leave town; the mayor had demanded his resignation in the wake of publicity following the incident. The police chief's trailer home was also burnt down amidst what appears to have been a hate campaign put into operation by unknown elements. Some suspect he was 'set up' for the alien contact by hoaxers out to make him look ridiculous and thereby lose his job – the 'alien' could have been a normal human wearing a fire-resistant suit.

However, Greenshaw has always claimed that the government sent investigators to visit him after his encounter and they had said that a UFO was tracked on radar and had come down near Falkville that night. They had documentary proof that would be released 'soon' to vindicate the policeman's story. Of course, no such evidence

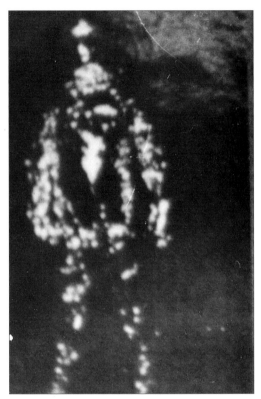

Alien or actor?
One of the photographs taken in October 1973 by Jeff Greenshaw, the chief of police of Falkville, Alabama. Was he the first man to successfully film a living alien or was he the victim of a cruel hoax?

was ever made public and Greenshaw was naturally furious that the government had failed in their promise to back him up and had lost him his job. In 1979 Greenshaw said: 'You can try to forget it...but it isn't really possible. Not when you did your duty and your life changed for ever.'

Exactly a day after Greenshaw's fateful encounter, the four-man crew of an Army Reserve Huey helicopter almost collided with a UFO over the town of Mansfield, Ohio. The object, which was shaped like a submarine,

THE SPACE PROGRAM

In 1973, NASA was still reeling from the public disinterest in space activities that had developed after the moon landings. Its scientific endeavours were being treated more as a matter of academic interest rather than making front page headlines.

Nevertheless, interesting developments were taking place. On May 14, Skylab 1 put into orbit the first semi-permanent space station. Three crews of astronauts went up during the year and each set a progressive record for the length of time in space. These missions were set up to research the effects of prolonged exposure of humans to the gravity-free environment of space. If mankind was ever to conquer space, then journeys of the order now being developed on Skylab would be essential.

An equally seminal event occurred on December 3. After voyaging for several years, the unmanned space probe Pioneer 10 passed Jupiter.

Gateway to the stars
A launch gantry and rocket at Cape Canaveral, Florida. It was from here in 1973 that NASA launched its Skylab 1 space station and the Pioneer 10 space probe. Pioneer passed Jupiter on route to becoming, in 1983, the first vehicle from planet earth to leave our solar system. It still flies on, and will continue to do so.

THE FIRST CROP CIRCLES

The 'saucer nest' at Wokurna, South Australia, as photographed by Peter Horne. The similarity with later British crop circles is undeniable. UFOs were often sighted around these 'nest' formations in the 1960s and '70s.

The fisherman's tale

The most dramatic encounter in the southern US states that autumn occurred on the Pascagoula River in Mississippi. Charles Hickson and Calvin Parker had their fishing expedition interrupted by three aliens.

headed straight for them and stopped dead in its tracks; it was close enough to fill the helicopter's windscreen. What happened next defied all the known laws of aeronautics. A green beam swept down from the UFO and seemed to hold the helicopter suspended in mid-air. This weird beam was also seen by several witnesses on the ground.

The UFO then flew away and the crew of the Huey felt the helicopter being sucked upwards by an invisible vortex. This was despite the fact that the pilot had the controls positioned for a gentle descent. After a short while, the controls returned to normal and the startled crew were left to file an official report with the military authorities.

Sceptics have claimed that the UFO was a meteor, but this seems ridiculous given the size of the alien craft and the three-minute duration of the encounter, not to mention the unexplained behaviour exhibited by the helicopter. UFO investigator Jennie Zeidman conducted a major inquiry into the incident and, after reviewing the witnesses' accounts, came to the conclusion that this was one of the most impressive cases of a UFO sighting on record.

Fisherman's tale

This alien wave also produced a remarkable case involving two fishermen, Charlie Hickson, aged 42, and Calvin Parker, aged 19. At around

9pm on October 11, Hickson and Parker Strange were reeling in catfish from an abandoned shipyard at Pascagoula, Mississippi, when they heard a strange 'zipping' noise coming from somewhere behind them. They turned to see an oval object with windows and blue lights that had come low down over a nearby clearing.

A door opened and three figures floated out. Hickson and Parker got the same odd impression as the woman in Somerset – that these creatures were robots. They stood 5 feet tall with claw-like hands and drifted silently towards the shocked men. Two of the beings grabbed Hickson by the arms and he felt a stinging sensation in his shoulder. Before entering semi-consciousness, he saw that his young companion had fainted and was in the process of being dragged towards the object by the third figure.

Memories of what happened during the next 20 minutes are dim. There were bright interior lights, a feeling of suspension and the sight of an eye-like object that moved across their bodies as if it were scanning them. Then the men were deposited back by the riverbank.

Just before the object took off, Hickson claims he heard a voice 'in my mind' say, 'We are peaceful. We meant you no harm.' He claimed to have heard this several times afterwards and felt that the aliens wanted him to stress their benign intent.

Hickson and Parker now sat in their car for 20 minutes composing themselves before going into town. They called a local Air Force base but were told that the US government had stopped investigating UFOs and they should contact the police. The Sheriff asked them to make a statement and they were closely questioned for two hours.

The men impressed Sheriff Fred Diamond and his officers with their sincerity and very obvious terror. Almost from the start they insisted that they should take a polygraph (a lie detector test) and demanded a promise (which was sadly not fulfilled) that the police would give them no publicity.

Intriguingly, the two men were left alone in the interview room and, unknown to them, secretly tape-recorded. The trick was set up with the expectation that their private conversations might reveal their story to be a hoax. But the tape shows no change in behaviour. The men talked to each other in the same shocked tones, Parker telling Hickson he wanted to leave to consult a doctor and Hickson repeating that nobody could be expected to believe them. When left briefly on his own the teenager can be heard praying, 'Oh god, it's awful.'

Utterly stunned by these events the sheriff then arranged for the men be taken to the nearby air base where they could be given a thorough medical examination. A strange 'cut' mark was found where blood samples could have been taken from the witnesses. Parker and Hickson were also interrogated at length by military officers who were left just as impressed as the Sheriff had been by their evident sincerity.

A few days later Charlie Hickson took a polygraph test, after which operator Scot Glasgow said, 'This son of a bitch is telling the truth'. He went on to say, rather more reflectively, 'I am convinced that he believes he saw a spaceship.'

Meanwhile, Calvin Parker was in a nursing home, having suffered a nervous breakdown attributed by medical staff to the stress of the terrifying encounter. He recovered only gradually.

In 1987 I met Charles Hickson. He struck me as being a simple, honest man who had never sought attention.

'I had to learn to accept what happened,' he said, 'because I saw what happened to a man who could not accept it. This thing almost destroyed his [Parker's] life. I was offered all kinds of money to let them do a movie. I declined. I am still declining. Making money is not what this experience is about.'

1974: Euro Rendezvous

Up the wall

During this winter Belgium and Holland had their first major wave of alien-contact sightings. Some were rather unusual.

As the old year ran out at Vilvorde in Belgium, a man paying a late-night visit to the lavatory got the shock of his life – instead of total darkness, a green glow illuminated his back yard and a scraping noise was heard. Walking across some loose rubble was a 4-foot tall being dressed in a one-piece suit and a backpack. It was holding an object like a metal detector but more the size of a vacuum cleaner, sweeping it over the ground as if searching for treasure.

Desperate to see more, the witness shone his flashlight at the being and illuminated large round eyes. The alien responded by holding up his hand and displaying a 'V' (for victory?) sign with its fingers! Holding the device in front at arms' length, the being then promptly moved towards the wall and literally walked up the stonework and over the top in complete defiance of gravity. As it climbed the wall, its body was sticking out at a 90-degree angle as if magnetic boots were holding it firmly in place. After it climbed over the wall, a hissing sound started from the open land beyond. Within moments a small object with a transparent cupola on top appeared, having risen just above the height of the back-yard wall. Suddenly sparks shot from it, the sound increased and the object sped away. A few weeks later a similar object appeared above the man's car as he, his wife and cousin were

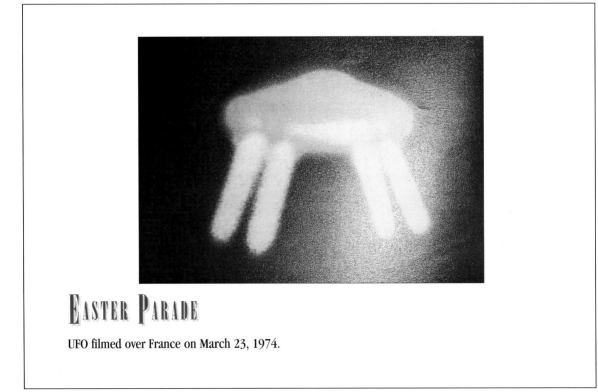

Easter Parade

UFO filmed over France on March 23, 1974.

driving near Koningslo. The engine and lights of the car failed, but when the object flew off they started for themselves again.

Car trouble was also reported at Warneton near the French border on January 17. The driver was baffled as the engine spluttered, the lights dimmed and the cassette player stopped working. He then noticed that an object shaped like an army helmet had landed near by. Two beings were walking across the fields towards him. They were about 4 feet tall with pear-shaped heads and grayish skins. Their eyes were large and rounded.

One of the beings wore a suit like the 'Michelin Man' formed of rolled material. The other was more robotic in nature and had a glass helmet. Both walked in a peculiar, stiff gait and came very close to the car. They stared in at the occupant as if he were an exhibit in a zoo. Despite his fear, the car driver could not escape. A peculiar buzzing sensation was tickling the back of his head.

There was then a noise from the road and the beings swirled around together, clearly attracted by it. It turned out to be an approaching car, which immediately caused the entities to return to their craft. Moments later it took off and the car regained all power.

A man got out of the other car and introduced himself to the stunned driver as a resident of a nearby village. He said that he had seen the UFO and entities and would gather some villagers to search for evidence. If they found any, then he would go public. If they found nothing he would remain silent. As this witness was never heard from again we can only presume that no proof was discovered.

An observed abduction

After the disappointments of the Maureen Puddy case in Australia, it began to look as if there were never going to be independent witnesses to UFO abductions. However, a case on March 23 in the small Swedish village of Vallentuna was a different matter.

Anders – son of a local electrician – was walking home towards Lindholmen late at night when a beam of light shot from a small hillock beside the country path. He lost consciousness in the blinding light and awoke some time later outside his own house. His wife was tending to burns on his body and asking him what had happened. Anders could not remember.

Dr Ture Arvidsson from the local hospital cared for Anders and hypnotized him to try to discover what had happened. This revealed a story of Anders being sucked up into the air by the blinding light and finding himself in a strange room. There were tall beings who used instruments to study his skin. Then they told him they would not allow him to remember any more but would drop him off at home – saving quite a walk!

Interestingly, Anders never thought that he had encountered a UFO or aliens. Such concepts were not discussed in this remote part of Sweden, where alien abductions had never been debated in 1974. His view was that he had met local trolls who, legend had it, lived in the hills. There had been centuries of stories of people meeting trolls and being taken away.

What makes this case even more intriguing is that there were several other witnesses to the UFO that night, including a woman who was walking on the road on the far side of the same hillock. She saw the beam of light that struck Anders, but did not see him – meaning that he was not there any more or she missed him in the dark. Unfortunately, this means we cannot answer the question as to whether the witness really was taken away (by aliens or trolls)!

Abduction UK

What was then thought to be Britain's first known abduction case happened later that year and proved to be highly significant.

The date was October 27 and a young family from Aveley in Essex were the victims. They had been out to see relatives near by and were hurrying home to watch a play on television. It was 10.20 pm and they were nearing their house, with John Day driving, his wife Sue in the front seat and their three children (aged between 4 and 8) half asleep in the back.

A blue light appeared briefly in the sky and they wondered what it was. Then, rounding a bend on the country road, they drove straight into a bank of green mist that straddled their path. There was no way of avoiding it, but they were only inside for a moment or two before they emerged out of the far side with a bump. Inside the mist the radio set started to splutter and crackle and John, fearing a short circuit, instinctively yanked out the wires.

Moments later they were back home. John, annoyed with himself, stayed in the car to fix the wiring. Sue went to put the children to bed and when she switched on the television she could only get an off-air signal from the set. The play was long finished and bafflingly the clock read 1 am. Sue was so astonished that she called the speaking clock to confirm the time. It was true. Over two hours had disappeared in the final few hundred yards of their journey home.

In the months that followed, the family's life changed drastically. They became fascinated by new-age ideas and altered their diet and lifestyle. Various paranormal phenomena such as poltergeist outbreaks occurred in the house and they all started to have nightmares in which a horrible monster-like face would appear. The children were especially terrified by these shared visions.

Eventually the family sought help from Dr Leonard Wilder. Despite his lack of knowledge about UFOs, Wilder was a skilled regression hypnotist and took both adults (the children were too young) back to that night. Later sessions were carried out at the Days' home and I attended one of these in early 1978 – my first direct taste of an abduction. During the session I was able to interview Sue Day and talk through her to the aliens, a quite bizarre experience.

The Days described how their car was stopped inside the mist and they were taken aboard by tall figures in silver suits with cat-like eyes. The horrible faces from the dreams were of small trained 'examiners' who studied the witnesses. Whilst inside the UFO the Days seem to have been 'out of the body' and even saw themselves inside the car in the middle of the UFO while they 'floated' outside with their alien captors.

The aliens revealed that their world was blighted by an environmental disaster, and showed holographic images of it. They had been watching humans for many years, regarding us almost as their protégés, and noted that we were part of a genetic experiment which seemed to involve children in some way. These aspects all fit the developing pattern of an ongoing alien plan.

Alien assault

At about the same time as the Aveley case was being investigated,

The Aveley abduction
The family who were abducted at Aveley in Essex became Britain's first 'spacenapping'. Their adventure began when they drove into this bank of mist.

THE WORLD SAYS WOW!

With the dramatic new spate of alien-contact cases flooding in from around the world, scientists had a new wave of enthusiasm in their search for alien signals from a distant star.

A new SETI programme was initiated by Bob Dixon at a research site in Ohio, scouring the universe for messages. Unlike the previous failed attempts, this one had a brief moment of success. One signal was recorded which showed signs of being artificial in origin. Scientists checked it over and there seemed to be no doubt. This really was a constructed signal – a message of some sort – being beamed across the light years from a source far across the universe. So stunned was Dixon that he wrote the letters WOW! across the chart recording the signal.

Unfortunately, the so-called WOW! signal was never repeated. Despite scientists making frequent searches through the same part of the sky, nothing like it was ever picked up again.

So what was the truth? Was this a freak effect – a natural signal that resembled a message? Was it just a one-off transmission that we happened to intercept? Or was it yet another example of the confusion that seems to dog this subject?

Nobody knows, but at least the WOW! signal gave new impetus to those who sought radio signals from space. It was now clear that this sort of project was not a vast waste of time and money and that signals from space were possible after all.

Barry King and Andy Collins were following up an encounter from the previous year.

In this case an Italian emigree woman driving on a country road near Langford Budville in Somerset found that her car had stalled. As she got out to investigate, she was assaulted by a tall robotic being that struck her on the shoulder and caused her to lose consciousness.

What followed next is astonishingly like the Villas Boas case from Brazil in 1957. The woman awoke inside a room surrounded by men of average height with large round eyes. She was totally naked and laid out on a table, with cubes and other devices being moved across her body as if they were taking readings. Samples of nail and blood were then painlessly extracted and a suction device was placed over her genitals, causing a pulling sensation.

The woman felt as if she was being studied like a laboratory animal by entities who showed no emotion. One being stuck a pin in her thigh and she felt her throat go sore. She was utterly paralysed as the man raped her in a mechanical fashion. Throughout this time she kept her eyes closed. He then helped her from the table and she collapsed.

Her next memory is of being near the car completely clothed, with the UFO no longer in sight. She drove home in total despair and broke down when telling her husband what had happened. After much discussion they decided not to make the story public as they felt that nobody would believe them and the woman felt too ashamed of the affair. When the story did emerge it was with great reluctance and an insistence on anonymity.

As time went by, the family had further encounters with UFOs and aliens but they have chosen to remain quiet – they have never tried to cash in on the money and notoriety that such a story could easily bring. Indeed, this tends to be very much the way abductees go about things. Gain or publicity of any kind is the last thing on their minds: they simply want to purge their lives of a terrifying memory.

Yet again we have a case of some sort of alien genetic experiment on a terrified witness. When this case was documented in 1977, even UFOlogists were still not aware of the pattern behind such cases. It is very difficult to imagine that all these witnesses could independently have made up stories that wove together so readily.

1975: GLOBAL ENCOUNTERS

Restricted access

Although there was now a steady flow of alien contact stories from Europe, Australasia and both North and South America, there were gaps in global sightings. Very few cases were emerging from vast areas of the world, including India and China. Although communications with the west were poor and many sightings may simply not have been reported, it was as if aliens had restricted access to a few places.

On February 14 an interesting case occurred on the island of Reunion in the Indian Ocean. A 21-year-old shop worker called Antoine Severin came upon a domed object that had landed in a field near Petite Ile. A number of small beings, under four feet tall, had emerged from it and were busily engaged in examining the local flora. Antoine was spotted by the beings as he approached them and one of them immediately projected a beam of light from his belt. This light beam knocked him to the ground, leaving him dazed and paralysed. Meanwhile the aliens gathered up soil samples, climbed back into their UFO and took off skywards.

The stunned witness was left unable to speak and with poor eyesight for several days. According to a psychiatrist who helped the man regain his health, this was a reaction to the shock of the encounter.

Local police investigated the matter and took him seriously. In conclusion, Lieutenant-Colonel Lobet, who was in charge of the case, summed it up by terming the man 'well balanced' and 'well behaved' and seemed to rule out any possibility of a hoax.

UFO MOTORS OVER TOYOTA

UFO filmed at Toyota City, Japan, on August 3, 1975.

Not what they seem

Elsewhere in the world aliens may not be recognized because what we might interpret as alien visitations tend to be regarded differently by the cultures of local populations.

Cynthia Hind has investigated several stories from tribal villages in mid-Africa in which glowing beings and balls of light have been described. These remote outposts have generally never heard of UFOs and aliens and consider their encounters to be meetings with ancestral spirits. But there are undoubted similarities with alien contact.

Fascinating reports have also emerged from Indonesia and Malaysia which contain features common to many alien abductions. These include encountering small human-like beings, bright lights, being taken to a 'house' where time flows at a different rate and noticing how all sounds of the environment disappear during the presence of the visitors. This is the classic 'Oz Factor', which has been reported during so many alien-contact cases.

In one case from Bandjar in Java, a man was taken to such a bright 'house' and a female entity indicated that she must have sex with him. The witness was unable to refuse and then lost consciousness, finding himself outside with no clothes on – these were found up a tree. Rather than rush to the nearest hypnotist to reveal the truth about an abduction by the grays, the witness was put under the care of the local shaman, or medicine man, whose task it was to heal his soul.

Such encounters are thought in Indonesia to be with a group of beings known as the Bunian, who co-exist with us on earth in a realm where time and space follow different rules.

Do aliens mould themselves to take a form that is culturally relevant? This might be suggested by the differences found between cases around the world. There are undoubtly broad similarities. But their actual appearance (such as Nordics or grays) and the way they are interpreted by the contactees (ranging from folklore creatures to beings from another planet) seems to depend upon the culture that is involved.

Jellymen have landed

Has anyone really seen what these beings may look like? Perhaps one case from July 22, 1975 offers a clue. The after-effects on this witness should be compared with those reported by the man on Reunion a few months earlier, as they are intriguingly similar.

Trevor was a teenage boy on holiday with his family in Dovey Vale, Wales, near the town of Machynlleth. He climbed Wylfa Hill at sunset and was astonished to see an amazing sight on the grass. It was a dome-shaped object with a transparent surface and made up of weird colours that were totally unfamiliar to him. The colours were pulsing in and out of visibility, as were two beings that were small but otherwise little more than lumps of jelly – or more like blood corpuscles in a constant state of flux. When one of these entities began to come out of the dome-shaped object Trevor ran down the hill to urge his father to return with him. He ran back up the summit, assuming that his father would follow.

At the top of the rise the object was still visible but the 'jellyman' was back inside. The craft then began to fade in and out of reality in a way that Trevor found almost impossible to describe three years later when he came forward. He likened it to a chameleon blending into the background. The odd colours suddenly became grass green, sky blue and so on, and the craft shimmered into nothingness.

Trevor suffered horribly after this encounter. Within 24 hours he lost his voice and then his sight. It took months of care from doctors and psychologists to steer him back to health. They were sure that a severe mental shock had somehow brought about this hysterical response in a psychosomatic illness.

Was that because he had seen the aliens as they really were and watched them disappear?

The American wave

At the end of October and beginning of November, the USA experienced another rash of alien contacts, two of which were to prove of great importance.

On October 27 (a year to the day after the Aveley abduction) two men in woods at Oxford, Maine, were listening to music late at night when they had a protracted encounter with strange lights flashing exotic colours. A bank of fog from nowhere surrounded the car and they lost a period of time, regaining awareness elsewhere in the forest. The links with other cases here are very clear.

When they arrived home, the two men spent 48 hours hallucinating, something they freely admitted and which tricksters were hardly likely to do. As an example, they saw snow falling indoors. They were also unable to co-ordinate their speech or body motions. It was as if they could not switch back into normal reality after their encounter with the UFO.

One of the men was so upset that his whole life had changed that he moved 2000 miles away from the woods. The other was treated by Dr Herbert Hopkins and agreed to be hypnotically regressed. Under hypnosis he recalled being taken to a strange room by small beings with heads shaped like lamps and cat-like eyes. They made him lie on a table and extracted hair and blood samples, but were not unkind during the process. They told him that he would meet them again and said they had planted tasks into his subconscious mind which would be awoken at a later date. He would only remember to do these tasks when the time was right.

Dr Hopkins and his family then found themselves victims of bizarre visitations at their home from what appear to be 'Men in Black'. There was a man and a strange woman who seemed ill at ease in human form. They left after asking odd questions about the case, saying that they were running low on energy.

In another forest thousands of miles away, a group of young men had one of the most famous alien contacts of all on November 5. To this day the arguments rage about whether it was just a scam to make money or escape a logging contract that was proving too difficult. The witnesses have always denied this and they passed lie-detector tests to back them up.

The scene was the Sitgreave National Forest near Snowflake, Arizona, and the witnesses were a logging crew in a truck driven by Mike Rogers. On their way home, they observed an object that looked like two pie tins stuck together; when they stopped for a closer look, one of the crew, Travis Walton, leapt out of the truck and ran towards the UFO. It was now emitting a beeping sound (a rare feature of alien-contact cases that is also found in the Hill abduction). A beam of light then shot from it like lightning, striking Travis on the chest and tossing him through the air. Convinced that he was dead, the other men fled from the scene.

Some minutes later, Rogers insisted that they return to help their stricken friend. There was no sign of the UFO or of Walton. Back in town, the Sheriff suspected a hoax, but when a search on horseback, then with helicopters, failed to find the missing woodsman, his thoughts turned towards the possibility of foul play. Was the UFO story a cover for misdeeds, or possibly even murder?

Five days later, Walton phoned his brother in a disorientated state from a phone booth at nearby Heber. He claimed to have awoken in a strange room where he was given a medical examination by small beings with heads like overgrown foetuses and very large eyes. He was shown 'film' of stars and saw UFOs in a giant hangar but recalled little else about the previous five days.

Police were unconvinced and medical opinion was split about the case. It is very different from almost every other abduction story. Travis Walton and Mike Rogers themselves seemed amiable and believable. Walton wrote two books and a movie was eventually made about the case 18 years later (although it

BETTY AND BARNEY ON TV

Worth noting in connection with these American cases is that the movie *The UFO Incident*, which was made for US television in 1975 and aired in late October of this year, just as the wave unfolded. This was a well told and fairly accurate dramatization of the Betty and Barney Hill abduction case from 1961. As such, it was the first movie that was based upon an actual UFO case and it set new standards in this genre.

Of course, the appearance of the movie had another effect. Prior to late-1975 there were few people aware of the details of the alien contact. Stories had been told in the press and in books, but millions had now seen them dramatized, including the form of the grays, the medical examination and hints about genetic experimentation. No abduction case reported after October 1975 could be immune from the possible contamination that *The UFO Incident* introduced. The way in which abductions are carried out was no longer an open secret.

This allowed critics to ask whether the 'beeping' heard in the Walton abduction was proof that the abduction really had taken place (because it mirrored the Hills' experience) or whether an element of conscious or subconscious copying was at work? The line between fact and fiction is blurred within the abduction mystery because at heart it is a phenomenon of consciousness. After the Hill movie, however, no abduction story could be taken at face value, at least not without reference to its possible, if subtle, influence.

Another extraordinary revelation occurred in 1975 with the publication of research by Robert Temple into the Dogon tribe of west Africa. Reliably dated artefacts had proved a centuries-old tradition that the Dogon had been taught secrets of astronomy by what they termed a race of beings from a planet around the star Sirius. The Dogon knew things that scientists only discovered in modern times – such as the fact that Sirius was a multiple star system and Saturn had rings.

Controversy continues over the interpretation of this evidence but it is hard to study the Dogon traditions and not suspect they knew things long ago that could only have been told them by aliens who had seen our solar system close up. The Dogon also describe the alien ship arriving in a way that sounds stunningly familiar. Remember that this account was written centuries ago:

'The ark landed and displaced a pile of dust raised by the whirlwind it caused. The violence of its impact roughened the ground. It is like a flame that went out when it touched the earth.'

seriously distorted the 'on-board abduction' sequence to make it look different from other cases, apparently on orders from the studio!).

The year also produced another intriguing alien abduction at Alamogordo in the New Mexico heartland where someone, or something, had been spying on top-secret American defensive technologies since 1947.

At 1.15 am on August 13, USAF sergeant Charles Moody was observing the spectacular meteor shower visible in the northern hemisphere each year around that date. Suddenly he saw something that was no meteor: in fact, it was a huge metal disc.

Seeking escape Moody leapt into his car but it would not operate. All power was gone. Meanwhile a high-pitched hum filled the air and a strange numbness began to overpower his body. Just before he lost consciousness the USAF officer could see humanoid forms moving behind a window in the disc.

Moody awoke to see the UFO departing. It was now 3am. His car worked perfectly and he drove back to base for a long sleep. Next day, however, he developed aching pains and a rash and his doctor, not suspecting what had happened during the missing two hours, proposed hypnosis to ease the problem. In fact, under hypnosis Moody recalled being examined on a slab inside the UFO by one small and two tall entities, all with bald heads and pale skin. They told him they would return to make closer contact with the Earth and reveal their presence in about the year 1995.

1976: THE ALIEN ARMADA

Spain opens its doors

The increasing awareness of UFOs was beginning to have a political effect. In 1976, US President Jimmy Carter was elected and the 1977 Freedom of Information Act released thousands of documents from the archives of the USAF, CIA, FBI and other intelligence agencies.

Other countries followed suit. Robert Galley, the French Minister of Defence, revealed that French Air Force planes had pursued and tracked UFOs on radar without catching them. He set up a scientific investigation team, known as GEPAN and based at the space centre in Toulouse. Set up in 1977, it is the only officially funded scientific UFO group in the world.

Spain was next in line. On October 20, 1976, government files on UFO cases were released to the public. This included a detailed report into a dramatic event over the Canary Islands.

On June 22 a Spanish naval vessel – the *Atrevida* – just off Punta Lantailla on the island

UFO over Gran Canaria
Spain was invaded by UFOs during 1976 at the Spanish government opened up its files. They included this photo of a UFO over the Canary Islands also witnessed by dozens of other people. Aliens were seen inside the UFO.

of Fuerteventura had spotted a yellow-blue light coming off the island and heading out to sea. A beam projected from this onto the sea creating an arc of colour. After hovering for a while, it moved off towards the island of Gran Canaria.

On this island Don Francisco-Julio Padron Leon was the doctor at the town of Guia. The son of a sick woman had come to collect him that night and the two men were travelling by taxi through Las Rosas when the huge ball of electric blue light appeared and hovered near by.

The men told a military enquiry that it was like a giant soap bubble. It hovered for 20 minutes. They observed two beings over 7 feet tall, wearing red clothing like diving suits of a shade none of them had seen before. The heads were pear-shaped and they moved tubes up and down inside the sphere whilst touching what seemed like instruments.

Eventually the UFO climbed upwards and began to expand in size. It changed into a whitish-yellow spindle or saturn shape and headed away towards the island of Tenerife, making a whistling noise.

The doctor explained how he had tested whether the incident was an hallucination by insisting that the aliens had worn blue suits. The other witnesses refused to accept this, saying that the colour was red, and the doctor then realized they had all seen the same being.

There were other factors that persuaded the Air Force that this was real alien contact. Firstly, a field of onions at Galdar near Las Rosas was found next day in which a wide circular area, 100 feet in diameter, had been destroyed by high temperatures.

Just as importantly, photographs were taken of the object by the passengers and crew on an inter-island ferry. The photographs show a huge

THE SOUND OF SPACE

The event of the year was undoubtedly the brilliant NASA success in making a soft landing on Mars in July. Colour photographs of the red desert landscape and sky with clouds were more like earth than had been expected. The hope that Mars might host some form of life after all was resurrected. When chemical experiments carried out by the lander seemed to reveal microbes in the soil, scientists thought the quest for alien reality was over. But the reactions stopped minutes later and it was eventually decided that this was just a chemical response that imitated life and not life itself.

Perhaps even more more important was the message picked up by the radio astronomy project known as Cyclops on February 14 this year. It contained a complex pattern of fluctuating sounds and rhythms not unlike music but incredibly advanced and expressionist in nature. Some notes were beyond the range of human hearing as if the message was not intended for our ears at all. Indeed the (as yet unrepeated) message came from Ophiuchi, a star 17 light years away and a prime candidate for habitable planets given its similar nature to our own sun. But this alien 'song' was by-passing earth altogether and aimed at another star – Eta Cassiopeiae, which lies some 18 light years beyond us!

yellow globe hanging over the coastal town. The object was also detected by military radar.

Shoot-out

Within days, the Spanish Government faced a new case on a military base at Talavera La Real near Badajoz on the Portuguese border. On November 12 at 1.45 am, two sentries on guard duty heard a high-pitched whistling sound. By the time they had gone to investigate, it was so intense that it hurt their ears.

The noise was heard three times in total, each lasting about five minutes and a few minutes apart. On the third occasion, a bright light illuminated the area for about 15 seconds.

These two men (Jose Trejo and Juan Lujan) were now joined by a third guard, Jose Hidalgo, who brought one of the Alsatian guard-dogs to sniff out any intruders. They called out the rest of the security force whilst Trejo, Lujan and Hidalgo went to search with the dog.

Hidalgo sent the dog to investigate bushes where a 'whirlwind' had started up and then suddenly ceased. It ran from the bushes whimpering and covering its ears. It was sent into the bushes twice more, with the same result. Then it began to circle the guard in a way it was trained to do when sensing danger.

Suddenly an eerie phosphorous green glow was seen. This materialized into a half-formed figure, arms outstretched, but with no feet and seeming to float near the ground. It was made up of tiny dots of light.

As Trejo raised his automatic rifle to shoot, he felt paralysed, then grew weak and collapsed onto the ground. As he fell, he warned the others, 'Down! They will kill us!' He remained conscious but quickly began to lose his sight.

Lujan and Hidalgo shot 50 rounds at the being. Being only a few feet away, they should not have missed. The bullets seemed to pass right through the apparition and there was a huge flash. The being then vanished.

Trejo was dragged off, semi conscious and with a pain in his chest. Not a single cartridge case was ever found and a stone wall behind where the figure had stood showed no marks. Air Force munitions experts did, however, confirm that the two guns (Z-62s) had been discharged as the men had claimed.

The bright glows (the colours are similar to those seen in laser-produced holograms) and the whining noise do suggest an electronically created apparition – perhaps a form of living hologram. But a hologram produced by whom and for what purpose?

1977: INVESTIGATIONS

The wave continues

As the 30th anniversary of the UFO mystery arrived, it was Britain that found itself in the thick of a new wave. Between March and May 1977, the Pennine Hills became active as one of Europe's busiest window areas, with dozens of close encounters reported.

A fascinating case in April occurred at Worrall on the outskirts of Sheffield. A young courting couple who had parked in a lovers' lane had never heard of the cases at Dakelia barracks or on the Spanish Air Force base at Talavera just five months earlier. But they saw something chillingly similar.

Suddenly their car radio began to fill with static and ahead of them was a giant hemisphere, not unlike the one that had flown over the Canary Islands the previous summer. It glowed a vivid orange colour. Inside this hemisphere was a tall being, again very like the one encountered on Gran Canaria. It was dark in outline and appeared to be walking towards the couple. As it did so, the hemisphere moved in their direction, floating like a hologram or projected image. They decided not to hang around to see any more and backed rapidly out of the lane. Moments later, daring to take another peek from the security of the main road at the bottom, they found that the lane was now empty. The weird apparition had simply disappeared.

Gone away

That same week one of the strangest abductions of all occurred in Chile at 3.50 am on April 25 on a frozen plateau 12,000 feet above the town of Putre. It befell a group of six conscripted soldiers camping out on a training exercise, with regular soldier Corporal Armando Valdes in command of the troop.

Pedro Rosales, who was on sentry duty, first spotted some purple lights that were projecting a glow onto the ground as they descended. When alerted, Valdes quickly put his experience to work, ordering the men to douse the camp fire because it could be an attack. The purple glow – one big central light and further lights at each side – had now landed on the slopes ahead. After telling his men to cover him with their weapons, Valdes said that he would go to investigate.

After a few moments the Corporal was swallowed up in the darkness of the mountain side. A few seconds after that, the purple glow had disappeared and the young men were left in a state of shock, wondering how to deal with this situation.

After about fifteen minutes of confusion, there was a noise behind them and the soldiers turned round to see their leader staggering through the gloom in their direction. He seemed to be in a daze or trance and was muttering – as if to himself – 'You do not know who we are or where we come from. But I tell you – we shall return.' He then collapsed onto the ground beside his men.

As dawn arrived over the mountain, Valdes was still in a state of shock and semi conscious. But the soldiers had a new riddle to confront them. They saw that their commander had suddenly developed a heavy beard growth as if he had not shaved in days, yet they knew that Valdes had been clean shaven the night before. Even more remarkably, his digital watch had stopped at 4.30 am, with the date setting on April 30 – five days ahead of the actual date.

The group took their officer down to the nearby town where the schoolmaster took charge and began to conduct investigations.

CE3K

This was a vintage year for science fiction, particularly with the release of *Star Wars* – the hugely popular movie that spawned sequels (and is still doing so as the millennium approaches!). More significant was the epic by Steven Spielberg, *Close Encounters of the Third Kind*, which was both a box office and critical success. It remains, in the opinion of many, the ultimate 'true life' movie about UFOs and aliens, with magical special effects and an intelligent storyline that have never been bettered.

'CE3K', as it is known affectionately to UFOlogists, is a fictional tale of a man obsessed by his UFO encounter and driven by some psychic impulse to get involved with the government cover-up of an imminent landing by aliens. It is very firmly rooted in UFO reality. Spielberg, personally very interested in the subject, worked with UFOlogists such as Allen Hynek and Jacques Vallee. Indeed, the film is in many ways a dramatization of Hynek's book, *The UFO Experience.* The data classification system from this book (as already widely adopted by the UFO field) provided the odd title and Hynek appeared in cinema trailers explaining it to a baffled public. Vallee's role was more subtle. The key character of a scientist leading the government study and musing about psycho-social factors was named Lacombe (played by actor François Truffaut). Many people were bemused as to why a Frenchman was running the otherwise very obviously American Government show. The reason is that Lacombe was based on Vallee. Hynek actually appears, Hitchcock-like, as himself in the climactic scene of the film meeting the aliens. In out-takes they were seen to stroke his beard!

Many of the scenes in the movie were recreated from actual cases such as Aveyron and Valensole. The aliens were designed to resemble the 'little men' so frequently seen. The entire movie is so rich in UFO metaphor and legend that it takes many viewings to take it all in.

There was huge public interest in this epic for many months. Stories about UFOs in the media reached unprecedented levels between late 1977 and early 1978 when it premiered around the world. But there was no new wave of alien contacts created by it – a kick in the teeth to sceptics who said that this film would make people see UFOs by the truckload. In fact, sightings actually fell in numbers for a short while afterwards.

Spielberg later edited the film into a 'special edition', adding a million-dollars' worth of new scenes – extra footage of the alien contact inside the UFO. For a time he was even planning a sequel. The sequel has never happened – but Spielberg's interest in UFOs persists to this day.

Welcome to Earth
One of the final scenes from *Close Encounters of the Third Kind* – a blockbuster Hollywood movie, directed by Steven Spielberg. Spielberg based much of the film on true-life accounts of alien encounters and Dr J Allen Hynek, Director of the Center for UFO Studies, actually took a cameo role in the film.

Once the army appeared, they soon put a stop to that, dragging Valdes away and stating that he was not going to talk in public.

There are clearly missing elements to this case. The full truth has never been revealed. General Julio Canessa, Vice-chief of the Chilean Army, explained that the only way to get Valdes to talk was on direct orders from President Pinochet himself. All that the corporal would say was that he did not recall the 'missing time'. It was 'a void in my mind. I do not even recall the words I spoke when I returned, but the kids in the patrol maintain I said them. We must wait. I shall talk one day.' We are still waiting.

1978: WE ARE NOT ALONE

Take-aways

The global nature of alien contacts was brought home in 1978 with reports of incidents coming in from all continents – including places that had not generated sightings before. That autumn, the Prime Minister of Grenada pushed through the first ever debate on UFOs at the United Nations to emphasize the worldwide nature of the issue. He spent so much time setting this up that he was deposed by a coup back home and the UN moves went no further than an impressive debate that featured astronauts and scientists like Hynek and Vallee backing calls for action.

On March 11 three young women were skywatching in the Waimata Valley near Gisborne, New Zealand, an area that had produced many UFO sightings. Camping out in their car on the warm night, they heard strange sounds and felt sensations of pressure on their bodies. Two hours of time were later found to be unaccounted for.

Several hypnosis sessions followed, during which a complex story emerged which implied that the women had been abducted – or rather two of them had been abducted, while the third was left behind.

The two who were 'taken' describe waking in a strange room on slabs upon which they were placed by human-like beings with pointed chins and large, dark, slanted eyes. One of the women was probed with instruments whilst the other was left alone. She reacted in fury, screaming at the aliens because of their 'degrading' medical examinations and said they were treated like guinea pigs.

There are remarkable parallels between this little-known case, which has had almost no publicity even within the UFO field, and several others, both before and after it.

On January 6, 1976, three women were abducted from their car at Stanford, Kentucky. One was not taken, a second was basically left alone and the third was given a painful medical examination. All three were devout Christians who insisted on taking lie detector tests to back up their story and all passed.

A few years later, in July 1981, three women were in a car near Telford, Shropshire, when they also lost a period of time and immediately drove to see the police. Hypnosis sessions with several different doctors gradually pieced together a memory in which one was left in the car, another was abducted but not medically examined, and a third was given a painful gynaecological study with samples taken.

The comparisons between these three cases on three different continents are so remarkable that they must either be direct copies of one another (for which there is no evidence whatsoever) or else they represent a genuine encounter which follows a clear and unusual pattern. Coincidence does not seem to be a factor here, especially given a fourth case which happened a few months after the Waimata Valley contact.

Red star abduction

The Soviet Union's first known abduction followed in May, 1978, at the Pyrogovskoye Lake. A young man named Anatoly, who was serving with the military, was walking along its shores when two beings appeared and communicated with him via a form of telepathy. They took him to a strange room – a description offered by many witnesses, who actually recall entering a 'UFO' much less often than you might imagine. They usually wake up in this odd white place with light oozing from unseen sources.

Anatoly spoke for some time with these human-like beings in shiny 'cellophane suits' and attempted to recruit their help to fight the evils of the world (including capitalism!). But they tried to explain why this sort of intervention was not possible. 'It would not be of any value if we helped the poor. Because then we would have to help the poorest of the rich and then everybody.'

These aliens were visiting from another galaxy and awaiting the time when the earth was ready for full contact. They gave him a drink which was said to be an amnesia-inducing agent. It has cropped up in other cases and witnesses say it tastes like salty lemonade.

Anatoly asked the aliens why an advanced civilization such as theirs did not drink alcohol – no doubt hoping for some vodka to wash down the foul taste of their brew. The beings replied with one of the few known examples of an extraterrestrial joke. 'Perhaps if we did then we would not be such an advanced civilization.'

The next thing the young man knew, he was lying alone by the lake. He walked home in a daze, feeling disorientated 'as if in a dream' (yet another common feature of these cases). His wife did not want him to talk about the incident for fear he would be locked away by a disbelieving government. But he had not done a job that he was assigned to do during the abduction period and so had no alternative but to report the events to his superiors.

Understandably, the Red Army thought that Anatoly was making the story up to evade a court martial for failing in his duty. However, after psychological analysis, hypnosis, batteries of tests and a lie detector scan they were persuaded that he was telling the truth.

Bush Aliens

During October and November – immediately prior to the UN debate – sighting levels really took off. South Africa provided a fascinating alien encounter in a remote area of the Groendal nature reserve between Despatch and Uitenhage. Four young men hiking in the reserve were witnesses. Three of the men spoke only Afrikaans, but one, the son of the local doctor, was able to speak good English.

Cynthia Hind followed up the case on site after an investigation by the local police had left them baffled. Two geologists from the University at Groendal also went into the bush to study physical evidence left behind.

The youths never used the terms UFOs or spacemen. They had no familiarity at all with alien-contact stories or science-fiction movies. In fact, they called the landed object which they had first seen through trees a 'shiny stone' and the two beings – whom they both argued did not walk, but glided 'as if on a trolley' – were 'silver men'.

The beings were tall and wore shiny aluminium foil and carried a box as they proceeded to ascend a steep hill without bending or stooping. Then they simply disappeared along with the 'stone'. Subsequent study by the police and university geologists found that the hillside was completely impenetrable and no human could have climbed it in the way described. However, the thick bracken had been flattened by something descending from above. There were also holes in the ground as if probes had been used and unusual footprints that experienced trackers said did not belong to any human or animal.

Police also logged various reports of UFOs over the reserve that same weekend, including a disc-like object seen to take off by a native woman who lived inside the remote bush.

Yet again, this case had a remarkable parallel half way around the world. Indeed, I was one of the first on the scene after service engineer Ken Edwards had encountered a man who appeared to be dressed in some sort of silver foil almost exactly as in this South African case. Ken's encounter had been on March 17, 1978, on a quiet access road at Risley in Cheshire in the north of England, outside an atomic energy plant.

The figure was seen to walk down a steep, bracken-filled embankment at an angle that was physically impossible for a human to duplicate. I tried it and if the witness was telling the truth (as I believe he was) then whatever was on that slope had to be floating, not walking. At the top of the embankment was a research building used in sensory deprivation experiments.

When the silver being reached the middle of the road, it stopped and faced Ken Edwards' van. Beams of light emerged like lightning and the figure walked on straight through a 10-foot-high security fence. It then simply vanished – just as the boys say the 'silver men' did in Groendal.

As with the South African case, the police were called and investigated. They were puzzled after they had tried to trick the witness in a failed effort to prove that he saw a man in a fire-resistant suit.

Ken Edwards' van radio receiver would not work after the encounter. An enormous power surge had been picked up by his aerial and had blown it apart from within. Soon afterwards, Ken also developed multiple cancers, from which he died at an early age. It is not possible to prove that the cancers resulted from the energy beam that struck his van. But if it did so much damage to his radio it surely could not have been good for his body.

Sayanora UFO

Japan's first known alien contact followed within 48 hours of the Groendal case. This was on October 3 on a mountain above Sayama City, where CB radio enthusiast Hideichi Amano had gone to 'tune in' free of interference. His young daughter Juri was with him for the ride.

Suddenly the car had filled with light and the engine and radio set were drained of all power. The witness turned to see what was happening and found that an orange beam was shining on his daughter's abdomen. He then felt a pressure pushed against his right forehead and Amano saw a small being with large ears staring in at him. A series of high-pitched noises and images

flashed through his head like a slide show in overdrive. Again, this is a frequent feature described by witnesses during their abduction – and is also intriguingly similar to the 'life review' often reported by people who claim to have a near-death experience.

The comparisons between such near-death experiences and alien abductions are marked. Both experiences commonly involve beams of light, a trip to a strange well-lit place, the appearance of wise beings who know all about the life of the witness, a promise of a future return and often a legacy of psychic phenomena and changed lifestyles. The only difference is in how we interpret them.

When Amano had regained his senses on the mountainside, both the light and the being had vanished and his watch had stopped, making it impossible for him to judge if there had been a time lapse. The car now working perfectly, he sped off, admitting that he never even looked back to see if Juri was alright until she asked for a glass of water because her throat was dry.

Amano says that something was planted into his mind during this encounter (another ongoing theme of such cases) and that somehow he knew that this would 'vibrate' when the time was right for him to perform a certain task.

The frightening image of an army of alien-programmed zombies in their millions all around us waiting (perhaps without knowing it) to be stirred into action emerges quite spookily from many cases of this type.

Psychic legacy

Many of the features that were cropping up in alien contacts by 1978 came together in an impressive case on November 22 at the village of Church Stowe in Northamptonshire, England.

Here, teachers resources manager Elsie Oakensen was returning from work when she drove underneath a dumbbell-shaped object that nobody else appears to have seen above a busy road. After turning off onto a country lane, her car was surrounded by flashing lights and its

MIRACLE REALITY

Throughout 1978 Spielberg's movie spread its message of friendly contact around the planet on a wave of public euphoria and vast commercial success. It said nothing about terrifying medical examinations and genetic experiments to create a human/alien baby. If the alien contact phenomenon was a fantasy provoked by changes in the collective unconscious, there is no doubt that the cases in 1978 and afterwards would have responded massively to the friendly, awe-inducing images of *Close Encounters of the Third Kind*. Instead, they continued the pattern that had gradually developed for over 20 years and which Spielberg had simply missed (as indeed by 1978 had most UFOlogists).

Yet there was one truly remarkable science-fiction story that year. It was a novel published around the world by British author Ian Watson entitled *Miracle Visitors*. It remains in many people's opinion (myself included) the best attempt yet to dramatize the extraordinary complexities of alien contact without resorting to clichés of little green men and spaceships.

In his wide-ranging novel, Watson conceived of something that he called 'UFO consciousness' – an altered state of reality in which many paranormal phenomena seem to change from being in a state of flux into a kind of semi-permanent reality. They are channelled into this dynamic and transient form by alien-contact witnesses who act almost in the same way as psychic mediums. Their abilities transform the other-dimensional reality into a sort of true reality that the rest of us are able to share temporarily.

Watson told me that during the writing of the novel, UFOs appeared frequently near his home as if to emphasize his case. When the novel was published, Watson lived in a small Northamptonshire village not far from the site of the encounters that befell Elsie Oakensen and the four women at Preston Capes. An alien contact had appeared immediately in the wake of this amazing novel and went a long way towards supporting its 'fictional' explanation for the close encounter and abduction phenomenon!

---

engine and lights stalled. Like Hideichi Amano in Japan, she felt a tightening sensation around her temples and her next memory is of being in her car further down the road, with the strange lights having vanished and a period of time unaccounted for.

Elsie later recalled a scene in which she was 'scanned' (and apparently rejected) by floating forms inside the light. She returned from her experience with renewed spiritual awareness and a belief in future contact.

About an hour later on a road at the nearby village of Preston Capes, four women travelling by car found themselves paced by a very similar object. Knowing nothing of Elsie's experience, they found their car engine and lights fading but believe that they just drove on and escaped the clutches of the UFO. All four women have resisted further investigation, preferring to forget whatever it was that happened that night.

Whether a deeper memory lurks in the subconscious of these other women we may never know. But the way in which Elsie Oakensen was apparently rejected for medical study (possibly because she was beyond child-bearing age at the time) and then four younger women in the same area were targeted in almost identical fashion so soon afterwards does seem very difficult to explain in any way other than as a concerted plan by some form of intelligent life.

Today Elsie Oakensen is a fine ambassador for fellow witnesses. A prime mover in a support group to represent their needs, she has tirelessly campaigned through the media to get their experiences taken more seriously. In 1996 she published a book describing her sighting but focusing just as much on the way the public and the media treated her because of her alien contact. It was given the name One Step Beyond by her publisher, but I think Elsie's own title – Why me? was far more appropriate.

1979: Angels or Demons?

The mince pie Martians

On January 4, angels came down to a British housewife and led to a case that has since been dubbed 'the mince pie Martians' affair. It also generated one of the more imaginative headlines afforded an alien contact – not 'Take me to your leader', but 'Take me to your larder'.

The location was Rowley Regis, a small town near West Bromwich. Jean Hingley had just seen her husband off to work when she noticed a light in the garden. Thinking he had left the light on in the carport, she went outside but saw nothing untoward.

Coming back indoors to feed her alsatian dog who had been in the garden, she noticed that he had flopped down beside her, glassy eyed and looking as if he had been drugged. Then there was a strange 'zee-zee' type noise and several small winged beings with waxy faces and dark eyes flew in, hovering just above the ground in shiny silvery suits.

These beings emitted a blinding light that 'floated' Jean a foot or so off the ground and through to her lounge. They drifted around the room inspecting the Christmas decorations and communicating with her by telepathy.

The conversation was most odd. They told her (helpfully) that 'we come from the sky'. She explained about the decorations and Christmas and they added, 'We know all about Jesus'. They said that they came 'to talk to people but they do not seem interested' – at which point Jean, ever the hospitable host, offered the aliens a drink and mince pies. They declined the water but took a mince pie (without eating it). When she then lit a cigarette, they fled in apparent horror, taking the mince pies with them. Jean followed them to the back door, observing that they floated into an egg-shaped craft on the ground. This then vanished in a silent flash of light.

Mrs Hingley called the police, but they did not know what to do other than call in a local UFO group. Fortunately, this allowed much of the evidence to be studied quickly. This included a clock that had stopped during the encounter and cassette tapes that were now unplayable – both seemingly subjected to a strong magnetic field.

However, the most interesting feature was an outline in the snow in the garden. This showed a boat-like object at about the point where the UFO had landed. Some researchers think this may be caused by the disturbed earth on the site of an old garden pond which a previous owner may have filled in.

Debate has raged as to whether this is a genuine alien contact or whether some kind of earth energy connected with the nearby quarries and a local TV transmitter might have triggered an hallucination inspired by the Christmas festivities. We will probably never know.

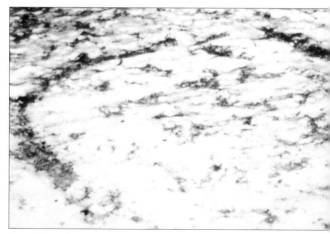

Touchdown!
The traces left in the snow at Rowley Regis, West Midlands, after the 'Mince Pie Martians' landing. Is the pattern the 'footprint' of an alien craft or the outline of an old pond, as sceptics suggest?

THE LIZARDS HAVE LANDED

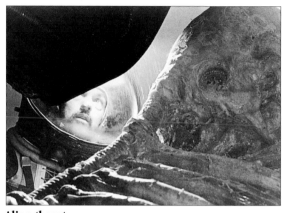

Alien threat
Ridley Scott's sci-fi thriller, *Alien*, captured the world's imagination with his story of an earth-shattering, alien nation.

The Ridley Scott movie, *Alien*, was a huge success in 1979, taking us away completely from Steven Spielberg's friendly aliens.

In the Hitchcock-style story, a horrible lizard-like creature stalks a spaceship, killing off the crew one by one. It has been followed by several sequels, though none matches the psychological terror of the original.

It is worth noting that no alien-contact cases have involved creatures of this type, despite the television series *V* (which followed the movie and adopted the same theme of evil reptilian entities). Once again, if alien contact cases were a reflection of – or a response to – popular culture, both *Alien* and *V* would have generated at least some lizard-alien cases in the early eighties.

The differences between celluloid fantasies and the realities of the ongoing alien contact saga could not be more obvious here.

The Devil Rides In

More devilish aliens appeared later in the year at Ponta Negra in Brazil. The case involved Luli Oswald, a celebrated concert pianist.

Luli was returning from Saquarema to Rio with a man to whom she had given a lift. As they drove along the coastal highway, a number of lights rose up from the water. They pulled the sea into a column before heading off towards the car, allowing the water to cascade back down.

As a pencil-shaped object with orange windows hovered near by, the car engine and lights began to fail. Three balls of white light then rolled down the hillside and surrounded the car; the couple passed out. When they regained consciousness, the car was now further down the road. Luli remembered that a nearby petrol station served coffee until late and, thinking it was only about 11.30 pm (as it had been when the UFO appeared), they drove there, only to discover that it was now 2 am.

Under hypnotic regression, Luli Oswald reported how the car and its occupants were sucked up into the UFO together. Her next memory was of standing by the car with several beings under 5 feet tall with pointed features.

Both she and the man were now naked and being probed by these creatures using beams of light. Hair samples were taken from Luli and a full gynaecological examination was carried out. The beings (communicating by telepathy) explained that she had been contacted because of her ability at ESP.

After the tests were over, Luli was informed that she was of no use. It was never explained why, but she was too old to have children and this might well have been the key. The man, who was aged 25, was apparently a good subject and, the aliens advised, 'will assist our research'. They examined his genitals and took samples of fluid.

Before returning Luli and this man to her car, the aliens told her that they came 'from a small galaxy near Neptune'. Her knowledge of astronomy was sufficient to know that this was nonsense, but, as she said, 'I can only tell you what they told me'.

1980: Back With a Bang

Alien secrets

When Aino Ivanoff was driving near Pudsjarvi, Finland, in the early hours of April 2, 1980, little did she know that she was about to learn the secrets behind the abduction mystery.

Suddenly her car was engulfed in a bank of mist that came from nowhere and caused her to lose consciousness. Her next memory was of awaking inside a strange, well-lit room where she was surrounded by small beings not much over 4 feet tall.

Aino was placed on a long table where the aliens were prodding her with various devices. They attempted to talk to her 'mind' and explain that war was evil and that she should join peace movements to try and make the world a better place. They wanted humankind to improve as a race but only we could achieve this for ourselves; they could not directly intervene.

Rather wistfully, the aliens looked at the young woman and explained that they were sterile in their own world. 'We cannot beget our own children', they emphasized. It was implied that they were hoping that humans might be able to help in the survival of their race – perhaps by a mixture of genetic material.

This case received little publicity in Finland and was little known elsewhere. But once again it emphasized the recurrent themes that were emerging from these cases but which, despite all the clues, no UFOlogist had managed to piece together.

Circular madness

Between June and August 1980, the first mysterious crop circles were found in an oat

The crop phenomenon
This aerial view of a Wiltshire crop circle displays the unusual design into which the flattened crops appear to have been manipulated. Two principal circles and two minor circles align with a key-like formation.

field near Warminster, Wiltshire. During the 1960s, this had been a location to which UFO buffs from all over the world had come to look for lights in the sky. It was, in effect, the Mecca of the UFO world. It is highly unlikely that these areas of gently flattened crop were appearing here by accident.

There were only three circles that summer and two were photographed by UFO experts. Over the next few summers, however, more circles would regularly appear in the fields around Wessex, initially attracting just a small number of local enthusiasts. It would be six or seven years before the circle mystery really caught the public's imagination, with media stories around the world and regular summer vigils. Those early circles also tended to be simple in design.

Even so, there was already tension between researchers certain that these circles were natural phenomena (citing other cases from many years ago such as those in Australia in the 1960s and '70s) and those who felt they represented a message laid down by the aliens to try to get the world to think more harmoniously. Of course, there were also the hoaxers who saw the opportunity for free publicity and a whole lot of fun that the fledging mystery had brought.

The price of fame

The first really big UFO wave since the release of *Close Encounters of the Third Kind* struck Britain in November and December l980. It produced a number of classic cases, including what would become the Britain's most famous alien abduction.

At 5.15 am on November 28, police officer Alan Godfrey was on duty at the small mill town of Todmorden, West Yorkshire, a highly active window area in the Pennines. He was looking for some cattle that had been plaguing a housing estate and taking one last trip in his patrol car before clocking off, he saw an object ahead that appeared to be an early-morning works bus. He then realized it was a dome-shaped craft spanning the road and spinning so fast that kerbside trees were shaking.

As Godfrey propped up an accident sketch pad to draw the object, he experienced a blink in reality and found himself – as had so many others before him – further down the road, without any indication of how he had got there. The UFO had vanished, but on driving back to the spot where it had hovered, Godfrey found the wet road surface to be swirled dry in the manner that the crop fields of Wessex had being forged by some unknown force.

When the policeman returned to base, he discovered that his heavy duty boot was split as

if he had been dragged along the ground without his knowledge and also that perhaps 15 minutes of time on his journey were unaccounted for. There are quite disturbing comparisons between this case and the abduction of Nebraska police officer Herb Schirmer almost exactly 13 years earlier, including Schirmer going off on impulse to seek out some distressed cows.

Whilst this UFO encounter is firmly supported by hard evidence, Godfrey was reluctant to be hypnotically regressed. He eventually agreed in Manchester seven months later, under the supervision of UFOlogist Harry Harris and a local psychiatrist. However, Godfrey admits that he read UFO material in the interim and cannot be as certain of the story he told under hypnosis as he is of his sighting of the UFO.

Under hypnosis, the police officer told how his car engine had been stopped by the UFO and a beam of light was then fired at him. He lost consciousness and awoke to find himself inside a room, on a table or bed where a human-like being with a beard who called himself 'Yosef' was supervising a medical probe. This probe was carried out by robot creatures the size of 'little lads' with heads like lamps. There was very little recollection of what these beings did to him because of pains the witness kept getting in his head. But Godfrey was promised a future visit by Yosef, who seemed to know the officer in some way.

Alan Godfrey suffered terribly for deciding to talk openly of his encounter. The West Yorkshire police force appeared somewhat uncomfortable with having a celebrity abductee on duty and Godfrey was sent to see various doctors, evidently in the hope that they might find him unfit for duty. The doctors declined to do so, but on their advice Alan took voluntary retirement thanks to a minor medical injury that he had incurred whilst on duty. He had by now surmised that his superiors found him an embarrassment and that he may as well go with honour whilst he could still do so.

Woodland mysteries

Undoubtedly, the most extraordinary case of the wave came in woodland east of Ipswich near two NATO bases, Bentwaters and Woodbridge. In the early hours of December 26, numerous witnesses – from courting couples in the forest to a USAF military patrol – all saw something crash from the sky into the trees. It was tracked on radar heading for Rendlesham Forest by several different units around East Anglia. Two USAF patrol men were sent out to discover what the object was and found themselves face to face with a landed UFO. The craft seemed to distort time and space in its immediate vicinity, making it almost impossible to walk towards it.

The site where it had landed was found next day to contain a set of triangular imprints and radiation levels ten times higher than normal.

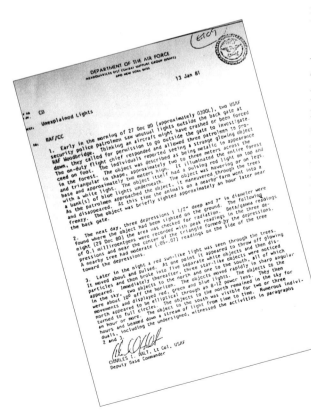

Indeed, some of the witnesses seem to have suffered mild radiation sickness and the dog of one witness (which stood with its master directly beneath the UFO) became seriously ill within hours and died soon afterwards.

Two days later, on the night of December 27–28, strange lights returned to Rendlesham Forest and numerous senior personnel – including the deputy base commander, Colonel Charles Halt – had a close encounter with a triangular craft. Some men claim to have seen small aliens with large heads and big eyes floating in the woods.

There was talk that the UFO had been captured by the military and numerous unscheduled flights came into the base soon afterwards. These were allegedly associated with Project Moon Dust – a secret intelligence operation known to be responsible for recovering objects from space. Woodbridge also operated the Aerospace Rescue and Recovery Squadron specially trained by NASA to help recover any capsules or astronauts that had to be brought down in European waters.

If something strange and heavily irradiated was recovered, where would it have been taken? Thirty-six hours later, on the evening of December 29, three people in a car inside a pine forest at Huffman, Texas, had an oddly similar close encounter. They were not far from the main NASA centre at Houston and observed a triangular object very like that seen in Rendlesham Forest. It was giving off huge amounts of heat and was eventually shepherded away by military helicopters.

Three witnesses – two women and the grandson of one of the women – suffered effects that certainly resemble radiation

What really happened?
The official report submitted to the British government by the base command at the NATO base in Rendlesham Forest, describing the devastating events of late December 1980. This file was 'covered up' by the British government for three years until it was released in the USA via the Freedom of Information Act.

THE EDUCATION PROGRAM

'About as credible as the three stooges in orbit', was how one noted movie commentator described the low-budget 1980 movie *Hangar 18*.

This was the latest attempt by an increasingly feeble Hollywood to portray the reality of the UFO subject. It played on the recently revealed legends about the Roswell crash in 1947 which had just emerged from 30 years of cover-up after Major Jesse Marcel had chosen to tell his story in public upon retiring from the USAF.

Hangar 18 was the legendary name of the location at Wright Patterson Air Force Base where the crashed UFOs and alien bodies were reputedly taken. Unfortunately, the corny science fiction and ludicrous plot of the movie stretched the truth way beyond breaking point. Cinema audiences were doubtless baffled by the cast list which credited actors as playing 'MIB 1' and 'MIB 2' etc. The idea of Men in Black (MIB) was well known to UFOlogists, but non-UFOlogists would probably have struggled to fathom out who these people were.

The release of this movie shortly before the landings in Rendlesham Forest may have been responsible for strange rumours that this UFO had crashed in the forest and been retrieved by the military. These rumours seem to have been planted into the UFO community in Britain by the USAF intelligence forces who may have hoped that the silly publicity over the *Hangar 18* movie would kill off any serious interest in what had really happened in the Suffolk forest.

True or not, these stories coincided with the first claims that an 'education programme' was under way. UFOlogists everywhere began to receive supposed leaks from official sources that a plan was afoot to break the cover-up. This was down to intelligence operatives who were frustrated by the years of silence. The public were to be gradually prepared for the ultimate revelation, by funding set in place for the production of movies that emphasized the reality of alien contact.

This was to become a regular talking point throughout the 1980s. When documents were fed out to UFOlogists purporting to show the workings of these secret operatives, and allegedly released by some of the disgruntled intelligence staff, it did look as if the education programme might be a reality. Unfortunately, it soon became obvious that these documents were as likely to be part of a disinformation operation as actual information. The end result was more confusion than elucidation.

sickness, including vomiting, sore eyes and headaches. One of the women had stood in front of her car for some minutes whilst the other woman stayed inside comforting the child. This first woman was the most seriously exposed and became so ill that she spent some weeks in intensive care. Her red blotches and clumps of hair falling out were unmistakable symptoms of severe radiation sickness.

These three witnesses eventually sued the Government for damages to cover their medical bills on the grounds that it was either responsible for the irradiated object or should have protected its citizens from it. Unfortunately, they ran out of money after a year or two after being chased through the costly judicial system by the US Government.

Dark skies and early warnings

Sightings of large, dark and unmarked helicopters have been seen flying over UFO landing sites within hours and before any public knowledge of the landing. They appear to be a modern update on the big black cadillac once favoured by government agents known as the Men in Black.

Whether they in fact belong to the UFO phenomenon or are operated by some secret element of the Pentagon's UFO investigations network remains a puzzle. Officially, they simply do not exist – that is they are not publicly revealed on the defence budget. Some people suggest that even the President, let alone Congress, might not 'need to know' – in which case who does sanction their missions?

1981: ALIEN INTERLUDE

A French connection

GEPAN, the team of scientists set up at the French space centre, faced their toughest test of all on January 8, 1981 – only a few days after the irradiating objects were encountered in Rendlesham Forest, England, and at Huffman, Texas. The French landing was inside a busy window area at the village of Trans-en-Provence. It, too, had serious implications because of its strong radiative properties.

Landowner Renato Nicolai heard a strange whistling noise at dusk and saw an object like two dishes joined together land on the steep terracing behind his house. After a few moments, the whistling began again and it took off, slowly at first, then rushing away at speed.

Next day, Renato and his wife found two circles on his land where the object had touched down. These were inside each other and coincided with markings he had seen on the underside of the object when it had taken off. He called the gendarmerie who took samples and recognized the importance of the case. They sent their results to the scientists at GEPAN who decided to visit the landing site for themselves.

The delegation from Tolouse was headed by then leader of GEPAN, Dr Alain Esterle. A huge battery of psychological tests were carried out on Nicolai, who proved to be a rustic man who had almost no awareness of UFOs – a situation that must have been almost unique by 1981. The very idea of alien spacecraft had to be explained to him, but he was adamant that the UFO had to be a secret device flown by the French government. GEPAN was able to establish that this was not the case.

Samples of the affected soil were sent to the science labs working in association with GEPAN for analysis. Dr Michael Bounais of the National Institute of Agricultural Research was so intrigued by the results that he spent two years pursuing the case and ten years later launched a follow up survey with Dr Jaques Vallee on behalf of the *Journal for the Exploration of Science*.

As a result of their work, Esterle stated that for the first time GEPAN really had a case where all the evidence fitted. When the GEPAN scientists visited Britain on a private fact-finding mission in May, 1983, it was even hinted that they were now willing to concede that cases such as this one were causing them to support the idea of alien contact.

But why? No aliens were actually seen by Renato Nicolai. The key comes from the findings of Dr Bounais and the lab tests. The soil inside the landing site had been changed drastically in comparison with control samples taken outside the area where the UFO touched down. A massive reduction in chlorophyll content was found, with the leaves prematurely aged by some form of radiation. Tests to find the precise sort of radiation involved had failed, although some type of electro-magnetic field was hinted at. If gamma radiation were involved, there would have been serious environmental consequences as the dosage would have been huge.

GEPAN were soon in action once again investigating physical traces left after a UFO encounter. This produced an even more in-depth case study than the one at Trans-en-Provence, one of the final reports to emerge from the scientists at Toulouse before the clamps came down.

On June 12, a farmer ploughing his field of maize at Le Guery came upon a huge flattened circle over 60 feet in diameter. In addition to the compression of the soil there was a series of holes in the ground. The plant life had been badly affected and there were indications that an

ORDINARY PEOPLE, EXTRAORDINARY TALES

The first signs appeared in 1981 that researchers were at last beginning to recognize a pattern within the alien-contact data. New York artist Budd Hopkins published a book entitled *Missing Time* through a small art company. It was not a huge success at the time but it revealed the six years work he had spent collecting half a dozen or so cases of abduction, usually via hypnosis carried out by local university psychologist, Dr Aphrodite Clamar.

Hopkins reported the pattern of standard American 'gray' type aliens and the ever-present medical examination. He even noted the first stories about implants reputedly placed into the bodies of witnesses by aliens. However, he had yet to see the 'genetic experiment' or 'alien-human hybrid baby' theme present in a lot of the data.

Nevertheless, this book went a long way to making UFOlogists probe more deeply into suspected abductions and to search for hidden patterns. It also initiated genuine scientific interest, thanks to the comments of Dr Clamar. She insisted that the subjects she had worked with were not pathological. Her afterword to the book termed abductions a 'real problem' and she urged her colleagues to take the matter seriously. As far as she was concerned, these witnesses were ordinary people who came together through an extraordinary and remarkably consistent set of encounters that were 'markedly different from most of the fantasies found in psychological literature'.

Following advice from Dr Clamar, she and Hopkins devised an experiment. Elizabeth Slater, a vocational psychologist who vetted people for important posts that required stable personalities, was asked to perform her five standard tests on nine individuals. She was not told anything about them and naturally assumed the work was to gauge their suitability for a sensitive job.

Slater found that there were no signs of psychopathology in any of the individuals that she tested. She did note that they shared a rich inner life that could work advantageously in the form of creativity or become overwhelming. Time was to prove this a critical finding. She added that there was also a sense of inner vulnerability as found in people who felt themselves victimized by outside forces. However, she could not have regarded any of these people as unsuitable candidates.

The truth was then dropped on the psychologist like a bomb. She was stunned to learn that all nine people all shared the conviction that they had been abducted by aliens. After reading their accounts and talking with Hopkins and Clamar about the evidence, she penned a further report.

This addendum firmly rebuffed the explanation that Slater expected her peers would make, namely that the claims of abduction 'could be accounted for strictly on the basis of psychopathology – i.e. mental disorder'. She also noted that the tests revealed no sign of paranoid schizophrenia, pathological liar traits or hysterical characteristics in the patients and stated that if the reports were to be explained as fantasies, she would expect to find such indications. Moreover, the patients displayed precisely the after-effects one might expect to encounter in victims of a genuine alien abduction. The after-effects included the same sort of depersonalization and isolationism found in just one other group of individuals – those who had been subjected to major psychological traumas such as rape.

---

unknown, high-intensity heat source had struck the site. The holes were aligned in a precise geometrical pattern – a trapezium – as if to indicate that they had been placed there to form a message, the farmer suggested.

Baffled gendarmerie called in by the farmer called in a team of GEPAN scientists, who spent 48 hours conducting a full survey of the unusual physical evidence. Investigation revealed that on the night these marks formed, believed to be June 10–11, a strange whistling noise had been heard over the field. GEPAN concluded that a very localized 'thermal and/or intense electromagnetic effect' had been associated with this aerial phenomenon and produced ground traces difficult to reproduce by any known cause. Although nothing was seen at Le Guery, the similarities with the Trans-en-Provence case were strong enough to imply that the same object may have been involved.

1982: THE OZ FACTOR

A breach in defences

Germany has, for some reason, generated fewer close encounters than most countries in Europe, but a major case did take place on March 12. It happened at Messel near Darmstadt and involved a clear breach in the defences of what was then one of the tightest security zones on mainland Europe.

Two teenage girls reported how they were 'attacked' as they walked home. A huge light swept from the sky and dive-bombed them to the ground. The girls fled into a nearby youth centre as the object seemed intent on striking them.

A number of youths ran out from a disco at the centre and saw the UFO now hovering above a sports field. It was illuminating the area with light as bright as daylight. The witnesses describe the object as being dome-shaped with a transparent cupola on top from which emanated a greenish-blue glow; beams were sweeping the ground. A humming noise emerged from the craft as it hovered, followed by a sudden explosion and flash of light, after which the object rose upwards and disappeared.

By now several of the youths – including the two girls – had run home. Their mother confirms they were white with fright upon their return and refused to go outside for weeks after the event. Some of the parents had also seen the UFO and had called the police. Chief officer Thomas Welland arrived in a patrol car and was amazed to find this was not the expected crank call. He immediately sent for back up and three further police cars – bringing a total of eight officers – all arrived in time to see the spectacle.

As the UFO shot away, all the radios on the patrol cars were swamped with static interference and the local houselights dimmed. Residents over a wide area reported that they lost their TV pictures at the same time.

The location was close to the Ramstein Air Force Base, the USAF HQ in Europe and the location to which the film evidence of the Rendlesham Forest landings had been immediately taken some 15 months earlier. The defence radar here picked up the object as it sped away and the power company also noted that circuit relays were tripped by an enormous surge of energy at this point.

Not even the usually circumspect German media could ignore the case. It led to increased interest in the phenomenon in a previously sceptical nation.

More abduction clues

In Australia, social care worker and researcher Keith Basterfield was studying his first alien contacts and proposed what he called 'the image hypothesis'. This suggested that the events were similar to 'false awakenings' – a kind of vivid dream in which the person believes that they are awake. He took heart from the words of Elizabeth Slater that the abductees seemed to have a rich inner fantasy life, but some underlying reality was proving difficult to dismiss.

In early September a new case in Britain was a perfect reflection of Elizabeth Slater's findings but is almost impossible to square with Basterfield's concept of a waking dream.

21-year-old Ros Reynolds was driving with her boyfriend to Corby to visit some friends. On the way, at Haverhill in Suffolk, they suddenly came upon a strange object above the electricity power lines. It was like a rampant jelly fish with tendrils of energy dangling down. Terrified, they drove on to escape the nightmare. But it was only just beginning.

Moments later, blue lights engulfed the car and a weird silence descended. This is what

BACK IN BUSINESS

Ten years after the damp-squib ending to the Apollo missions, NASA was back in business with the first true voyage of the new space shuttle.

Unlike all previous rockets which had used fuel tanks that burnt up in stages to boost a tiny capsule into orbit, this shuttle was re-usable. Its fuel tanks fell into the ocean off Cape Canaveral in Florida and were picked up by ship to be refilled and attached to another flight. The shuttle itself went up into orbit and then returned to earth, landing on an airstrip just like an aircraft – or, more correctly, like a glider.

With the launch of the first shuttle mission, a new era of space travel had begun. Indeed, the flights soon became so commonplace that they were barely thought newsworthy. When I first saw a shuttle launch in November, 1983, the local people had already become quite blasé about the process and said that they only bothered to look out for night launches which were more visually spectacular!

The earth had now become a planet of accomplished space travellers and accustomed observers.

Launch site
The first Shuttle mission landed in 1982. Here the space shuttle sits on the launch pad ready to blast off for one of its now routine flights from Cape Canaveral.

UFOlogists call 'the Oz Factor'. It indicates the onset of an altered state of consciousness. Next, the car engine and lights failed and they coasted to a stop. The lights in the sky were still near by so they desperately tried to restart the vehicle. Suddenly the car headlights came back on and they could no longer see the UFO. Relieved, they drove on to Corby, only to find their friends in bed. It was not 9pm as expected, but 1am; four hours of time had disappeared.

This experience drove a wedge between Ros and her boyfriend, for she suffered exactly as the US psychologist had indicated (even though Slater's work had not been published in 1982 and so Ros Reynolds cannot possibly have known about it). She locked herself in her room for weeks, felt somehow tainted and began to have terrible nightmares about a frightening gray face with large eyes.

Eventually Ros was forced to seek help and underwent regression hypnosis. This was a big mistake, for although the barriers came down in her mind, the images that poured out were shocking. She saw herself being medically examined by small beings with large heads, all under the supervision of one taller, more human-like entity. A gynaecological study was then conducted and samples of body fluids were taken. She felt abused by these entities over whom she had no control. There were also memories of a fantastic propulsion system inside a UFO. Ros, whose artistic talents were enhanced, sketched recollected images as a way of trying to relieve some of the trauma she had experienced.

It was some years before Ros' life returned to a level of normality. During this time she experienced a series of paranormal phenomena, although she would not consider herself psychic. She put a lot of energy into a business caring for animals and met a man who understood what she had been through. However, they were unable to have children; doctors believed that this was the result of a trauma that Ros had experienced when younger. Believing that she had been abducted to take part in alien medical experiments would certainly fit into this category of trauma.

1983: ALIEN REJECTS

Too old and infirm

In the early hours of August 12, 1983, Alfred Burtoo became one of the oldest witnesses to an alien abduction. At 77 years of age, he broke what had become a very obvious pattern – namely that over 80% of known abductees were aged between 18 and 35. Indeed, the older you are, the less likely you seem to be to have an alien contact.

Burtoo was fishing by a canal in Aldershot near a British Ministry of Defence base. He had his dog with him and had just poured some tea from a vacuum flask when a brilliant light appeared in the sky and landed on the tow path. Although he heard no sound, he assumed that the object was a helicopter and so continued to sip his tea. But the dog was now snarling at two 'men' who were walking through the gloom towards them from the direction of the landed object.

The dog was oddly calm as the beings gestured for Burtoo to follow. He noticed that they were well under 5 feet tall and were dressed in green coveralls with visors over their faces. He put down his tea and set off with the men towards their craft. (He later explained to investigators that he had felt no fear because at his age 'you can only die once'.) As Burtoo climbed some steps into the craft, he had to duck his head because the ceiling was too low. One of the beings told him to stand beneath an orange light and then asked him his age. After a few minutes he was told, 'You can go. You are too old and infirm for our purposes'. Burtoo then found himself being unceremoniously ushered outside.

As he walked back along the canal path towards his waiting dog, Alf saw the UFO climb silently upwards, its top half rotating as it did so.

The story told by Burtoo charmed all those who met him. He came across as being a completely sincere, no-nonsense old man who was utterly unphased by these rude aliens. Having total recall of all phases of his abduction is exceptional. Indeed, there are very few other cases on record like it.

The theme of witnesses being rejected by aliens is a remarkably consistent one. It is worth noting that the people who have been told that they are 'unsuitable for alien purposes' have almost always been beyond normal child-bearing age. This is very much the rule – as if procreation is somehow vital to the equation.

Another thing that struck investigators about Burtoo was that he had led a rich life that included braving wolves in the Canadian wilds. If he was going to make up a story about encountering aliens, it seems virtually certain that he would have cast himself more in the role of a hero. This is certainly the way psychologists would expect such people to behave.

In any case, the aliens were sadly correct in their pronouncements and Alf Burtoo died not long afterwards.

Intriguingly, there had been another oddly similar (but unpublished) canal-side alien encounter earlier that year, on January 27. This had been at Bloxwich in the West Midlands where a 39-year-old man saw a craft that looked rather like a mirror descend.

The man was approached by two beings who spoke cultured English and asked him to accompany them on a journey. He declined, saying that he did not want to leave his wife. The aliens promised that they would bring him back, but he still refused. They then offered him an unspecified reward. After turning this down, the man expected to be met with force – but the beings simply walked off and left him.

FANTASY PRONE?

In l983, two American psychologists, Theodore Barber and Sheryl Wilson, published some results that were soon seized upon by those striving to find a mind-based solution to the alien contact issue.

Barber and Wilson studied 52 excellent hypnotic subjects and discovered (rather as Slater had noticed about her nine abductees) that they had very rich, fantastical imaginations. Indeed their imaginations were at times so vivid that these people had difficulty separating reality from fantasy. The doctors surmised that good hypnotic subjects needed this inner capacity to create images in order to be guided toward the creation of a memory or fantasy by the hypnotist. Noting that about 4% of the population fitted into this category, they created the label 'fantasy-prone personality' to define such people.

FPPs – as these people came to be known – told how they had images in their heads so realistic that they seemed to be experiencing a three-dimensional movie. They had a tendency to experience psychic phenomena throughout their lives and to see strange figures popping up that were often regarded as apparitions. Several actually said that they sometimes had to stop driving when on quiet roads because figures would appear out of nowhere in front of the car, figures that they later realized were not really there, but which seemed too real not to stop for.

Researchers like Keith Basterfield saw the relevance of this to the alien-contact controversy and began a research programme with psychologist Dr Robert Bartholomew from Australia's Flinders University. They asked whether abductees were simply one version of the fantasy-prone personality in action.

Their work found that witnesses who claimed alien contact tended to share many of the traits of FPPs; people akin to the contactees of the l950s or who acted like Maureen Puddy, who had seen entities on the Mooraduc Road near Melbourne when others who were present definitely confirmed that nothing was actually visible. However, the researchers had more trouble making the pattern fit the abductees.

That abductions are not simply products of the imagination is strongly inferred by the links between cases which are so subtle that copycat reporting would be nigh impossible. Of huge importance here are cases such as that of Alf Burtoo and other alien rejects.

If you study all of the known examples where people allege that they were dumped by the aliens after abduction, a staggering consistency emerges. Burtoo was told he was 'too old and infirm'. Elsie Oakensen was 'rejected' for being above child-bearing age and several younger women were then selected in the same rural area almost immediately afterwards. Luli Oswald in Brazil was told she was no use for alien purposes (again being above child-bearing age) but her young male companion was seized upon for sexual tests and sampling. In another case, US hunter Carl Higdon from Wyoming was seemingly turned down at the age of 41; he was told that he was unsuitable for the aliens 'breeding programme'. Higdon had had a vasectomy.

It seems hard to believe that this pattern is a coincidence. I know of no case of an older person being accepted. Psychologists note that few humans would be likely to demean themselves by reporting how they were dumped by the aliens as being over the hill. People would be ill-disposed to make this up. If abductions were fantasies, they would not follow such a chillingly logical course.

Alien artistry
Clues began to emerge from abductees that they were creatively gifted more often than chance should dictate. US abductee Judith Starchild, for example, was an artist. Others were poets, wrote novels, and expressed an inner desire to communicate the 'alien message'.

1984: Star Children

A woman's story

Karen from Warrington, Cheshire, had undergone many strange experiences in her life. These had included ghosts and poltergeists as well as vivid dreams and ESP phenomena. Karen was the kind of individual that is sometimes referred to as a 'fantasy-prone' personality – although, of course, she regarded her strange experiences as being completely real.

Along with her boyfriend Gary (now her husband), Karen had also had a number of UFO encounters, the most interesting of which had occurred at Newquay in Cornwall where they were working in the summer of 1979. In September of that year, Karen and Gary were walking together in a country lane at Pentire when they heard a humming noise which was followed by a rustling in the bushes. A blinding light then shot from a field skywards, leaving behind a blast of wind that rocked them 'like a high-speed train'. They were paying little attention to the time as it was a late-night stroll and they were winding down after a hard day, but there are hints that a time lapse may have occurred. If so, there could well be unrecorded memories of an abduction here.

After returning north, Karen discovered that she was pregnant. Soon afterwards she had a

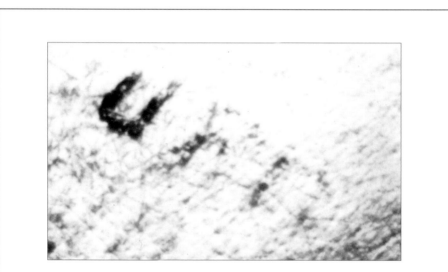

Written in Blood

Marks and implants in the bodies of abductees came to prominence during 1984. In this astonishing case a witness in Birmingham had a vivid 'dream' of a close encounter – lights of which were seen by neighbours. On waking, the letters UFO were found etched in blood on his hand.

WISE BABY DREAMS

A year after these events, but when none of them had been published on express request of the women involved, Budd Hopkins produced his first report leading up to his second book on abduction research. This would eventually appear in 1987 under the title *Intruders*.

Hopkins told of a case that he began to investigate in late 1983. It involved a woman called Debbie Tomey from Indiana but the researcher had not published anything about it until he had verified some of its wilder aspects through other cases. What Hopkins told me of his work stunned me because it matched exactly what had emerged from three British women and their abduction stories. Debbie Tomey (and several other American women) had been abducted several times. They believed that samples were taken from them to allow the aliens to develop an alien-human hybrid baby. They insisted that this grew inside their womb and was then removed in a subsequent abduction. Often the first they knew of this came via

dreams of the odd-looking babies (which Hopkins called 'wise baby dreams'). They also subsequently told of being shown the older baby by the aliens in an abduction perhaps several years later. The 'phantom pregnancies' terminated in a show of blood at between two and three months.

There is absolutely no way that any of the British women could have known about Hopkins' research until his book appeared several years after they spoke to me. Equally, I know that I did not tell Hopkins about these three British cases and did not document any of them until I told Karen's story (with her permission but under a pseudonym) in 1987.

Yet they are clearly all talking about the same thing. Unless this is the most fantastic coincidence, once again it is almost impossible not to presume that these women were describing events that really happened to them – that they had conceived star children on behalf of the aliens.

terrifying dream in which the baby was born and was possessed by an incredible intelligence. It began talking immediately after being born and appeared to be like the devil. The dream scared Karen but she soon wrote it off as the normal fears of any future mother. However, the dream kept recurring. Then, on December 26, she found blood in her bed and tests revealed that she was no longer pregnant. It was assumed that she had miscarried and Karen interpreted her dreams as a premonition of the miscarriage.

In the summer of 1984, Karen awoke to hear a humming noise just like the one that had filled the bushes in Newquay five years earlier. Going to the bedroom window, she saw a white light directly outside. There was a door facing the window and a woman stood in this opening. The entity was 6 feet tall with china-white skin and slanted eyes. Its hair was very blonde, but it was hard to tell whether it was male or female. This is a comment often made by abductees. The being invited Karen into the light and she

asked if she could bring her husband but was told that he would not wake and she should come alone. As she stepped towards the object that floated in mid-air, Karen recalled feeling cold and seeing lights, but she remembered nothing more about her encounter when she awoke the next morning.

Some months later, Karen recalled how she was awoken by tiny fingers pressing her hands. They felt like those of a little child. Calling to Gary to switch on the light, she noticed a tiny light floating upwards and disappearing through the ceiling.

By the beginning of 1985 I had personally investigated 10 alien abductions, six of which involved female witnesses. Three of these six women had told me how they had unexpectedly become pregnant immediately after their abduction and had then seen the pregnancy end after three months with blood on the bed at night. It seemed hard to imagine that this was yet another coincidence in the alien-contact story. But I had no idea what it all meant.

1985: STRANGE ENERGIES

An arctic window

Window areas turn up in the oddest of places and one of the most difficult to investigate was found around the Arctic Circle in the Hessdalen Valley near Trondheim in Norway.

Reports of strange lights had been made by locals for some time before a group of Scandinavian UFOlogists braved the bitter temperatures to camp out in the mountains and obtain photographic evidence. They raised money for 'Project Hessdalen' from within the UFO community and were loaned expensive equipment such as lasers and radar by Swedish defence authorities and universities.

The result was the most detailed investigation of a window area ever mounted and some truly impressive evidence for their efforts. In January 1985, Dr J Allen Hynek flew out to join them for the second wave of investigations, recognizing the importance of their research, but by this time sightings were already tailing off. Window areas tend not to be active all of the time and with so few local inhabitants and a remote rural location, this one was more difficult to monitor than others.

Glowing lights were seen and filmed on various occasions. Speculation as to what they might be was split between two possibilities. The first was the spectrographic analysis that suggested they were plasma – a sort of ball of energy that drifted along magnetic currents. Some people felt that this meant that they were natural in origin, akin to the theory of 'earthlights' which was gaining ground as the likely cause of other phenomena being seen within many window areas. However, the other possibility was that the lights were intelligently controlled.

In one experiment, laser beams were shone at the lights and they clearly appeared to respond in an intelligent manner as if attempting some sort of communication. Beams were fired down at the researchers' feet as if imitating the laser. The possibility that the plasmas could react to the human mind in a sort of interactive process was debated, while others felt that the energies might be the by-product of an alien craft.

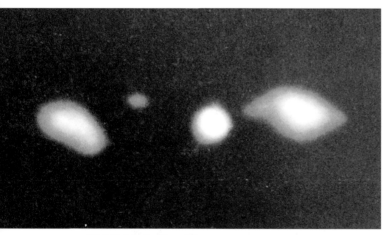

Highlights in Hessdalen
Some of the strange lights filmed over the Hessdalen Valley in Norway during scientific expeditions to hunt the source of countless UFO reports in the 'window area'. The glows are some form of atmospheric plasma of unknown origin, but how they form is unknown.

Little children

Whilst lights in the sky can certainly be regarded as natural phenomena, alien contacts are much harder to explain in this way. There were certainly encounters of this type within the window area.

PSYCHIC ALIENS

Two movies in 1985 epitomized the growing debate amongst UFOlogists, some of whom were tiring of the old-fashioned idea of extraterrestrials flying to earth in spaceships. The excellent movie *Enemy Mine* graphically illustrated the difficulties of contact between two wholly alien cultures in a 'two-hander' played like a psychological thriller set in an eerie alien environment.

Far more commercially successful was the movie *Back to the Future*, which, with its two later sequels, expressed scientific interest in the view that time travel might be feasible through a study of quantum physics. A few UFOlogists were sensing the opportunity that this now provided. Might alien contact involve visitors from our own future? If time travel ever became possible (even centuries hence), then there must be visitors coming from the future back to the present day. Otherwise we would be forced to conclude that time travel could never be achieved. Would time travellers pretend to be aliens, spouting nonsense to those they met?

However, quite the most interesting fiction of 1985 was a British television dramatization of the John Wyndham novel, *Chocky*, followed by two specially-written sequels from Anthony Read. These adopted the new awareness of the role that children were having in alien-contact cases, as exemplified by a major case from Flint in Wales, where an entire family had undergone landings and alien meetings and the eldest girl had felt her life directed by two beings who befriended her during a benign abduction.

Chocky is a similarly friendly alien who is 'attuned' to the mental wavelength of children. The ESP mode of contact is easier here because children still have the ability to use the limitless capacity of the mind. This fictional story matched the growing awareness that alien-contact witnesses did experience many psychic phenomena and that abductions mixed readily with poltergeists, apparitions, paranormal dreams and other strange events in the lives of such witnesses from childhood onwards.

A strange banded object with a searchlight beam roamed the valley at Tynset on February 18. It seemed interested in children. Indeed, there were a growing number of cases in which children appeared to be the centre of alien attention. Most notable was an incident on October 28 at Honefoss in Norway, a case which seems to be completely unique.

Children aged between 7 and 12 from the village were watching an eclipse of the moon when an oval light descended from the sky and hovered near ground level. One of the children shone a flashlight at it, illuminating a gray metal surface. The object then responded just like those filmed by the Hessdalen researchers, projecting a blinding beam of light at the children's feet.

In the glow, the witnesses could now see an incredible scene. Underneath the UFO were dozens of alien creatures. These were basically humanoid but with box-shaped helmets. They were different colours (including white, brown and black), yet were only the size of large dolls! Once they had seen the children, the beings appeared to flee, but were witnessed at various points around the village over the next few hours. They seemed to play a game of hide and seek with the children.

Attempts were made to take photographs, but the aliens always hid from the cameras. Adults were called out but only one of them saw what the children were showing him and he insisted it was just a cat. After dawn, strange footprints were found near the site where the aliens had first appeared. However, a local dog went crazy when brought near the marks and destroyed the evidence in a frenzy.

When UFOlogists arrived on the scene, they easily found a dozen children in the village who all told very similar stories about the night. However, there was no evidence left to prove their claims.

1986: Big Bad Aliens

Alien healing

The psychic nature of some alien contacts was proving uncomfortable for some people, particularly for researchers in the USA, where the literal interpretation of an extraterrestrial kidnap was strongly preferred. However, it was almost impossible to ignore the mounting evidence.

John Evans was a classic illustration of the problem. From childhood he had undergone psychic experiences, notably vivid dreams and out-of-body sensations. In 1944, he had had a dramatic UFO encounter in which strange lights had been seen climbing an escalator that took coal slag up an artificial heap at Penywaun in south Wales. A weird UFO floated overhead into which the lights disappeared as if it were a black hole. Soon afterwards the slag heap collapsed.

A far worse disaster had occurred in October, 1966, at nearby Aberfan, when a terrible tragedy resulted. Slag that had become heavy with rain water gave way and crushed a school, killing many children. Once again there were reports of a cigar-shaped UFO being seen in the area shortly beforehand. Questions were raised by some as to whether aliens might be responsible. Or, perhaps, if we were being visited by time travellers from our own future, they were simply voyeurs observing a famous catastrophe?

In 1986, John Evans entered hospital in Cardiff for surgery on his hip. He believes that during surgery he saw the compassionate side of the aliens. As he was being wheeled into the operating theatre, he saw a tall being dressed in a shiny suit. He recognized the figure as an alien he had encountered in earlier 'dreams'. Evans says he was then 'sucked' upwards into a strange room where the being administered healing. As he floated over his body on return, he saw the doctors talking to one another, saying 'this man

has healed himself'. Then he awoke in his hospital bed.

The fact that this was more than just an hallucination was supposedly confirmed to John Evans by one of the doctors who explained that he had babbled incessantly while he was under the anaesthetic about aliens. The doctor confirmed that he did still have to fix the man's diseased hip, but otherwise he was found to be surprisingly well.

Then, when Evans was discharged, one of the theatre nurses asked him to go and have a drink with her. She did not wish to discuss this matter inside the hospital but insisted that she had seen a double ethereal form of John rise from his operating trolley and float through the ceiling. At first she thought he had died on route to the surgery and this was his spirit going to heaven. But he was clearly still alive, talking as if he were conversing with an alien. Some time later, after the surgery, she saw the same ethereal form float back into his body.

Researcher Margaret Fry, who investigated this case, argued that it showed how aliens use the psychic components of human beings during their contact. It matches other cases, such as the Maureen Puddy alien contact from Australia in 1972 and the Aveley abduction from 1974, where 'out-of-body' experiences are described by witnesses in the presence of aliens.

Some investigators, however, began to wonder if the clue was more subtle.

Near death in a UFO

University of Connecticut psychologist Dr Kenneth Ring was an expert in NDEs – near-death experiences. These are cases where people claim to float free of their bodies, enter a white light and, close to the point of death

THE CHALLENGER TRAGEDY

The frailty of human life was brought home in January, 1986, when the seemingly impregnable space shuttle blew up on take-off. All astronauts aboard, including the first true civilian (a school teacher who had ironically been sent into space to show the public how safe such flights now were) died.

This caused the NASA programme to be set back several years, particularly when revelations emerged that the crew survived the explosion but had no way to escape the craft as it plunged into the ocean. Unfortunately, the rise in tabloid sensationalism of the UFO mystery led to the apalling spectacle of UFO sightings miles from Cape Canaveral fuelling silly speculation that aliens had blown up 'Challenger' as a warning. In fact, the cause was soon determined as being in a faulty fuel tank connection and was very terrestrial in origin.

(during a surgical operation, for example), meet wise beings. The wise beings are believed by the witness, and by most researchers, to be voyagers on their way to an afterlife or heaven. Ring and others saw strong links with abductions. In the story of John Evans – whether it was fantasy or whether it really happened – there is a choice between a typical NDE or an alien abduction. It is likely that many people would regard the case as a brief excursion into heaven.

Nor was John Evans' case unique. I had already noted several where it was very difficult to know what to call this type of experience.

A man in a dentist's chair in Middlesborough suffered a reaction to the drug being administered and almost died. However, he saw himself float free of his body, through the ceiling and into a UFO where aliens told him about their involvement with earth. Then he was told he must fight his way back into his body, and he drifted back to see a very worried dentist desperately trying to revive him.

In another case in Leeds, an ambulance driver lying exhausted on his bed found tall beings with pale faces and dark eyes standing by the bed asking for his help to fix their broken UFO. He was floated up through the ceiling into a strange room, made to lie on a long table and given a medical examination with a giant eye-like device. Then he was given a typically confusing message and sent back into his body, where he lay on his bed paralysed and unwell for some time.

The patient never assumed that this was anything other than an alien abduction. However, it would not take too much stretching of the evidence to suggest a mild seizure (possibly a heart attack) and a near-death experience instead.

If the now quite numerous cases of overlap between near-death experiences and alien abductions suggest anything at all, it is that we should not adopt too dogmatic an attitude to whatever is going on. Something mighty strange is happening.

The Oz factor

The Oz factor is the name given to the sensations often described by witnesses around close encounters. These include a sense of isolation, lack of environmental sounds and utter disorientation of time and space. It is another clear illustration that there is a special 'UFO state of consciousness' into which the witness lapses.

One question remains unresolved. Is this 'aura' a mental state that triggers the experience – rather like a 'turning inward' of all conscious thought? Alternatively, is it caused by a physical force generated by the UFO – possibly its propulsion system warping space time so powerfully that the witness who gets too close feels the slipstream?

1987: SPACENAPPED

The turning point

Although UFOlogists had some warning, few were to realize just how critical this year would prove to be. It was to include the fortieth anniversary of the birth of the UFO mystery and big celebrations were planned – including a major international conference in Washington. But it was to be events on the alien-contact front that were to really change the face of the phenomenon for ever.

A noted horror fiction writer (whose novels had been turned into movies such as *Wolfen*) announced he was publishing a book for which he had been given a huge advance. At a stroke, this had taken UFO writing into the big league. However, the writer, Whitley Strieber, was not producing a new novel. He claimed that his story would tell the absolute truth about his own alien abduction.

It was a copy of my 1985 book (*Science and the UFOs*) that had provided this celebrated writer with a key. My down-to-earth book was based on an article in *New Scientist* magazine and dealt sensitively with abductions via an archetypal case. It also included the early stages of Budd Hopkins' research -– even though he had then published little outside UFOlogy.

GRAY DAY DAWNING

The image of the 'gray' alien came to dominate alien-contact stories during 1987. This sketch by a witness depicts the figure he saw in his bedroom inspecting his bedroom alarm. As a very practical man, he noted that it was not an hallucination because he had to screw up his eyes to see the figure – being shortsighted and not wearing spectacles at the time.

ALIEN SOAP

If the impact of Whitley Strieber's book was not dramatic enough, a popular television soap opera, *Dynasty* (and its spin-off, *The Colbys*), ensured that millions more around the world saw the reality that underpins the abduction phenomenon. One of their major characters, Fallon Colby, was spacenapped and the plot then followed the aftermath as she was probed by psychologists, suffered emotional trauma and was eventually regressed to reveal the truth.

This opened up the phenomenon to a whole new audience of people who would not normally be interested in UFOs or read Strieber's book. It was fascinating to see how its producers assumed that all abductions were alike. For example, Strieber had mentioned a smell of cinnamon connected with the aliens. This had not been reported before, but *Dynasty* included it. Following the television series, some cases referred to aliens smelling of cinnamon and investigators faced a dilemma. Was this a new clue uncovered by Strieber and now reinforced by the *Dynasty* fiction? Or had a hoaxer copied Strieber's story and, like the television series, imagined that this feature would make their contact more credible?

Even more important was the fact that the series dramatized the scene where Fallon was spacenapped, showing her walking up a ramp into the landed UFO. This had great impact for the viewers and is precisely the sort of scene that all science-fiction films depicting alien contact tend to include. It is also likely to be what someone inventing an abduction would conjure up to add to the drama. Unfortunately, in real abduction stories, it almost never happens.

The few cases where entry into the UFO is remembered are atypical ones, like Alf Burtoo's 'alien rejection'. Research into 700 well-recorded abductions by University of Indiana folklorist, Dr Eddie Bullard, had proved this by 1987. He had set out to show that these tales were a space-age myth and was shocked to learn that they did not follow any of the rules of mythology. What he called doorway amnesia – this inability to recall being taken into the UFO – was a significant clue that suggested to Bullard that abductions were more like reality than myth.

Experiments by Alvin Lawson in California and myself in the UK soon verified this. When asked to imagine abductions, eight out of ten witnesses told of being led aboard the UFO and came up with a wide range of types of alien, including the reptiles of recent television and movie lore. When they were asked to describe their memories of allegedly real abductions, under one in ten recalled entering the UFO and more than nine out of ten involved just the two highly consistent alien types – the tall, blond ones and the grays.

Strieber was given my book as a Christmas present, but he reacted in unexpected terror when reading it and peculiar images in his mind suddenly slotted into place. Throughout his life there had been oddities and time lapses. He had also recently been taken from his weekend residence in New York State and medically probed in a very painful fashion by little beings with dark black eyes and pointed chins.

After recognizing that these 'visions' might be real, Strieber went to see Hopkins, who lived near by in Manhattan. Hypnosis followed and within a year his blockbuster was written.

This case stirred up intense debate inside the UFO community. Strieber did not have a good rapport with some researchers for a variety of reasons. Both myself and Hopkins were two of those researchers, although I found him a fascinating man to talk with and recognized that he was much more advanced in his thinking than most of his American peers.

To many people, Strieber's story seemed too good to be true. He was widely attacked, especially in the very sceptical British media. I suspect his case is highly significant and the views he expressed in later books were quite sophisticated. But at other times they reflected the confusion that this mystery creates. This is not surprising; a man as intelligent as Strieber must feel swamped by these phenomena.

Writing a later novel on the Roswell crash certainly added to the difficulty some UFOlogists faced in understanding the author. But, like it or not, he had become a major player, even though he disassociated himself from much of the UFO community and expressed disenchantment with how it was dealing with the abduction phenomenon. Some of this criticism was actually very appropriate. Strieber reminded people that UFOlogy is built out of witnesses who count as people – not just as fodder for theories invented by UFOlogists from their stories.

Mass market

Because of his high profile and a brilliant publicity campaign, Strieber's book *Communion* was a huge success all over the world. For months he was on television chat shows and in newspapers, raising the stakes in the abduction mystery overnight.

Posters carrying the startling painting of the alien face Strieber had encountered appeared on walls and bus shelters as well as on the cover of his book. It was now impossible to escape the American version of the abduction story with little grays, medical examinations and time lapses. UFOlogists had not published some of the finer points of the spacenapping motif because they helped to judge the credibility of cases. Any witness could make up a story based on what they read in the media. But if they added features that the press left out but which UFOlogists had recognized from earlier cases, then these proved vital clues. Through the powerful reporting of his own experiences, Strieber had unintentionally changed the ground rules.

He received thousands of letters from all over the world from people who believed they had been abducted and were now seeking help. UFO groups also felt the backlash, getting countless requests from people with strange memories or odd events in their lives and requesting immediate hypnotic regression to reveal the facts about suspected hidden memories of abduction. Whilst some of these were doubtless genuine cases of desperate need, others were people who had convinced themselves they had been the victims of spacenapping as a result of trivial events in their lives. People remembered driving behind a car and seeing it disappear. Had it turned off onto a side road or had they had been spacenapped?

Other examples were bizarre. Because Strieber and Hopkins talked about 'screen memories' – more pleasant images substituted in the unconscious mind for the frightening alien face – people recalled seeing lots of rabbits in a field, for example, and now hoped that hypnosis might reveal whether the rabbits were substitute images for grays!

Within months, the UFO community was heading on a mad helter-skelter ride in which the abduction phenomenon was plastered across the media everywhere. It was the only area of research that anybody wanted to do. UFOlogists quit investigating UFOs and started doing their own hypnosis (sometimes with no medical qualifications). Even young children were regressed. This was the way to solve the mystery, researchers claimed. This was what thousands of witnesses expected of UFOlogists, they added, pointing to piles of letters talking about lights seen on a country drive 30 years ago. Of course, this was also the way to get book deals, television appearances and a high profile as a UFOlogist.

Because of his speciality, Budd Hopkins, too, suddenly found himself a mega-star. His own new book was a big hit and he was in constant demand from the media and UFOlogists. The UFO community now saw where the future lay and it was Strieber and Hopkins who had pointed them towards it.

All change

Alongside all this massive public fascination with alien contact, the phenomenon appeared to undergo a complete change of direction. Over the next few years, several major cases were to occur that overturned all the accepted rules.

One of the most extraordinary cases occurred on December 1, 1987. It involved a former police officer who was fell walking at daybreak over the White Wells area of Ilkley Moor in the Yorkshire Pennines; as already noted, this area of the Pennines was the UK's most active window area.

The policeman had his camera to take photographs of the village below when he spotted a figure beckoning from a rock. He took one shot of the entity, which had a green cast and large eyes, before it hurried off around an outcrop. He then saw a strange object climbing skywards.

Afterwards the man found that his compass was pointing south instead of north. He abandoned his walk and went down into the village, discovering from the church clock that about an hour and a half of time had vanished. Immediately getting the film processed, he visited the library and found my address from a book. The next day he wrote to me, explaining what had just happened.

This case proved baffling. After he and I met, the witness and I began a study of the photograph and Peter Hough conducted a major follow-up. From the start we were dubious. It was unheard of in such a case for the witness to photograph the alien involved. The 'little green man' image on the grainy shot was also suspicious. Yet the cameraman was completely disinterested in publicity, although he was quite happy to co-operate with an investigation. He has never appeared in the media. Indeed, he has resisted many chances to make money from the photograph and has signed over its copyright to Peter to allow detailed research.

Numerous studies have proven that it does show an entity about four-and-a-half-feet tall on the hillside. But investigations have not established whether the figure is that of a model, a child in a suit or an alien. However, it is certainly not an insurance salesman riding a bicycle and wearing an anorak – as claimed by one sceptic and quickly disproven! Computer enhancement of the photo is difficult due to its graininess and it is quite easy to 'see' things in the fuzzy results that are probably not there in reality. Claims about the creature wearing a back pack and having horns, which were made by some reporters, are frankly nonsense; although research has revealed a history of strange, goblin-like creatures being seen before in White Wells.

The man's compass was studied by a university, who found that it was possible to reverse the field with equipment like a hospital magnetic resonance scanner. The radiological protection board assisted with the site study but no abnormal radiation was found.

A clinical psychologist at a Lancashire hospital carried out tests and found that the man free from psychopathology and was telling the truth as he believed it. The same doctor performed regression hypnosis after the other tests were complete.

Hypnotic regression – as expected – brought out a story in which the man claimed to have been spacenapped, given a medical examination by the little beings, shown holographic videos of space, told deeply personal things about his life and implanted with things to do. It was the usual form of alien contact – if the word 'usual' can ever be used in this context!

Ten years on, the case remains as puzzling as ever. The witness still declines to be interviewed and insists upon the truth of his story. If it is a hoax, then the motive for it is obscure. Early theories that the witness was trying to 'test' investigator expertise seem hard to sustain after so many years. But if the case is genuine, then it certainly represents the first known photograph of an alien abductor taken by a spacenap victim. The very fact that this is so unique out of the thousands of abduction cases before it is prime evidence that the phenomenon underwent a major revolution during 1987.

1988: ALIEN REVELATIONS

Baby boom

In 1988 cases of genetic experiment and wise baby dreams appeared all over the world. On July 19, a graphic artist and her mother in Johannesburg, South Africa, had worked into the early hours finishing a creative advertising project. Exhausted, Debra drove her mother home, but a light approached the car and engulfed it. A mist surrounded them and the two women regained consciousness in a room surrounded by small hairless beings; the leader was female and called herself Meleelah. The women were scanned using bar-like instruments and samples of fluid from the abdomen were extracted. Although they did not realize it at the time, these women were reliving the by now completely standard female version of spacenap followed by a genetic experiment.

In Britain, a new case surfaced in Birmingham. The young woman was called Corinne and had been experiencing psychic phenomena , including out-of-body trips. During these she was sometimes found by her parents deeply unconscious on her bed. She also had visits in her bedroom from a 'little man' which began at the age of 18 months. The being had a white face and coal-black eyes. Corinne developed a phobia of standing by windows at night, which is the sort of clue that could mask a deeper memory. She also had a vivid 'dream' in which several of the beings flew through the window into her room and she attacked them with a can of hairspray. Soon after that Corinne had the first of her 'dreams' of giving birth to a super-intelligent baby with wispy thin hair. The small creatures told her that this was an alien-human hybrid and she must care for it during their visits because they wanted to test the emotional response of a human woman to their genetic creations.

Meanwhile, in Port Augusta, Australia, a nurse called Susan told of her frequent encounters with aliens since childhood. There were two types of beings involved, both of which ought to sound familiar. A seven-foot tall one that was very human in appearance, possessed psychic powers and spoke to her via telepathy. He was in charge of the small beings with large heads and dark eyes who performed medical tests on her. From the age of 14, these tests became overtly sexual in nature and the beings told her they were doing something to her ovaries. At 18, her periods stopped, her breasts became tender and she developed all the symptoms of a pregnancy; her doctor told her she was not. Then she found blood on her bed one morning and all was normal again.

In 1988, after another abduction involving samples of ova being taken, Susan was diagnosed as being pregnant – something she insisted was impossible as she had had no recent relationships. Then she had dreams of giving birth to a very intelligent but strange-looking baby and became ill. During treatment, doctors found there was no sign of a baby but there was a massive discharge of blood.

In Gulf Breeze

In early 1988 Gulf Breeze, a small town on the Florida panhandle across a channel from Pensacola naval base, took on the mantle of the UFO capital of the world and media and UFOlogists flocked there in droves.

The town's reputation was based on a local builder called Ed Walters who introduced yet another unprecedented type of UFO encounter – a siege by aliens lasting six months. The events had began in November–December 1987. Walters was not simply seeing UFOs night after

AREA 51

News began to spread around the UFO world that Bob Lazar, who claimed to be a scientist working at a secret government facility, had extraordinary news to report. Lazar was later joined by others who went on the lecture circuit and an entire folklore developed about 'Area 51' which persists to this day. A 1996 British TV advert for a new Ford car actually shows the vehicle entering the site, being abducted and taken into space to the strains of the tune 'Fly me to the moon'!

What is not in doubt is that Area 51 exists within the Nevada desert north of Las Vegas and is a very secret base where Stealth aircraft technology was developed. However, the debate rages over this place, nicknamed 'Dreamland' by its workers because of the fantastic technology test flown from there. Does it also house UFOs and aliens? People like Lazar claim that it does. In fact, he has seen the craft 'back engineered' by the US Government after unravelling the secrets of crashed UFOs. Other stories that have emerged from workers at the site have even claimed that aliens helped the US Government to develop this technology in exchange for an agreed quota on abductees and a pact of non-interference from the Pentagon within the alien's genetic experiments. Lazar has not gone as far as that, but his story of alien technology in Area 51 convinced many.

The region was soon the centre of huge attention from skywatchers who camped on local mountains. Even the nearby small town of Rachel cashed in as a tour centre. Then the US Government bought land surrounding the base and enforced a strict no-go area accompanied by a policy of arresting those caught in the area.

Aviation sources in the USA have told me that this caution is because the base builds tomorrow's top-secret aircraft, even using experimental nuclear motors. Many UFOlogists counter that these actions are all part of the cover-up and that the US Government was afraid of solid proof being captured that demonstrated their home-grown 'UFOs'. Indeed, before the ban was introduced, fascinating video footage was obtained of incredibly manoeuvrable craft flying over the desert. The argument remains as to whether these are secret aircraft or Uncle Sam's very own UFOs.

night – he was taking dozens of colour polaroid photographs of them. In 40 years of UFO study, this was unique and at first cast great suspicion on Ed's story.

For a time America's two leading groups, the J. Allen Hynek Center for UFO Studies and MUFON, were in serious conflict, with MUFON officers backing the case and the Center pointing out flaws. The Center later moderated their views. Doubts about Walters grew when plans of a model UFO were found in his house. He said that these must have been planted by those out to discredit him and had the support of many townsfolk who by now were seeing UFOs and taking more photographs. There is a suggestion that some locals (possibly from the naval base) were tricking skywatchers who gathered nightly by the Bay Bridge. They were building hot air balloons out of candles and plastic bags and launching them across the water in full view of watching cameras!

Gulf Breeze still has a huge reputation. While some of it is built on shaky foundations, some impressive cases have been reported. There is also plenty of support for Ed Walters and his photographs, notably from optical physicist Dr Bruce Maccabee, who built a special camera for Ed to use which provided more photographs that Maccabee considered impressive.

Ed had bizarre alien contacts with little creatures that smelled of cinnamon, but he never succeeded in filming them. Voices spoke in foreign languages. He was shown images of dogs and naked women and various incoherent messages were conveyed. A video was obtained by one local reporter showing Ed undergoing a sort of 'psychic contact' in his car, akin to that of Maureen Puddy in Australia. This was another weird departure for the rapidly escalating mystery of alien contact.

1989: TELL THE WORLD

The Manhattan transfer

That the phenomenon had changed dramatically since 1987 was already suggested by cases such as Gulf Breeze and Ilkley Moor. When a further major barrier fell in 1989, the new trend became obvious.

At last there was a clear example of an 'observed' abduction, the sort of case that all critics of the literal reality of alien contact were demanding. As they said, if a bank was robbed but there was no money missing and no passers by in the street saw the getaway car, would we believe that a crime had occurred based on just testimony of the teller alone? Yet this was the position of the abduction mystery. Hundreds of people were being spacenapped, they claimed, from bedrooms and cars. Yet nobody in the room or in another car driving past had seen the abandoned car from which the person had been snatched, or better still, had observed the alien kidnap as it happened.

The event that came to be dubbed the 'Manhattan Transfer' overcame this serious omission in the data and the nature of its observers provided further evidence that alien contact had entered a new dimension.

This case unfolded on November 30 in a high-rise apartment block in downtown Manhattan. The victim was Linda Napolitano, a woman who had already contacted local researcher Budd Hopkins to describe previous meetings with small, gray aliens with large black eyes. Hopkins had enrolled her in his new self-help therapy group. But her latest encounter had been terrifying; Linda had awoken to find grays in her bedroom. She had tried to fend them off by throwing a pillow at them, but she was then paralysed and awoke inside the white room undergoing medical tests.

Subsequent hypnosis brought out more terrifying details. Linda saw herself being floated through the apartment window in a beam of light and surrounded by the levitating forms of several small aliens. She recalled entering the UFO, even though this is exceptionally rare. When she was returned to her bedroom an unknown time later, her husband and children had been 'switched off' (in deep trance-like sleep states) and had not noticed she had been missing.

About 18 months after Linda told her story, Hopkins received the first of several contacts (by letter and tape) from two security guards. They were unburdening themselves of a terrible trauma. So deep had they been affected that one had suffered a nervous breakdown.

The men had been in a car protecting a 'world leader statesman' and driving him to the heliport after a meeting. They had stopped in the street (it seems as if subconsciously motivated to do so) and all three had witnessed Linda being floated out of her apartment above sleeping Manhattan, then transferred into the UFO, which promptly flew off under the nearby river and disappeared. They did not know who the woman was, of course, but told Hopkins they could pinpoint her apartment. The guard was wrestling with his conscience and had parked often by the building wondering if he could summon up the courage to see if the abducted woman was alive or dead.

Budd Hopkins did not let on that he already knew of Linda's story, but encouraged the guard to go and see her. Hopkins then shared this amazing news with the abductee so that when the man arrived sheepishly at Linda's door, she was expecting his visit! Needless to say, he was stunned.

This case has created huge controversy. It seemed too good to be true for many people,

WITNESS SUPPORT

The self-help therapy group set up in New York by Budd Hopkins was one of many that had been created. It followed ideas mooted by Whitley Strieber and noted that UFOlogists were not catering well for the emotional needs of spacenap victims. In Britain, BUFORA helped to create a 'Witness Support Group' and these gatherings allowed close-encounter victims to share their intimate experiences with others who had been through the same trauma without fear of their stories appearing in the tabloids. They operated not unlike 'Alcoholics Anonymous', based on the principle that people need support and that such support is best offered by others who have found ways of coping with the abduction entering their lives.

However, doubts were growing about the constant use of regression hypnosis to 'bring out memories' from the subconscious of abductees. Witnesses expected this to help them, but often faced more trauma from the uncertainties that these new memories brought (not to mention their frequently horrific nature). Hypnosis appealed to UFOlogists because it seemed to provide deeper stories of alien contact and so much material for new books. Although unqualified researchers were using it daily – sometimes even on small children – witnesses rarely felt better for it. However caring and well intended these experiments were, the witness was forced to live with the aftermath of the regression.

Psychologists were worrying about long-term consequences from hypnosis and one British man had an epileptic seizure during a hypnosis session, at which no medically qualified person was in attendance. So, BUFORA decided to act. It had already imposed strict requirements in its code of practice regulating the activities of its investigators. Now they voted for a moratorium banning the use of hypnotic regression altogether. Only Scandinavian UFO groups followed suit, with UFO Sweden issuing its own moratorium. Elsewhere in the world the use of hypnosis continued to spiral out of control and the outcome was a wave of thousands of apparent new abductions – most of which relied heavily on the dubious 'memory' (or 'fantasy') dispute that emerged via rampant hypnotic testimony.

especially when the guards resisted a meeting with Hopkins and the 'world leader' stayed silent. Speculation mounted that the encounter had been set up for this famous person to see. Indeed, as Hopkins told me three years later, 'This man is of such importance and has such credibility that if he were to tell the world what he saw that night, then the truth about alien contact would be established for all to see'.

Who this 'third man' was still remains a secret, although rumours are rife that it was a former secretary of the United Nations, Javier Perez de Cuellar. De Cuellar has never confirmed this story, despite being asked to do so. Officially, he was 'not in New York' on the night in question.

Other independent witnesses have since come forward, including a woman driving on the Brooklyn Bridge who says she also saw Linda being floated away. Some find it suspicious that all these people contacted Hopkins; his fame within New York, however, does not make it improbable. An independent study by three UFOlogists found that there were no witnesses from a busy news building opposite the apartment block despite their view that many should have seen what the three men in the car and woman on the bridge supposedly did. Hopkins has responded thoughtfully and in 1996 published a long-awaited book devoted to the case that has been dubbed as 'the big one'.

If this case is proved genuine and if the 'world leader' does talk, then it will be another example of the bold new direction taken by the phenomenon. Nobody disputes Budd Hopkins' integrity and no damning evidence on the honesty of other major players has been found, but many UFOlogists are hedging their bets before they commit themselves to this amazing close encounter.

Circular logic

Alongside the first news of this remarkable case, the crop circle phenomenon in Britain also took extraordinary new leaps forward. For a decade, simple circles and patterns had been forming in crop fields around Hampshire and Wiltshire as well as other rare examples around the world. But in the summers of 1989 and 1990, two things happened that turned a minor mystery into the talk of the planet.

Firstly, the phenomenon caught the imagination of the world thanks to a book called *Circular Evidence* which had many colour photographs of the patterns. Then the phenomenon responded by producing an ever more fantastic array of complex designs – nicknamed 'pictograms' – which ranged from glyphs or symbols to designs that varied from animals to computer-generated complex mathematical symbols akin to fractal graphics.

When the Hopi Indians of New Mexico announced that they recognized the symbols as coming from 'sky gods', the cry went out that this was a new form of undeniable alien contact. Along with the other new developments it seemed all too timely. As critics pointed out, however, the whole thing might be a massive hoax from someone reacting to the increased publicity by playing to the crowds. Hoaxers have come forward in abundance to claim the circles as their handiwork. Most notorious were Doug Bower and Dave Chorley, two retired Hampshire designers who alleged that they invented the whole mystery after seeing media reports about the 1966 patterns in Queensland, Australia. Although it is undoubtedly true that they – and others – have faked many circles and fooled a lot of people, there is much doubt that the entire phenomenon stemmed from human engineering.

Fields of vision
Crop circles began to appear in south-west England in the mid-1980s and became increasingly complex. The theories about them range from the 'plasma vortex' theory to suggestions that they are 'messages' from an alien culture.

Those who believe that a natural atmospheric effect is involved point to the fact that simple circles were discovered many years before the modern publicity, such as those dating back to the sixteenth century. These researchers insist that all complex shapes are hoaxes.

However, the belief that an alien message is being sent to earth is supported by the new-age community, ensuring that the crop circle mystery will not die.

The space shuttle and the UFO

On March 30, 1989, the front page of the British tabloid newspaper, the *Daily Star*, screamed: 'Shuttle Crew Saw Aliens'. Had NASA finally obtained proof that aliens were real?

Flight STS-29 has been launched in mid-March, involving the orbiter 'Discovery'. The story reported that the crew had encountered a strange craft that provoked electrical problems, leading to early termination of the mission.

MUFON UFO investigator Don Ratsch had tape-recorded a radio transmission in Maryland at 6.35 am on March 14. He had assumed that this was a ham radio interception of an earth-to-shuttle transmission. The crew had allegedly spoken the chilling words: 'Houston – we have a problem. We have a fire.'

At first glance it is hard to know why anyone would assume that this message had any other meaning. Fire aboard a space shuttle is not something about which NASA would be anything but honest. Indeed, it is known that there were some electrical faults aboard 'Discovery'.

However, Ratsch claims that seven minutes later he heard the far more sinister message, 'Houston – Discovery. We still have the alien spacecraft under observance.' The voice appears similar to that of John Blaha, the STS-29 mission pilot, but given the recording quality it is impossible to be sure.

The media suggested that 'fire' was NASA code for 'UFO'. Yet surely the crew would not waste precious time explaining to ground control that they had a genuine fire? Besides, if this was a code word, how come the phrase 'alien spacecraft' was spoken so openly?

On April 12, NASA responded to MUFON appeals for help. A full audio recording of the ground-to-space communications could be obtained 'for several hundred dollars'. NASA also stated that the tape was a hoax.

Meanwhile MUFON conducted a voice analysis of the tape. There were insufficient words spoken during the 'alien spacecraft' message for any assurance, but what checks were possible offered no evidence that John Blaha was the speaker. MUFON closed the file.

During May, the British UFO group – the IUN (Independent UFO Network) – contacted John Blaha and mission commander Michael Coats. Both insisted the story was 'pure fiction'.

Even though this case has not been proven, both 'Discovery' and Don Ratsch were to feature in a second riddle two years later.

On September 15, 1991, the same shuttle was over Indonesia when its cameras recorded white blobs of light that appeared to streak across the rim of the planet earth, seen below and ahead of the shuttle. They turned through right angles, bouncing into space at speed, exhibiting G forces that would be impossible for manned craft.

According to NASA's 'best guess', these are ice particles – a little like ice-borne meteors on the edge of the earth's atmosphere, skimming across earth's gaseous envelope. But the possibility that they are rather more than that is being taken seriously in at least some quarters.

Physicist Dr Jack Kasher of the University of Nebraska had worked on the 'Star Wars' programme, then moved to NASA in 1987 to take on the task of verifying the ice particles theory. He concluded that the theory was 'completely untenable' and the objects – whatever they were – seemed to be displaying apparent intelligent control.

The debate continues, but future 'Discovery' missions should certainly be worth watching.

1990: EXTRATERRESTRIAL TV

I want to tell you a story

When Alan from Hertfordshire contacted me, it was to request hypnotic regression. By 1990, most UFOlogists were getting pleas from such people all of the time. But, as Director of Investigations for BUFORA, I was responsible for its ban on regression and I had to tell Alan why it was not advisable.

Alan had experienced dreams and visions since childhood. These involved small creatures with gray skins and large heads who medically examined him to extract genetic samples from his body. It was only when he read books by Strieber and Hopkins that he came to see how these dreams matched an apparent reality described by others.

Of one of his experiences in which a device full of wires was placed inside his body causing it to vibrate, Alan told me: 'It was so prolonged and real that I thought it must have happened.' As with other spacenap victims, he felt that subconscious 'tasks' had been implanted in his mind waiting to be unleashed on some alien command. Like a growing number of people who were contacting UFOlogists the world over, these tasks were now unfolding and proving to be a wave of alien art and literature – professing new-age mysticism, cosmic philosophy and a blueprint for a better life on earth.

In Alan's case, a 64-chapter story about alien life and their mission on earth 'just tumbled out'. He was far from alone. I knew of many other abductees who had done the same thing.

Then Alan contacted me again to express relief that he had not been hypnotized. He felt that to do so would have locked him into the alien interpretation of his story. In the meantime, he had found some notes written immediately after one of his most profound experiences. These showed that he had adapted his memory in the wake of his reading into alien contact. He had not realized he had done this; it was entirely subconscious. But it substantially altered his memory of the event. Now he was sure these visions were internal psycho-dramas, perhaps expressing some sense of isolation.

Paradoxically, however, he was sure that the incident that had triggered all the visions was itself real. As a very young child he had awoken in the garden with a sense of paralysis, surrounded by 'little beings' and followed by a silent explosion of pure white light. For a time afterward he played a game – staring at the sky easing his mind with the words: 'the sun is my friend.' The process calmed him down.

Mass demonstration

As further complexities to the alien-contact story unfolded through this flood of alien literature, events in Belgium culminated in a case that remains one of the classics of modern history.

Sightings in late November 1989 and into December had been of gigantic 'football field' sized triangles of light. Triangles were by now already becoming the most common form of the UFO by far across the world – a pattern set to continue and escalate.

There had been hundreds of witnesses, including many police officers in the area around Eupen. Some UFOlogists argued that a new type of computer-controlled laser searchlight was to blame, reflecting off low cloud. This is certainly a possibility. There is also some evidence of secret mid-air refuelling exercises by NATO forces prior to bombing raids on the Middle East. Again, the unusual visual form of tanker aircraft and jets linked by umbilical cords and with a huge array of lights has similarity with the UFOs being reported.

ALIENS BOOST TV RATINGS

Television was now discovering the UFO mystery in a big way. The trend began in 1990 and over the next five years reached such a level that it was almost impossible not to turn on a set and find something about the subject being reported.

A series called *Unsolved Mysteries* in the USA set the ball rolling by adding occasional reports on UFO cases to its usual diet of reconstructed crimes. It was followed by *Sightings,* a magazine programme with weekly reports on the latest paranormal news.

These series were (and still are) shown around the world and spawned various offspring – such as *The Extraordinary* in Australia. Britain was one of the first on the scene with *Strange But True?,* dramatizing big cases using lookalike actors and mixing this with interviews involving real-life witnesses and researchers. A number of major cases – such as the events in Rendlesham Forest in 1980 – have since been portrayed. This programme provided a record TV audience for a British programme about UFOs, attracting over 12 million viewers.

Once-sceptical newspapers of high calibre, such as the London or New York *Times,* even the *Financial Times,* were now occasionally carrying favourable comment. Several books on the subject made the best-seller lists. Current affairs and defence specialist reporters began to cover the subject which had once been left to the tabloids and 'pulp' writers.

Some people, however, began to wonder whether this new respectability was all part of an alien plan. After all, aliens had allegedly told spacenap victims for many years that when the time was right an army of hidden abductees would be unleashed upon the world with a task to perform that was buried in their subconscious minds.

Was the escalation in unprecedented cases a sign of this? Were TV writers, producers, programme makers and media moguls also being stirred into action by a subconscious command? Indeed, was the planet being educated into the reality of alien contact through its most hypnotic medium – television?

Whatever the truth, the Belgian sightings generated huge public attention. On the night of March 30–31, 1990, UFO group SOBEPS joined forces with the media to stage a weekend 'sky-watch'. They had teams on standby at strategic points linked to police and Air Force controls using radar. Two F-16 fighters were put on alert and ready to launch if the experiment revealed new sightings. And it did.

Police at Wavre reported strange lights and the Air Force jets were scrambled. Their on-board radar picked up unusual readings and sophisticated computer equipment produced filmed proof, complete

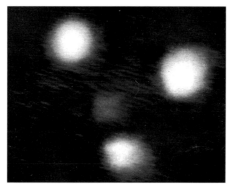

Belgian triangle
One photograph was taken of the triangular UFO seen over Belgium (and many other places since). It is thought by researchers to be an aircraft, but it looks just like the subject being widely reported.

with masses of hard data about the UFOs. The Belgian Air Force convened a press conference to release this material and admitted to being totally baffled. Some speculation centred on possible American 'Stealth jet' flights, but documents released by the Freedom of Information Act suggest that the US Government was just as puzzled as everyone else.

The fact that the F-16 pilots did not see the UFO detected by their radar may suggest it was 'disguised' (carrying no lights) or was some kind of natural phenomenon. Either way, the wave died down and the world was left with one more case to fathom out.

1991: New Frontiers

Braving the world

One advantage of the new mood of interest in UFOs was that witnesses who would formerly not have spoken out through fear of ridicule now chose to do so.

On June 16, l991, Bill, a highly successful and respected businessman, was returning to his Staffordshire home from a meeting in Chester. Because he was driving, he had consumed many cups of coffee whilst his colleagues who lived locally had consumed alcohol. This meant that when he reached Rushton near Rudyard Lake he was in dire need of a toilet. As it was 1.30 am and there were no conveniences in this isolated spot, he stopped to use some bushes near a place where he knew there was a neolithic site with standing stones.

Once in the bushes, Bill noted a bright light above the stones. At first he ignored it – but when it began to send a shower of golden sparks down towards the ground, he decided upon caution. Bill never considered the possibility of UFOs, but assumed that youths were playing about and he would be safer out of their way. Hastening back to the car he tried to start the engine, but both it and the vehicle's lights were dead. He got out to investigate, but as he was about to raise the hood a huge ball of golden light streaked towards him. Despite an intense desire to run, he was totally paralysed. He felt a sharp pain behind his eyes and lost consciousness.

Bill came to his senses on the ground in scrub at a spot he later found to be 600 feet from the car. He was disorientated, still groggy and terrified. But the object had now vanished. He also noticed that he was wearing his trousers, yet his shirt and shoes were missing. Brushing himself down, a brief shower of sparks emerged from his body, suggesting that he had been filled with static electricity.

In blind panic Bill hunted for the car. When he found it his shirt and shoes were there, warm to the touch. He tumbled into the car and it started first time. The dashboard clock read 3.05 am – an hour and a half had vanished.

Bill told his wife he had been in a car crash, but a few days later decided to come clean.

Eastward ho!

As the former communist states of eastern Europe opened their barriers to western culture, we found that alien contact was happening in these countries just as it was everywhere else.

One case occurred in the autumn of l991. A woman driving near Szekszard saw a blinding light swoop towards her car and she suddenly lost power before blacking out. When she awoke she was inside the Trabant but it was in a field surrounded by snow, and there were no tyre tracks to indicate how she had driven there.

Staggering from the car, the young woman headed towards a light which turned out to be a security guard post. The guards saw her distressed state, with legs bleeding as if she had walked through brambles. They drove her to the hospital suffering from dizziness and a high temperature, with puncture marks and blotches on her skin. All she could tell the doctors was her memory of the light. Meanwhile, police investigating her Trabant were baffled – the door handle had been subjected to such enormous heat that it was welded shut.

There was also a dramatic case of a 24-year-old woman who saw an orange ball fall from the sky, spiralling towards her like a flare. As it approached, she lost consciousness and awoke thirty minutes later wandering in a daze in the woods outside. Further experiences followed, which seem to be abduction memories.

HUBBLE TROUBLE

Exploration of the universe had taken a new step forward with the launch of the Hubble space telescope, put into orbit around the earth. Free of the limitations imposed by the atmosphere, it was able to see much further than any earth-based device.

Unfortunately, a problem arose with its mirror, making it far less useful than had been hoped. The new, reliable shuttle launches soon proved their worth when NASA astronauts were able to fix the telescope by, in a sense, fitting it with a pair of spectacles!

The results would soon come in from Hubble, revealing much about the distant parts of the galaxy and aiding the search for alien planets around other suns. We only knew for certain about our own solar system, where life was very improbable outside the earth. But if aliens were coming here, then they had to be travelling from a distant solar system light years from earth and if we could prove that they were commonplace, as many scientists believed, the odds in favour of alien life would become overwhelming.

There was some circumstantial evidence of the reality of other solar systems based on 'wobbles' in the orbits of suns believed to be caused by the tugging effects if planetary gravitation. But actual proof was almost impossible, because the vastly greater size and enormous glare of the sun would swamp any hope of seeing planets so far away. It was likened by astronomers to trying to pick out a speck of dust on a car headlight miles in the distance. At least now the hunt was on in earnest.

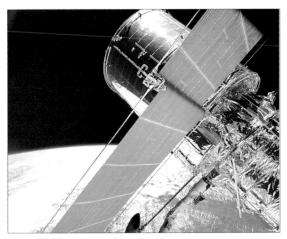

The Hubble space telescope
The space telescope was intended to view objects 50 times fainter and seven times further away than is possible with ground-based optical telescopes.

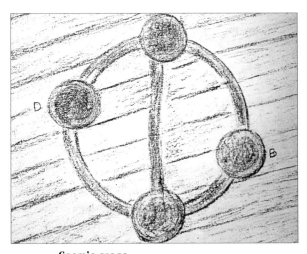

Cosmic crops
The spread of UFOs and related phenomena to Eastern Europe began as Communism fell. This is one of the first complex circle formations to appear in Bulgaria.

Shortly after this encounter, the woman unexpectedly found herself pregnant. She was sent to a hospital in Budapest and the findings were confirmed. After two months she began bleeding and was rushed back to see her gynaecologist fearing that she had aborted. An ultrasound scan was taken and the doctor looked stunned. It is alleged that he saw an image of an 'alien baby' with a very large head, but he has always publicly denied this. Indeed, as another gynaecologist stated, enlarged heads are not uncommon in scans of a foetus, particularly in the sort of disease that he suspected this case might have been. The Hungarian woman required surgery that same day and was told by her doctor this was to ensure all trace of the foetus was gone.

1992: UNDER THE INFLUENCE

Silent army

In early 1992, the Roper organization conducted a major opinion poll in the USA to discover the extent of abduction experience. It concluded that a staggering 2% of the American population may have been spacenapped.

This remarkable figure was only slightly modified when a survey was carried out on American mental health professionals. Of 266 of their patients, 43 claimed to have seen UFOs, the vast majority not having publicly reported them. A further 1.5% described incidents that suggested an abduction experience.

There is a huge problem with these figures. If we extrapolate to the general population then we would, for example, expect at least 800,000 British victims of spacenapping and about 4 million in the USA. The global numbers would be truly unthinkable. During a 1992 survey of British cases, I found there were only about 60 known examples of examples – less than one in ten thousand of those inferred by the surveys. Where was this silent army of abductees?

That was the subject for discussion at the first 'in camera' scientific symposium about abduction cases, organized by Dr Mack and an MIT physicist, David Prichard. The venue was the prestigious university of MIT in Cambridge, Massachusetts. It ran for a week in June 1992, and was by invitation only to the world's most experienced abduction researchers, plus a number of people working in related areas.

These areas included fields such as hypnosis, fantasy-prone personality data and a new cloud on the horizon – false memory syndrome. Psychologists were finding that in such cases a person could have an entire memory which they were certain was real, but which had been falsely implanted. Hypnosis was one way in which false memories could be induced.

The MIT symposium was a landmark in alien contact research. Among the positive results was the final disproving of the fantasy-prone personality theory as a working explanation for abductions. This came from numerous test results presented by several doctors. The problems of hypnosis were also highlighted but it was conclusively shown that this was not creating the abduction phenomenon, simply distorting some of its evidence.

New clues

Important new clues were produced from this mountain of research. For example, there was no longer any room to doubt that abductions primarily happened to people who had a life-long track record of other paranormal experiences such as out-of-body states, ESP and poltergeist attacks. It was also found that these people often had a very high level of visual creativity. Moreover, they frequently had an almost photographic memory and tended to be able to recall events from babyhood onwards – as opposed to the average first memory of most humans, which begins at about the age of three.

Did this mean that people were imagining abductions? The physical evidence and threads that bound these cases together seemed to dispute that idea. Or were aliens more able to contact people with a good visual capacity and a latent talent for ESP? Indeed, did the fact that abductees have such good memories explain the countless missing witnesses? Did only those with gifted recall know that it had happened to them?

Breakthrough

In November 1992, Houston hypnotist and abduction researcher Derrel Sims conducted a fascinating experiment to develop the lessons

IF ET PHONES...

With the Hubble telescope seeking alien life, a new project was launched by the US Government in 1992. It was designed to hunt for radio signals as in previous studies, but with sophisticated new computer technology a thousand times better than had previously been used.

Named 'Columbus' to coincide with the 500th anniversary of his discovery of the new world, this search for new worlds in space soon hit the buffers due to the huge costs involved in running the project. However, a NASA protocol was drawn up asking what to do should it pick up that elusive alien message. The protocol involved effectively dismantling the equipment to rule out the possibility of computer error, and then transferring the news to the US President for ultimate approval. The quaint idea that if ET called tonight we would all hear about it on the news tomorrow was quashed by these moves. The truth was that we would hear about it when the President decided, if at all.

learnt at MIT. He attempted to input a post-hypnotic suggestion into half a dozen spacenap victims who claimed frequent abduction memories. What he wanted them to do was challenge their alien captors with news that humanity was about to fight back and was seizing control of the situation!

Immediately, one of the abductees claimed that the method had worked. They were abducted and the suggestion stirred him to wakefulness during the experience. He then told the small grays that were kidnapping him: 'We know what you are doing. We know all about you.'

Within days, five of the six abductees recalled a new spacenapping. Independent follow-ups were carried out across the USA and Canada. Three of them spoke of the new abduction taking place on the same night – December 8, 1992. They all awoke to find blood on their pillows and there were suggestions that implants had been put into them to try to control their memories.

During hypnosis sessions, each of the abductees told very similar stories, but had somewhat different interpretations for the new features within them. One thought she had been to heaven and seen dead relatives. Another spoke of being in the presence of God. Two others told of similar events but placed them as being inside a UFO.

One of the most intriguing new features to emerge was that all of these abductees now described conversations with entities whom they had never met before – tall and more human-like beings. American cases in general had always provided less evidence of the tall ones. There is evidence that the grays are often supervised by the taller beings, but because the grays do the medical examinations while the tall ones usually stay in the background, a witness – especially under hypnosis – tends not to be aware of the more human-like figures.

In one case, a male abductee described to Sims how he had told the human-like being that the game was up and the abductees were regaining control. The alien asked the witness how he could recall his previous abductions since these had been 'blocked', and asked him to point to the subconscious mind in a model of a human brain.

Before he returned to his bed, this witness recalled hearing a debate between two of the tall entities now unsure as to whether their experiments could continue. These aliens blamed the grays for the problem and it was clear that there was major disagreement as to the correct approach between the two groups.

The media have emphasized the existence of grays to the almost total exclusion of the tall beings. As a result, anyone inventing an abduction would be unlikely to know that both entity types are common together.

1993: THE ALIEN OSCARS

By 1993, UFOlogists were receiving increasing numbers of videos submitted by witnesses who had filmed UFOs with their own camcorders. Rarely did these show anything very exciting, most depicting hazy lights in the sky that were not real proof of alien contact.

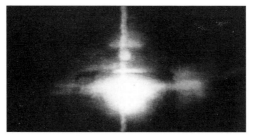

The Canadian video
A still from the video received by Bob Oeschler and which reputedly shows a UFO rotating near Carp, Ontario, Canada. The video was later retrieved by the authorities.

All that changed in early 1993 with revelations about a dramatic video taken in Ontario, Canada, that would capture the public's imagination. The tape arrived in the hands of ex-NASA researcher Bob Oeschler, who had established himself in the American UFO scene with firmly held beliefs about a US government cover-up. The tape came from an anonymous source known as 'Guardian', who had already passed on some rather implausible written reports of alleged UFO sightings.

The video tape was another matter altogether. When it arrived, it was subjected to intense investigation. It purportedly showed a UFO being 'recovered' near Carp, Ontario, with the first six minutes of the tape showing a well-lit, top-shaped object spinning and flashing in the dark.

Then came another 20 minutes of quite extraordinary footage. Unlike the UFO shots, these were montaged photographic stills. Lack of video film is one of the main arguments used by sceptics in this case. These images allegedly show a living alien recovered from the UFO! Unfortunately, all you can really see are cat-like eyes on a white beard and glowing hands. The rest of the body is black. The impression is not unlike mime artists who use a black backcloth in their acts. The being in the stills could easily be a human in a mask.

UFOlogy is strongly divided on this case. Many researchers think it is a hoax, noting that they have found no reliable evidence to support the story. Could someone have filmed this event and added the still mock-ups of an alien?

The real thing?
One of the controversial stills allegedly depicting a living alien recovered from Carp, Ontario. Unlike the UFO, which is shown in colour and motion on the video, these are black and white stills. Most UFOlogists are not convinced.

THE RACE FOR THE STARS

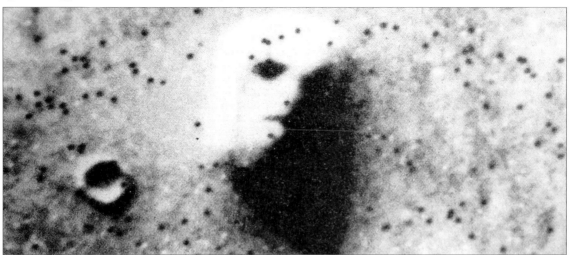

The face on Mars
The notorious 'face on Mars' as found by the NASA landing missions whilst in orbit. Is it proof of an alien civilization or an optical illusion, as NASA insist? In August 1993 NASA's Mars explorer was possibly about to settle the arguments once and for all. But then fate intervened.

In August 1993 the Mars Observer space-craft reached its destination after the long journey from earth. Its sophisticated cameras would provide the best photographic evidence about the red planet since the highly successful Viking landing missions of 1976.

Although Mars had become a fascinating world where the possibility of life could not be ruled out, NASA had seemed curiously reluctant to explore one of the strangest images from the Viking missions. Several photographs seemed to show what looked like a human face on the plains of Cydonia.

This object was a remarkable structure. A mile wide and facing skyward, it looked like an extraterrestrial equivalent of the sphinx. NASA laughed it off as a trick of the light – shadows reflecting from rocky surfaces and

human imagination. However, computer experts enhanced the image and concluded that the face was a genuine surface feature. Even Dr Brian O'Leary, a NASA physicist and astronaut, told me how he was convinced by the mounting evidence.

It took a great deal of persuasion to get NASA to publicly consider filming Cydonia from the Mars explorer. The cameras on board were so good that they would quickly prove if the face was real or just an optical illusion. There were even worries that, for the first time, the photographs would be 'vetted' before being released to the media.

However, this debate was to prove academic. When the Explorer reached Mars, it began to power up its cameras. Then all contact was lost. Frantic efforts were made to regain control, but all failed. The billion-dollar spacecraft was lost without providing any data. No one knew what had happened – a meteor strike, an engine explosion, perhaps a computer failure. Of course, there were those whose eyes turned to the surface of Mars and sought a stranger explanation.

Oeschler himself seems uncommitted. Accepting that the incident contains dubious elements, he claims to have found a circle at the site where the microwave energy had bleached the soil. Samples of a black powder taken from

here proved to be the rare metal titanium. Several local people also told him about seeing odd lights and military activity in the trees. An anonymous woman living nearby informed Oeschler about two small beings with pale faces that she had seen inside a craft that came down in the woods. But she lost consciousness and remembers nothing after that.

The jury is still out, but this is an astonishing new development for the alien contact story.

second, yet three separate images appear on the film of a disc-like object. The camera had recorded three different 'manifestations' of the object. Considerable analysis followed as UFOlogists attempted to understand the physics

of alien contact from the photograph. But researchers made one fundamentally flawed assumption – that the 'triple image' photograph depicted one single object that was moving upwards. It did not.

The 27-year fake
The 'triple UFO' photographed over Diamond Peak in Oregon, USA. It had been widely considered one of the most important cases on record and scientists attempted to understand the physics of the flight of the craft that produced these three 'simultaneous' images. The astonishing truth was revealed by researcher Irwin Wieder in 1993. The famous UFO was nothing more than a roadsign, with the motion of a passing car and the fast camera shutter speed producing the triple image.

The Williamette Pass controversy

One of the most impressive daylight UFO photographs was taken at Williamette Pass, Oregon, in October 1966.

The photograph was taken by a micro-biologist who wanted to remain anonymous, but who gave no suggestion that he was not telling the truth. This man had been trying to film the Diamond Peak beauty spot from his car when he saw an object shoot upwards.

Instinctively, he took a photograph. When it was processed, the print showed what appeared to be a UFO climbing up from the tree-line, trailing powdered snow in its wake. This fitted in well with eyewitness accounts of cases such as the South-Australian 'saucer nests'.

Yet there was a problem here. The camera lens had been open for just a fraction of a

UFOlogist Irwin Wieder had been pursuing the case for some years and he had a theory. He went to the Williamette Pass and tested his theory with reconstructions that attempted to duplicate the 1966 picture. In 1993, he published his findings in the *Journal of Scientific Exploration*. It was to be quite a shock for the UFO community.

Wieder proved beyond any possible doubt that there was only one object on the photograph and that it had not moved at all. The illusion of movement had actually been created by two elements: the motion of a passing car combined with a fast shutter speed on the camera. More astonishingly still, the 'UFO' in question turned out to be nothing more than a roadsign!

Nobody could have imagined that this well respected case would have such a simple explanation. Perhaps the witness knew the truth all along; maybe he was fooled when the photo was developed. Either way, this is a perfect example of how even the best evidence is sometimes not immune to misinterpretation!

THE SCIENCE-FICTION YEAR

Although only a couple of alien-themed movies appeared in 1993, it was a year when drama was destined to have a major influence on the UFO story.

The most intriguing film was *Fire in the Sky*. This was a fictional rendition of the famed 5-day-long alien abduction case from Snowflake, Arizona, in November 1975, with D.B. Sweeney taking the key role of real-life spacenap victim, Travis Walton. The movie was penned by Tracey Torme, who was responsible for some of the *Star Trek: The Next Generation* episodes. While most of the film dramatizes the abduction exactly as it was then recorded, the final scene aboard the UFO bears little resemblance to Walton's memories.

According to Torme, the switch was forced upon him at a late stage because of the appearance of the US TV series *Intruders* the year before. This dramatized other real alien-contact claims and, because such phenomena are closely similar, *Fire in the Sky* may have looked derivative. So producers insisted that their abduction had to be more gruesome.

Those sceptics who argue that abduction stories derive from sci-fi movie plots should bear this in mind. However, there is actually much more of a symbiosis – one medium moulds and shapes the other. Real life creates fiction, which in turn influences real life.

There is an extraordinary example of this process at work, suggesting that at times it borders on the magical.

Mainstream coverage
Fire in the Sky is probably the most realistic account Hollywood has ever produced of a case of alien abduction and remains a seminal film.

In the years before and after the actual Travis Walton abduction, there was a hit TV series called *The Waltons*. This long-running drama was based on the real-life childhood of writer Earl Hammer. Yet its fiction came to reflect subsequent reality in rather eerie fashion.

The TV *Waltons* involves brothers in a wood-cutting family in a rural area. Both Travis and his brother Duane in the real-life Waltons fit this description. In two episodes made shortly before 1975 a fiery UFO plunges from the sky, and in another, Mrs Walton talks idly about a small town she has seen on a map – the otherwise very missable Snowflake, Arizona!

Strange but True burst onto the scene in March 1993 – a title aptly describing this chain of coincidental events. Some may feel that co-incidence is the wrong word and that clues about the nature of reality are really being offered. In any event, this British television series presents factual dramatizations of paranormal cases and had huge success with its UFO episodes, including a record 12.5 million viewers for a recreation of the 1980 Rendlesham forest case.

1993 also saw the birth of the extraordinary US drama series *The X-Files*, which was to have an outstanding effect on public perception of UFOs in the following year.

Artistic licence
In this scene from *Fire in the Sky*, Travis Walton, played by D.B. Sweeny, is comforted by Doctor Kayle (Julia Ariola) and his girlfriend Katie (Kathleen Wilhoite) after having been abducted by the alien beings. The most disturbing final images, however, were more gruesome than in the real story.

1994: Not Going Mad

Highway robbery

Yet another barrier came down in 1994 with the discovery of a case that was seemingly an observed abduction. There had only been the controversial Manhattan transfer incident during which independent witnesses had reported an abduction as it happened. Now a new case offered further evidence, ironically from a spot quite close to the most famous example of a non-observed abduction – Maureen Puddy's 1972–73 encounters.

Young mother Kelly Cahill and her husband had been returning home in Melbourne, Australia, late on the night of August 8, 1993. They were passing through Belgrave in the foothills of the Dandenong mountain range when an orange light appeared on the road ahead. As they neared it they could see that it had a transparent dome on top and what appeared to be dark figures inside. Then a brilliant light filled the windscreen and they panicked. Kelly's husband asked her what she was going to do and she said she would drive right through it. Their next memory is of the light having vanished and the couple talking confusedly to one another of a UFO that they had both expected to confront. They dismissed the thought.

Driving onward, they reached home at 2.30 am. Kelly insisted that this was impossible and that it should only be about 1 am. Her husband said they must have left later than expected and the entire episode of this close encounter was written off as being of no importance. Besides, Kelly had more pressing concerns – as she put it, she felt 'pretty crook'. Not only was there a red triangular mark on her abdomen, but she had stomach pains and was sick. Then she started spotting blood.

Several weeks later, Kelly was rushed into hospital with an infection of the womb. The doctors stated that such an infection could only occur in one of two ways – if she had recent gynaecological surgery or if she was pregnant. Neither applied, but the hospital brought the infection under control and Kelly never connected the incident with her now barely recalled 'strange light'.

It was in January 1994 that the story took on a dramatic new edge. Kelly had been struggling to get her husband to even admit they had seen a UFO. He did not want to talk about it. She had had a series of dreams in which she saw a black suited figure over 6 feet tall and herself being paralysed and forced onto a table or bed inside a strange room.

Then she had driven down the same road again and had a panic attack. Recreating that August night brought its memory flooding back. Now she clearly remembered that the orange object had landed by the road and their car had been stopped along with another vehicle she did not recognize. She, her husband and some other humans were in the field surrounded by the tall beings and being told not to be afraid as no violence was intended. She was screaming that these entities were 'monsters' who intended to 'steal our souls' and felt herself hit in the stomach by a blow and thrown onto the ground. Then she heard the entities saying they meant no harm and one adding – as if talking to an unseen human – 'I could not harm her. She is my daughter'. Kelly then found herself back in the car.

Call for back up

Taken on its own, the Dandenongs case is a typical alien contact. Sceptics would term it a fantasy, perhaps based on something real such as seeing a light in the sky. But the critical difference is that Kelly could be regressed to the

ALL IN THE MIND?

The Dandenongs case was not researched by sceptical psychologist, Dr Sue Blackmore of West of England University, when she presented a BBC science documentary for *Horizon* about the phenomenon of abductions. This was stimulated by the decision of the Harvard psychiatrist and Pullitzer prize winner, Professor John Mack, to publish his book-length report into personal abduction investigations and to reveal that he believed that some genuine alien contact may be occurring.

Blackmore seemed to side with a Canadian neuropsychologist called Dr Michael Persinger, who for 15 years had been working with 'earthlights' researchers. Although Blackmore's programme gave British UFOlogy none of the credit it deserved for this work, she found that Persinger had equipment to duplicate the intense electro-magnetic fields generated by these energy balls at window areas. By exposing human guinea pigs to them, Persinger believed that he could show how the lights triggered hallucinations, possibly in the brain's temporal lobe. Those who saw an 'earthlight', then thought it a UFO, would face a subsequent hallucination based on modern cultural interpretations of that UFO – as an alien contact. Centuries ago they would have interpreted the glowing light differently and so would have had an hallucination of some other phenomenon such as a trip to fairyland.

Despite such powerful evidence for alien abduction as the Dandening case presents, John Mack was still to suffer considerable peer pressure to abandon his research. Indeed, his methodology was reviewed by the Harvard medical school which, according to some sources, might have threatened his career.

After some time the review appeared happy to allow Dr Mack to continue provided that he continued to apply scientific protocol. He has expanded his research and travelled the world bringing both his charm and medical expertise to the aid of baffled and concerned witnesses to alien contact.

While the value of regression hypnosis as a tool to investigate abduction cases is debatable, the need for a professional of Mack's stature to volunteer time and energy to assist people too often ignored by his colleagues is all too clear. It is welcome news that John was not deflected from his research.

Twenty, or even ten years earlier, he would have faced such severe censure from his peers that he might well have been forced to give up. This, above all else, is a measure of the progress that has been made.

night and describe the licence plate on the second vehicle that had stopped beside the UFO. From this it proved possible to find the car and its three occupants – a husband and wife and young female friend.

Bill, the husband in this trio, reacted intriguingly like Kelly Cahill's husband. He was, in effect, 'switched off' during the encounter, recalling seeing the UFO and 'black figures' inside, but not seeming to have experienced an abduction. Both the women spoke of going into the UFO, although, interestingly, they felt that they did so willingly. Is this why Kelly Cahill remembers screaming at people whom she could not see, desperately trying to persuade them not to trust the aliens despite their protestations of friendship?

Again, both women displayed physical after-effects. The symptoms included a vaginal infection present in one woman, and a rash on both women's thighs. More detail has since emerged from this case and, according to investigator Bill Chalker, the witnesses have yet to go public with regard to these aspects of their story.

As Chalker rightly points out, this event seems to be an ideal case of spacenapping. Potentially it is of huge importance in proving the reality of the phenomenon outside of the mind of a single person. At least it confirmed mounting evidence from tests by psychologists in the wake of the MIT symposium. These results proved clearly that abductees were normal people and were not going mad.

1995: Proof at Last?

Roswell: The movie

In late 1993, a few UFOlogists in Britain began to hear stories that the ultimate proof was on its way. It concerned the Roswell case and was actual film footage from the official US military archives that depicted the autopsies conducted on the recovered bodies during late 1947.

The news was kept within a small group of people for more than a year at the request of BUFORA officer Philip Mantle, who explained that delicate negotiations to buy the footage were under way between a British businessman who had been offered it by a retired military cameraman in the USA. Mantle seemed to have been approached as a sort of consultant by the businessman to confirm that there really was a Roswell case and that film of these bodies was thus conceivable.

In early 1995 the dam broke and the news of this amazing footage came out when rock singer Reg Presley stunned presenters by referring to it during a BBC TV interview. Presley's song 'Love is all around' had just been a massive worldwide hit and he announced that he planned to spend his earnings on research into UFOs and crop circles. This inevitably put him in the spotlight. It turned out that the businessman was a rock video and music entrepreneur called Ray Santilli, and he had just shown Presley, singer with The Troggs, the footage that he had finally purchased.

Surprisingly, this revelation did not lead to immediate headlines, but a series of leaks followed in the national media, citing researchers such as Mantle and thus hyping the product. Mantle also secured a deal whereby Santilli agreed to give the public premier of the footage at BUFORA's major conference in Sheffield in August 1995. As the story of the film grew ever more complex, this decision was questioned by many within UFOlogy, who argued that BUFORA was putting financial advantage above its principles. They had not been allowed to conduct scientific research into this piece of evidence and its authenticity was increasingly in doubt. BUFORA council countered that they were simply facilitating a debate by allowing its screening. Unfortunately, no debate took place at the conference and incredible security precautions were demanded to ensure that nobody took hidden cameras into the screening! As feared, the conference became a PR exercise for the footage.

Real or hoax?

Was the Roswell footage genuine or not? By the time stills from it appeared in the tabloids and the world saw it on television a few days later, there was already widespread disenchantment. Numerous leading UFO experts, including several key figures in the Roswell case investigation, had been publicly calling it a hoax. There was dwindling support for its authenticity when the footage went on sale as a video and Santilli's marketing company carefully worded the package to say that, although they thought it to be genuine, they could not prove beyond all doubt that it really was footage showing an alien autopsy.

In essence, the film runs in black and white on jerky footage for some minutes and shows a small, but surprisingly human-like body on a table being cut open by masked doctors. The being's cranium is large but this is not a gray of alien-contact lore, nor particularly akin to any of the accounts of the bodies supposedly recovered from the Roswell crash. Indeed, the figure much more resembles a deformed human than it does an alien. Various organs are seen being

ROSWELL REVISITED

Not to be outdone, a movie based on the Roswell story entitled Roswell also made its debut. Made for TV, it was a faithful dramatization of the story that placed Jesse Marcel in the role of a crusader upon his retirement in 1978 and then refused to accept the cover-up imposed upon him from above for 30 years.

Marcel was played by actor Kyle McLachlan, who had starred in the enigmatic series *Twin Peaks* as an FBI agent. He was rumoured to be in the running for the lead role in *The X Files* which had gone to David Duchovny (another who was also in *Twin Peaks*).

As a reflection of a UFO case, Roswell proved an excellent movie – by far the best UFO-related screenplay since *Close Encounters*. Its chief consultants were Kevin Randle and Don Schmitt from the J. Allen Hynek Center for UFO Studies, who themselves had cameo roles in the movie. It was based on their two books about a new investigation they had mounted, notably *UFO Crash at Roswell* (1992). Indeed this Paul Davids film went some way to compensating for the negative factors that the case had accumulated during 1995.

extracted from the body but these are fuzzy shots and it is difficult to tell if they are of any significance.

Other brief sequences depict the supposed wreckage at Roswell, but whilst there were stories that the cameraman had filmed the US President walking through the debris field, we simply observe lumps of metal set out on a table. There is a beam with hieroglyphic-like symbols on it, but this wreckage is not akin to any of the eyewitness reports or the model of the debris and symbols produced by airline pilot Kent Jeffrey under the direction of Jesse Marcel's son. He had seen the debris for himself back in 1947. As one of the few surviving eyewitnesses to Roswell, the fact that Marcel's detailed description does not support what is on the Roswell film is one of many reasons why Jeffrey is certain that the film is a hoax. The beam on the footage even has letters that seem to spell out 'Video OTV' – which is either a coincidence or, as some people have claimed, a clue that was deliberately left by whoever hoaxed the footage.

Nobody suggests that Santilli faked the footage. He claims to have paid big money for it from some still anonymous source in the USA. This source alleges that it was not collected from him by the US Government after he was

contracted to film the autopsy. He was selling it to help out his family. As to whether this mystery man was the hoaxer, or he himself was fooled, nobody is certain. But the limited evidence in favour of the footage (that the film stock may well date from 1947) is balanced against the numerous problems. For a start, it has not been properly authenticated and it seems inconceivable that just one man would film the autopsy (and in black and white) when major military events were being filmed from multiple angles and in colour well before 1947. Experts in film techniques also say that there are clear signs on the footage that it is not authentic. Miles Johnston – a Sky TV worker who watched it with me in Sheffield (and who is a firm believer in aliens) – said with great disappointment: 'I knew within two minutes this was not genuine.'

Disinformation?

The Roswell autopsy film created massive public interest for a time but the story faded from popularity quite quickly when its status was left in limbo. Throughout 1996 there were many rumours of new footage releases and nobody is betting that we have heard the last of this story. But even the TV series *The X Files* created a spoof 'autopsy' episode which seemed unwilling to take the evidence seriously and a book, due for release in April 1997, is awaited in which the full story will allegedly to be told.

Although the film may prove to be genuine, very few people, be they special effects experts, photographic specialists or UFOlogists, seem convinced. If it is a fake, the quest to find who hoaxed it and why has also failed to come up with damning evidence.

Some wonder, for example, if the footage could be real military film from 1947, but the claim that the bodies were of aliens might have been made to the cameraman as a ruse to mislead him. This might have been disinformation to hide horrible medical experiments being conducted on humans – possibly research into the genetic effects of radiation. After all, captured Nazi scientists were helping the USA to build rockets at this time; the Nazis got up to some pretty awful medical experiments as well. What if some of these were also continued?

The question of disinformation also figures because of other events in the Roswell case that occurred during 1994 and 1995, exactly matching the timetable for the release of this footage. These began when US Senator Walter Schiff was persuaded by UFO researchers to take action and the GAO (General Accounting Office of the US Government) agreed to a major document search for records on the case. This was the closest thing in 47 years to an independent study of the case.

Whilst the GAO mounted their investigation, the US Air Force pre-empted it almost immediately in August 1994, by announcing new records on the matter. Something had crashed at Roswell and it was not an ordinary weather balloon. The UFOlogists were right in charging that this story had been a cover-up. It was not, however, an alien spaceship – the wreckage was of a balloon used by a top-secret project known as Mogul. The project was concerned with searching for any evidence that the USSR had successfully exploded an atomic weapon, a crucial question for the Americans in the years following World War Two.

When the GAO enquiry findings emerged a year later, the furore over the Roswell autopsy footage and the widespread feeling that it was a hoax muted the public attention this mammoth report might otherwise have got. Although the GAO found no proof that a spaceship crashed at Roswell, they seemed to agree that it was more than just an ordinary balloon. The Mogul Project was considered feasible, but they had discovered that crucial records covering the period had been taken from the archives. Nobody could now find them and this prevented any clear judgement on the matter.

Whether by accident or design, the dubious autopsy-footage saga was an excellent distraction from this GAO quest. If the powers-that-be, unsure precisely what this enquiry would turn up, had wanted to engineer a discrediting of the Roswell case in most people's eyes, then the furore over this film could not have been more timely. Perhaps they were just lucky.

Alien airways

On January 6 1995, a remarkable encounter took place over the Derbyshire hills of northern England. It involved a British Airways Boeing jet inbound from Milan to Manchester Airport. Above the small town of Whaley Bridge an object was seen both by the pilot and first officer, rushing at great speed towards their cockpit. There was little time to react, other than to duck instinctively. Within five seconds, the object had vanished.

After the two pilots swapped notes and realized that they had both seen more or less the same thing, they filed a report with air traffic control. The first officer appears to have described the object as a wedge shape with what might be windows on the side. The pilot's report describes a mass of light, which may have been reflected from the Boeing. But the similarities between their reports outweighed

COSMIC CLUES TO ALIEN LIFE

News broke in May of this year that strange results were being recorded from tests on a meteorite found in Antarctica some years before. This was believed to have been ejected from the surface of Mars when it had been struck by a comet or large rock and the projectile had eventually crashed on earth. These tests were suggesting that organic processes had been fossilized inside. If proven, this might be the first true evidence of life beyond the earth.

Comets were also in the news in 1995. Comets are gaseous clouds of particles. Often they have a solid ice core that burns off as they pass around the sun and are projected like slingshot into the further reaches of their orbit. The return trajectory may take anything from just a few years up to several centuries. There is even a remote possibility that earth may be in line for a direct hit one day.

Such a strike is a rarity but it does happen. One such strike occurred on Jupiter when the Shoemaker-Levy comet made one of its return visits just as it had done so many times before across the aeons. Only this one, during the summer of 1994, had been different. So close did it come to Jupiter's massive gravitational pull that the comet was literally shaken apart and broken into fragments. Some of these plunged to their doom in a pyrotechnic spectacle caused by the heat of the friction as they entered the Jovian atmosphere.

Other fragments escaped to wander the solar system and may have been responsible for a dramatic increase in 'fireball meteor' activity which was visible from the earth's northern hemisphere a few months later. During the winter of 1995 many of these brilliant balls of glowing light trailed across the heavens and were mistaken for, and reported as, UFOs by startled witnesses.

the differences, and this led to a civil aviation authority investigation that lasted a year. The investigation viewed the incident as a possible near collision – which is certainly how the air crew considered the threat that they had faced. It was difficult to estimate the distance between the jet and the UFO in the darkness and there was no evident 'wake turbulence' left by its passage, suggesting it was not quite as close as it had seemed.

UFOlogists are divided on this case. Some feel the jet encountered an alien craft. Others believe that it was some sort of secret earth technology – possibly a rogue flight of a pilotless aircraft which strayed into the airline's. If so, then somebody covered it up and the aviation authority enquiries failed to discover the truth. Indeed, the object was not even detected on radar by Manchester airport – only the British Airways Boeing being visible during the close encounter.

For this reason, amongst others, I suspect that it might well be possible that the object was

a bright fireball meteor known as a bolide, miles high in the atmosphere, only appearing to be much lower and closer. This opinion is controversial and seems to be disputed by both the air crew and the aviation enquiry – even though there is no indication from the published report that they ever considered this as a possibility. It is also true that during 1996 the 'secret aircraft' theory gained ground due to other events, as you will see shortly.

As for the civil aviation authority, they created a ripple of astonishment when, for the first time in an official report, they took seriously the idea that the object seen by the British Airways pilots might have been an 'extraterrestrial' visitor.

The authority's investigators did note that it was not their province to make such a judgement, but the fact that they were willing to discuss it as the possible cause of a near mid-air disaster shows just how far we had come by 1995 to accepting alien reality.

1996: ALIEN ARTEFACTS

An inside story

Some of the expected rumours about new Roswell revelations surfaced in April when pieces of metallic debris were received by a museum set up in the town. Later, more pieces were received by a journalist. The anonymous note claimed that this was actual debris from the Roswell crash. However, tests revealed that these fragments were very terrestrial materials and had not been anywhere near the vacuum of space, let alone a distant alien planet.

Far more curious was the discovery made by abduction researcher Derrel Sims. He had persuaded a doctor in California to risk his licence and perform surgery on two abductees, one from the USA and one from Canada. Both believed that aliens had placed objects inside their bodies as monitor devices.

Small, strange-looking objects were extracted from the bodies of the two witnesses and two were very similar. Electron-microscope studies revealed a complex structure like fibre optics, but their exact nature could not be ascertained. More research was ordered. The doctor noted that in both instances the patient had shown a physical response when he touched the objects before he had removed them.

It was possible that these would turn out to be further dramatic evidence for alien contact, but nobody was getting too excited in case another explanation materialized.

Triangular UFOs

Throughout 1996, the prominence of reports of triangular UFOs grew throughout the world. These triangular objects were reported to hover then speed off at amazing rates of acceleration. In the UK there was a massive wave of such sightings on the Lancashire coast, involving unexplained power cuts around Fleetwood and video footage of the object taken in Knotty Ash, Liverpool and in Morecambe.

Speculation mounted that a British Aerospace plant at Warton near Blackpool (right in the middle of the area of these sightings) was somehow responsible. It was likened to a British version of Area 51 and the possible test site for new secret aircraft – or alien-inspired craft.

They were also sighted in many other areas, including the Peak District between Sheffield and Derby. A British Airways aircraft crew claimed they had almost collided with one over Whaley Bridge in Derbyshire.

Then, on September 23, 1996, one of the triangular objects with lights on each corner was alleged to have landed at Freuchie in Fife, Scotland. According to eyewitnesses, several strange entities emerged from the object. They comprised one dark being that was over 6-feet tall and a number of smaller grayish-white creatures; they were seen doing menial work under the supervision of the tall one. They appeared to be digging in the ground and creating mounds of earth. In daylight, these strange physical traces were found.

Throughout 1996 evidence mounted for these triangular craft, including a spectacular photograph taken over Rivington Pike near Bolton in the north of England. Witnesses who saw it were baffled. The tabloids wrote up their stories as potential alien encounters. But if what they saw really was terrestrial in origin rather than extraterrestrial, then the extraterrestrial explanation was a perfect smoke screen for a secret project above a populated area where test activity would otherwise be impossible. It almost seemed as if UFOlogists were being used by the authorities as convenient agents of disinformation.

LIFE ON MARS — AND BEYOND

In the summer, Dr Sue Blackmore announced that two years of research into alien abduction stories at the University of West of England had vindicated her view that they were hallucinations. She had found evidence that the paralysis reported by witnesses was not caused by aliens but was a well known physiological consequence of the mind's nocturnal limit on control over the muscles known to psychologists as sleep paralysis.

Dr Blackmore, whose 1993 theory of the Dying Brain had dismissed near-death experiences as visions brought about by neural breakdown when the body was seriously ill, received similar criticism from abductees as she had then from NDE witnesses. Nobody could understand this phenomenon by studying it in the laboratory — it transcended attempts to wish it all away.

As the media used Dr Blackmore's conclusions to try to show that alien contact was not possible, the year was providing extraordinary scientific proof to the contrary.

Deep space scans had revealed the first confirmed existence of other solar systems around distant stars. By March, new planets were constantly being revealed. This vastly increased the probability that alien life must exist on one, perhaps on many, of these distant worlds.

In August, NASA convened an astonishing press conference and announced to the world that they had indeed found fossil life in the Martian meteorite. It was now strongly believed that primitive life (possibly even more advanced life) had lived on this planet millions of years ago. It might still be there today and those who had championed the cause of the Face on Mars photographs were delighted.

Soon afterwards the first signs of possible life on a moon of Jupiter were detected.

Then, in December 1996, a NASA probe found a lake of ice water on the moon. It was deep in a crater and had long gone undetected, but its presence on a world that was widely considered sterile and dead was astonishing. Water was the key to life. Whilst its presence does not mean that life exists on another planet, it greatly increases the probability.

Suddenly within a few months the odds against the existence of alien life both inside and beyond the solar system had been drastically cut. It showed the folly of making too many presumptions based on the opinion that science knows everything of importance already.

Of course, if life existed somewhere out there, then the fact that it might well be able to come here and contact us (possibly to spacenap us) was a good deal harder to deny.

On October 26, huge explosions and flashes of light were witnessed by inhabitants of the island of Lewis, off the west coast of Scotland. Something was seen to plunge into the ocean trailing smoke. A major search and rescue operation was launched, but no civil or military aircraft was reported missing. Flights of US stealth jets were checked to see if a secret mission might have gone down. It had not.

Yet the search continued. The following day, UFOlogist James Sneddon, who was monitoring the radio transmissions of the search, heard a description of what appeared to be the discovery of a small object. Soon afterwards a Lynx helicopter was flown to the site. Hours later a major NATO 'exercise' brought several military vessels into the area and they stayed there for a week. Officially this was a 'routine' event, but a local politician was later told by a fisherman that he had seen one of the ships 'haul something' from below the surface.

The official story was that the sighting was probably just a bright meteorite or space debris fall. But with Flyingdales and Norad radar sniffing around the case from both sides of the Atlantic, and organizations such as the Sandia laboratories in New Mexico standing by to analyse data, suspicion was mounting that there was a lot more to this case than met the eye.

Did a flying triangle crash on October 26 1996? Or was this — almost 50 years on — a new Roswell story, destined to gather momentum as the years roll by? Was it, in fact, just the latest in a long line of alien contacts?

1997: Are We Ready?

Is the world ready for what a rising number of scientists consider the inevitability of alien contact? Most still deny that it has happened already, although the probability that it has is described in this book. Even so, the chance that it will happen, possibly quite soon, is taken very seriously indeed.

1997 has brought the 50th anniversary of the saga of alien contact, a story that has gone through remarkable twists and turns. A barrage of movies about UFOs and aliens have been made to coincide, including *Men in Black* – about government agents of disinformation to hide the truth – and *Contact*, from the novel of alien contact in space by Carl Sagan. Sagan was one of the men who sat on the US Government commission into UFOs in l966 and who six years later edited its first scientific book.

These fictional renditions go some way towards preparing the ground. Indeed, they have provoked speculations about a gradual education of the population to ensure we will not face the culture shock that alien contact might provoke. After all, what will it do to religious beliefs to learn that aliens have been studying us, possibly even intervening in our history in a way that many races have interpreted as divine? How will the money markets, technology, and many other areas of our lives be affected by the new science and philosophy that a more advanced race could bring in an instant?

Must we assume that alien contact will actually be to our advantage? Two of the biggest movie hits of l996 and one of the first movies of l997 certainly did not. In *Star Trek: First Contact*, an evil force takes over the earth by controlling time and space. In the blockbuster *Independence Day*, the cover-up of alien reality is blown when they finally land en masse and the earth defeats them thanks to the technology retrieved from the Roswell UFO kept under lock and key in Area 51. *Mars Attacks* was even less subtle, preying on the fears of what life on this red planet might be like if it is rather more than the microbes that most scientists predict.

The experiences of Michael Knighton reported as the New Year dawned showed that we still have some way to go. He is a highly successful multi-millionaire businessman and chairman of Carlisle United football club. His team were doing well, but he made the mistake of attending a meeting about UFOs from which the local paper discovered why he was so interested in the subject. Knighton and his wife had seen a UFO descend over a petrol station in the Pennine Hills on the Lancashire-Yorkshire border during the massive 1977 wave. It was also right inside the window area where more alien contacts have been recorded than anywhere else in Europe. As the UFO descended, Knighton had heard a seemingly alien voice telling him not to be afraid.

As this book shows, he probably did not have anything to fear from the UFO or its possible alien occupants. Whatever they are doing, however we might struggle to understand their motives, it seems that the open warfare of *Independence Day* and *Mars Attacks* will remain fiction.

However, what Knighton may instead need to fear is the public attitude he had to face, possibly born of such irrational fears. It is an attitude fuelled by media hysteria that heaps ridicule on brave witnesses for simply relating what they saw. It is an attitude that must change if we are to handle alien contact when it finally happens beyond any shred of doubt. That day is coming. Bet on it.

FURTHER READING

There are countless books about UFOs and aliens, covering a wealth of ideas. The following selection is divided into a number of key topics. Whilst I by no means agree with the contents of all of them, they do provide an important aspect of coverage in the area concerned. As with any issue, breadth of awareness is crucial to true understanding which is why I have included some books that are openly sceptical. Much as you want to see why researchers adhere to one theory or another, it is just as important to appreciate why some people do not believe. After all – they might be right!

Early days
The Coming of the Saucers
Kenneth Arnold & Ray Palmer
(Amherst, 1952)

UFOs Exist
Paris Flammonde (Ballantine, 1977)

The Roswell Incident
William Moore & Charles Berlitz
(Grafton, 1980)

UFO Crash at Roswell
Kevin Randle & Don Schmitt
(Avon, 1992)

History
The UFO Controversy in America
David Jacobs (IUP, 1975)

UFOs and Outer Space Mysteries
James Oberg (Donning, 1982)

The Complete Book of UFOs
Peter Hough & Jenny Randles
(Sterling, 1996)

UFO Encyclopedia Project
Jerome Clark (3 vols.)
(Omnigraphics, 1996)

UFOs 1947–1997
(Ed) Hilary Evans & Dennis Stacy
(Fortean Times, 1997)

Government studies
The Report on UFOs
Edward Ruppelt (Ace, 1956)

Clear Intent
Barry Greenwood & Larry Fawcett
(Prentice-Hall, 1984)

Above Top Secret
Tim Good (Sidgwick & Jackson, 1987)

Open Skies, Closed Minds
Nick Pope (Simon & Schuster, 1996)

A Covert Agenda
Nick Redfern(Simon & Schuster, 1997)

MIB: The Men in Black Phenomenon
Jenny Randles (Piatkus, 1997)

Scientific research
Flying Saucers
Carl Jung (Routledge & Kegan Paul, 1959)

Anatomy of a Phenomenon
Jacques Vallee (Regnery, 1965)

UFOs? Yes!
David Saunders & Roger Harkin
(World, 1968)

The Scientific Study of UFOs
Edward Condon (Ed)
(Bantam, 1970)

UFOs: A Scientific Debate
Carl Sagan & Thornton Page
(Cornell, 1972)

The UFO Experience
J. Allen Hynek (Regnery, 1973)

Space-time Transients
M. Persinger & G Lafreniere
(Nelson, 1976)

UFOs: The Public Deceived
Philip Klass (Prometheus, 1983)

Science and the UFOs
Jenny Randles & P.Warrington
(Blandford, 1986)

The Omega Effect
Kenneth Ring (Morrow, 1992)

The UFO Mystery Solved
Steuart Campbell (Explicit, 1994)

SETI
We Are Not Alone
Walter Sullivan
(Hodder & Stoughton, 1965)

Messages from the Stars
Ian Ridpath (Fontana, 1978)

Other Worlds
Paul Davis (Dent, 1980)

Where is Everybody?
Edward Ashpole (Sigma, 1997)

Case Investigations
The Interrupted Journey
John Fuller (Souvenir, 1978)

Project Blue Book
Brad Steiger (Bantam, 1978)

The UFO Handbook
Allan Hendry (NEL, 1980)

UFOs: African Encounters
Cynthia Hind (Gemini, 1982)

The Evidence for UFOs
Hilary Evans (Aquarian, 1983)

UFOs and How to See Them
Jenny Randles
(Sterling, 1993)

From Out of the Blue
Jenny Randles (Berkeley, 1992)

The Oz Files
Bill Chalker (Duffy &
Snellgrove, 1996)

Something in the Air
Jenny Randles (Hale, 1997)

Crop Circles
The Crop Circle Enigma
Ralph Noyes (Bartholomew, 1990)

Circles from the Skies
Terence Meaden (Souvenir, 1991)

Crop Circles: A Mystery Solved?
Paul Fuller & Jenny Randles
(Hale, 1993)

Abductions
Missing Time
Budd Hopkins (Merak, 1982)

Intruders
Budd Hopkins
(Random House, 1987)

Abduction
Jenny Randles (Hale, 1988)

*UFO Abductions: A Dangerous
Game*
Philip Klass(Prometheus, 1989)

Perspectives
John Spencer (Macdonald, 1990)

Dark White
Jim Schnabel (Hamilton, 1994)

*Close Encounters of the
Fourth Kind*
C.D. Bryan (Weidenfield &
Nicholson, 1995)

Alien Discussions Various
(the MIT symposium)
(North Cambridge Press, 1995)

*The Truth about Alien
Abductions*
Peter Hough & Moishe Kalman
(Cassell, 1997)

Many magazines are currently
available to further UFO research.
Their quality is often far less
predictable than the books. Most
of the major UFO groups listed
below produce their own
publication and these are a very
safe place to start. The leading
UFO journals in the world often
come from these sources – most
notably International UFO
Reporter (the J. Allen Hynek
Center for UFO Studies), UFO
Times (BUFORA) and MUFON
Journal (MUFON).

There are also some worthy
independent titles. This list is by
no means exhaustive but it does
include what I regard as some
very useful publications.

Enigmas
29 Kent Road
Alloa
Clackmannanshire
Scotland
FK10 2JN

Irish UFO Journal
Box 3070
Whitehall
Dublin 9
Ireland

Just Cause
Box 176
Stoneham
MA 02180
USA

Magonia
5 James Terrace
London
England
SW14 8HB

New UFOlogist
3 Selbourne Court
Tavistock Close
Romsey
England
SO51 7TY

Sceptics UFO Newsletter
404 N Street South West
Washington DC
20224
USA

The Sceptic
Box 475
Manchester
England
M60 2TH

**Information service and
reports of sightings**
In the UK only, a weekly updated
news and information service is
produced on behalf of BUFORA.
This covers all the latest news,
highlights forthcoming lectures
and conferences around the
country and describes recent
sighting activity. Known as UFO
Call, it is available on the BT
network at premium line rates
(39p per minute off peak in
1997) Dial: 0891 12 18 86.
For full reports of regional
sightings in the UK plus the latest
news and forthcoming
conferences and events – or,
indeed, should you wish to report
your own encounter to the author
of this book – I recommend:

Northern UFO News
1 Hallsteads Close
Dove Holes
Buxton
Derbyshire
SK17 8DS

UFO ORGANIZATIONS

The following are some of the more reputable UFO organizations in the world. Once again, this is by no means a complete list and no slight is intended should a credible group not be featured. But if you wish to get in touch with an organization, either to expand your own knowledge or to report a sighting, you cannot do much better than any of the following:

Africa
UFO Afrinews
Box MP 49
Mount Pleasant
Harare
Zimbabwe
Africa

Australia
Australian UFO Centre
Box W42
West Pennant Hills
NSW 2125
Australia

Belgium
NUFOC
Tien Esteenweg 78/401
B-3800 Sint-Truiden
Belgium

France
Ovni Presence
SOS OVNI BP 324
13611
Aix-en-Provence
Cedex 1
France

Germany
CENAP
Postbox 520231
D-68246
Mannheim
Germany

Italy
CISU
Corso Vittorio Emmanuelle 108
I-10121
Torino
Italy

North America
Canada UFO Research Network
Box 15
Station A
Willowdale
Ontario
M2N 5S7

J Allen Hynek Center for
UFO Studies
2457 West Peterson Ave
Chicago
Il 60659

Mutual UFO Network
103 Oldtown Road
Seguin
TX 78159-4099

UFO Research Centre Canada
Dept 25
1665 Robson St
Vancouver
British Columbia
V6G 3C2

Sweden
AFU/UFO Sweden
Box 11027
600 11 Norrkoping
Sweden

UK
British UFO Research Association
BM BUFORA
London
WC1N 3XX

Northern Anomalies Research
Organization
6 Silsden Avenue
Lowton
Warrington
WA3 IUE

Scottish Mysteries Research
35 Fountain Road
Bridge of Allan
Stirlingshire
FK9 4AU

Welsh Federation of UFOlogists
Box 43
Rhyl
Denbighshire
LL18 IYW

INDEX

A

abductions 16–17, 23, 24, 34, 42–43, 45, 54, 69, 70, 75, 77–78, 79, 81, 82, 86, 88, 91, 93, 94, 95, 99, 100, 103, 105,111–112, 113, 114, 116, 123, 124–125, 130, 131
  doorway amnesia
  implants 69, 90, 104, 120, 125, 136
  observed 116–17, 130–1
  post-hypnotic suggestion 125
  research 124, 131, 137
  screen memories 112
Adamski, George 25, 27, 28
aggressive encounters 26, 30–1
Air Force Scientific Advisory Board 12
aircraft, disappearance 23
aliens
  see also humanoid forms; monsters
  appearance 19, 20, 26, 27, 34, 111
  dead bodies 9, 10–11, 15, 23, 46–7, 132
  grays 10, 16, 26, 27, 55, 59, 69, 81, 83, 99, 110, 112, 137
  message protocol 125
  Nordic/tall type 26–7, 36, 55, 58, 125, 137
Amano, Hideichi 90
American Association for the Advancement of Science 65, 71
Apollo 63, 64, 67, 69
Appleton, Cynthia 36–7, 45
Area 51 115, 138
Arnold, Kenneth 8
atomic weapons 13, 15, 29, 33, 134
Australia 33, 52, 64, 68, 69, 70, 100, 114, 130
  UFOs 33, 52, 64
Aveyron, France 56, 87
Aztec, New Mexico 10

B

babies 37, 45, 62–3, 91, 94, 103, 104–5, 114, 123
Basterfield, Keith 68, 100, 103
Bender, Albert 22
Bigfoot 20
Blackmore, Dr Sue 131, 137
Blue Streak missiles 52–3
books 29, 35
  by abductees 112, 120, 121
  Chocky 107
  Circular Evidence 118
  Communion 112
  Flying Saucers and the Three Men 23
  Intruders 105
  Miracle Visitors 91
  Missing Time 99

Science and the UFOs 110
They Knew too Much About Flying Saucers 23
The UFO Experience 71, 87
UFO Crash at Roswell 133
  Was God an Astronaut series 63
You are Responsible 29
Brazel, William 8
breeding experiments 55, 60, 62–63, 79, 83, 94, 104–105, 114, 131
Britain 21, 26, 30–31, 42, 49, 51, 77–78, 79, 81, 86, 88, 89–90, 91, 94, 95, 100, 102, 104, 107, 108, 117, 118, 122, 136–137
BUFORA 117, 120, 132
Bulgaria 123
Burtoo, Alfred 102, 103

C

Cahill, Kelly 130
Canada 17, 23, 60, 126–8
Cape Canaveral 39, 109
cars, power loss 19, 33, 34, 56, 59, 77, 90, 93, 100, 101
Carswell Air Force Base 9
Center for UFO Studies 71
Chalker, Bill 131
Chavez, Sergeant 51
Churchill, Winston 21
CIA 23, 27, 30, 65, 84
cinnamon, smell of 111, 115
Clamar, Dr Aphrodite 99
CND 29
Cocconi, Giusepio 41
Coleman, Loren 57
comets 135
communication
  crop circles 118
  images in head 39, 90, 103
  language 16, 27, 28, 29, 50, 102, 115
  light beams 106
  radio 41, 47, 53, 61, 79, 85
  telepathic 29, 32, 34, 39, 55, 58, 59, 88, 92, 93, 94, 114
Condon, Dr Edward 60, 65
Condon Report 60, 65, 71
Cook, James 32, 34
crash landings 9, 10–11, 15, 29
creativity 103, 120, 125
crop circles 73, 94, 118, 123
CUFOS *see* Center for UFO Studies
cultural tracking 26

D

Day, John and Sue 78
de Luna, Leonardo 65
devil names 57

Dewilde, Marius 24
Dias Air Force Base 10
Dixon, Bob 79
Dogon tribe 83
Drake, Dr Frank 41
Drake, Raymond 63
dwarf forms 27, 32

E

earthlights 56, 106, 131
Edwards, Ken 89
Eisenhower, President 46
electricity
  earthlights 56, 106, 131
  electro-magnetism 131
  power cuts 19, 36, 38, 100, 136
  propulsion systems 34, 59
environmental concerns 71, 78, 120
equipment 25–6, 31
ESP 93, 104, 107, 125
Eustagio, Fernando 48
Evans, John 108

F

Facchini, Bruno 14, 16
falling-leaf motion 19
false memory syndrome 124
fantasy-prone personality 103, 104, 124
films 138
  Alien 93
  Back to the Future 107
  Close Encounters of the Third Kind 56, 87, 91
  Doomwatch 71
  Earth Versus the Flying Saucers 31
  Enemy Mine 107
  Fire in the Sky 129
  Hangar 18 97
  I Married a Monster from Outer Space 37
  Quatermass and the Pit 37
  Roswell autopsy 132–4
  Star Wars 87
  The Day the Earth Stood Still 19
  The Day of the Triffids 49
  The Flying Saucer 12
  The UFO Incident 83
  This Island Earth 27
  Zero Population Growth 71
Finland 66, 94
fireballs 15, 20
Flatwoods, Virginia 20
Flying Saucer Review 35, 45, 66
flying saucers 8, 15, 19
Ford, President Gerald 57
Foreign Technology Division 9, 23
France 24, 58

abductions 16–17, 54
  GEPAN 84, 98
  UFOs 56, 76, 84
Freedom of Information Act (1977)
  15, 84

G
GAO enquiry 134
Gatay, Georges 24
Gee, Doctor 10
Gemini 4, 55
genetic experiments *see* breeding
  experiments
GEPAN 84, 98
Germany
  captured alien 26
  UFOs 100
Gill, Father William 38
Glasgow, Scot 75
Gleason, Jackie 46
Glenn, John 47
goblin forms 27, 40, 66
Godfrey, Alan 95
Greenshaw, Jeff 72
Groendal Nature Reserve, South Africa 89
Gulf Breeze, Florida 114

H
Halt, Col Charles 96
Hargitai, Karoly 123
Hart, Carl 18
healing 108
Heinonen, Aarno 66
Hessdalen Valley, Norway 106
Hickson, Charlie 74–5
Hidalgo, Jose 85
Higdon, Carl 103
Hill, Betty and Barney 43, 83
Hind, Cynthia 81, 89
Hingley, Jean 92
Hollonan Air Force Base 32, 47
holograms 26, 60, 78, 85, 86, 113
Hopkins, Budd 99, 105, 110, 111, 112,
  116–17, 124
Hopkins, Dr Herbert 82
Hubble space telescope 123, 125
humanoid forms 9, 10–11, 14, 16, 17,
  18, 23, 24–5, 26, 27, 28, 29, 32,
  34, 36, 38, 40, 43–44, 48, 49,
  50–51, 54, 55, 56, 58, 59, 64, 65,
  67, 68, 69, 70, 72, 76–77, 80, 81,
  82–83, 84, 86, 88, 89, 92, 94, 95,
  96, 99, 101, 102, 107, 110, 112,
  113, 114, 116, 120, 123, 125, 126,
  127, 133, 137
Hungary 123
Hynek, Dr. J. Allen 38, 42, 50, 65, 71,
  87, 88, 106
hypnosis *see* regression, hypnotic

I
image hypothesis 100
implants 69, 90, 104, 120, 125, 136
Indonesia 81
interbreeding *see* breeding

experiments
investigations 13, 15
  Condon report 60, 65, 71
  GAO enquiry 134
  GEPAN 84
  MIT symposium 124
  Robertson report 23, 27
Italy 14, 16, 18–19
Ivanoff, Aino 94

J
J. Allen Hynek Center for UFO Studies
  71, 115, 133
Japan 80, 90
Java 81
'jelly' beings 81, 100
Johansson, Gideon 38
Journal for the Exploration of Science 98
Jupiter 73, 137

K
Keel, John 49, 56
Keyhoe, Major Donald 31
King, Barry 79
Kingman, Arizona 23
Kneale, Nigel 37
Knighton, Michael 138
Kopal, Prof. Zdnek 47
Kurz, Shane 62

L
Lagarde, Fernand 56
language 16, 27, 28, 29, 50, 102
laser beams 24, 26
Lazar, Bob 115
Libya 25
lightballs 56, 93, 106, 123, 131
Los Alamos, New Mexico 13, 29, 47
Lujan, Juan 85
Luna 3 39

M
McBoyle, Johnny 9
McDivitt, Brig. Gen. James 55
Mack, Prof. John 124, 131
Magee, Judith 70
magnetic propulsion 10, 56
Malaysia 81
Manhattan Transfer 116–17
Marcel, Major Jesse 8, 9, 97, 133
Mariner 2 47
Mars 50, 69, 85, 127, 135, 137, 138
Masse, Maurice 54
medical examinations 44–45, 68–69, 75,
  77, 79, 82, 88, 91, 93, 95, 99, 101,
  102, 109, 111, 113, 114, 116, 120,
  123, 130, 134,
memory 60, 124, 125
Men in Black 22–3, 52, 82, 97, 138
Menzel, Dr Donald 65
meteorite, fossil life 135, 137
Mexico 54
Michalak, Steve 60
MIT symposium 124
Mogul Project 134

monsters 20, 23, 27, 40, 49, 66, 78,
  81, 100
moon 39, 53, 64, 67, 69, 71, 137
Morrison, Philip 41
Mothman 20, 49
MUFON 115, 119

N
Napolitano, Linda 116
NASA 47, 48, 61, 96, 119
  message protocol 125
  Apollo 64, 67
  creation 39
  Discovery 119
  Gemini 4, 55
  Mars landing 85
  meteorite fossil life 137
  Pioneer 10, 73
  Ranger 7, 53
  Skylab 1, 73
  Viking 127
NATO 21, 30, 96
near-death experiences 108–9, 137
Neptune 93
'nest' formation 73
Netherlands 76
New Mexico
  alien bodies 10–11, 47, 133
  Project Twinkle 15
  research centres 13, 15
  rocket testing 11, 15, 29
  UFO sightings 13, 32, 51, 59
New Scientist 110
New Zealand 88
Nicolai, Renato 98
Norman, Paul 70
Norway 26, 106, 107
nuclear weapons 13, 15, 29

O
Oakensen, Elsie 90, 103
O'Brien, Brian 57, 60
Oeschler, Bob 126
O'Leary, Dr Brian 127
Orion 55
Oswald, Luli 93, 103
out-of-body experiences 56, 70, 77,
  108–9, 114, 124
Oz Factor 101

P
Page, Dr Thornton 65
Papua New Guinea 38
Parker, Calvin 74–5
Patterson, Col. Alfred 65
Pentagon 8, 9, 65, 115
Persinger, Dr Michael 131
Peru 54
Philippines 64
Pioneer 10 73
Pritchard, David 124
Project Blue Book 15, 27, 65
Project Hessdalen 106
Project Moon Dust 96
Project Ozma 41

Project Twinkle 15
propulsion systems 19, 101
    electrical 34
    electro-magnetism 59, 131
    magnetic 10
psychic forces 37, 55, 68, 108–9,
        114, 115
psychology 37
    abductee characteristics 99, 103, 124
    alien image 27
    hypnosis moratorium 117
    nuclear technology link 29
    research 124, 131, 137
Puddy, Maureen 70, 103
pulsars 61

Q
quasars 53

R
radiation 34, 39, 90, 96, 97, 98
radio signals 41, 47, 53, 61, 79, 85
RAF encounters 30–1
Ramey, General Roger 9
Ratsch, Don 119
regression hypnosis 43–5, 59, 61, 62–3,
        78, 82, 93, 95, 101, 103, 111,
        112, 113
    controls on 117
    research into 124, 125
religion 63, 138
Rendlesham Forest, Suffolk 96,
        100, 129
research 124, 131, 137
Reunion, Indian Ocean 80
Reynolds, Ros 100
Ring, Dr Kenneth 108
Robertson, Dr. H.P. 23, 27
robotic beings 75, 79, 95
rockets
    testing 11, 13, 15, 29, 52–3
Roestenberg, Jessie 26
Rogers, Mike 82
Rosales, Pedro 86
Roswell, New Mexico 8, 97, 132–4,
        136, 138
Ruppelt, Capt. Edward 27

S
Sagan, Dr Carl 57, 65, 138
Sandbach, Roy 17, 54
Santilli, Ray 132
Santos, Raimundo 40
Sarbacher, Dr Robert 47
satellites 32, 33, 39
Schirmer, Herb 59, 61
Scotland 31, 136
Scully, Frank 10
secret reports 13, 15
SETI programme 79
Severin, Antoine 80
sexual encounters 34, 37, 45, 79,
        81, 114
Simonton, Joe 52
Sims, Derrel 125, 136

Sirius 83
Slater, Elizabeth 99, 100
SOBEPS 121
South Africa 89, 114
South America 26, 27, 54
    Argentina 32, 49, 67
    Brazil 34–5, 36, 40, 48, 54, 55, 93
    Chile 62, 86
    Mexico 54
    Peru 54
    Uruguay 54
    Venezuela 26, 55
Soviet Union
    space craft 32, 33, 39, 53, 61
    UFOs 88
space craft 37, 39
    Columbus 125
    Hubble space telescope 123, 125
    manned 47, 53, 61, 63, 64, 69, 101
    planetary exploration 47, 73, 85,
        123, 127, 137
satellites 32, 33, 39
Space Shuttle 101, 109, 123
Surveyor 1 57
    UFO sightings from 48, 55
Spain 58, 67, 84–5
Sputnik 32, 33
Strieber, Whitley 110–12, 117
Stringfield, Len 10, 46
Surveyor 1 57
Sweden 29, 38–9, 77, 117
symbols
    crop circles 118
    on UFOs 9, 10, 51, 58, 133

T
technology 25–6, 31, 33, 115
telepathy see communication, telepathic
television 121
    Dr Who 49
    Dynasty 111
    The Extraordinary 121
    Quatermass and the Pit 37, 57
    Sightings 121
    Strange but True 121, 129
    The X-Files 129, 133, 134
    Unsolved Mysteries 121
    V 93
Teller, Dr Edward 13
Temple, Robert 83
Templeton, Jim 51–2
time travel 50, 86, 107
Tombaugh, Dr Clyde 13
Trejo, Jose 85
Trent, Paul 14

U
UFO groups 22
    BUFORA 117, 120, 132
    J. Allen Hynek Center for UFO Studies
        71, 115, 133
    MUFON 115
    SOBEPS 121
UFOs
    see also crash landings; landings

army helmet shape 77
banana shaped 43, 44
bell-shaped 38
cigar shaped 28, 29, 108
disc shaped 9, 10, 12, 21, 26, 31, 89
dish-shaped 98
dome shaped 80, 81, 95, 100
dumbbell-shaped 91
egg-shaped 25, 28, 50, 51, 54, 55, 64
first sighting 8
flying saucers 8, 15, 19
official investigations 57, 60–1, 65, 134
oval 30, 31, 40, 42, 46, 59, 70, 75
pencil-shaped 93
plate-shaped 66
shape 19
submarine shaped 72
taking off 19, 24, 51, 59
triangular 96, 121, 136
water collection 17
UMMO mystery 58
United Nations 88, 117
Uruguay 54
USA 8–13, 14, 15, 16, 18, 20–3, 27, 29,
        30, 31, 32, 33, 40, 42, 43, 46, 47,
        49, 50, 51, 55, 59, 62, 65, 71, 72,
        74, 75, 82–83, 84, 88, 96–97, 111,
        114, 115, 116–117, 128, 133, 134

V
Valdes, Corporal Armando 86
Vallee, Dr Jacques 16, 42, 87, 88, 98
Valley, Prof. George 12
Vandenburg, General Hoyt 15
Venezuela 26, 55
Venus 47
video evidence 126–9
Viljo, Esko 66
Villas Boas, Antonio 34–5, 43, 45
von Daniken, Eric 63

W
Wales 81, 107, 108
Walters, Ed 114–15
Walton, Travis 82, 129
Wanderka, Josef 28
Watson, Ian 91
weapons 16, 18, 24, 49, 80, 82
Welland, Thomas 100
Wieder, Irwin 128
Wilcox, Gary 50
Wilder, Dr Leonard 78
Wilson, Sheryl 103
'window' areas 37, 56–7, 68, 86, 95, 98,
        106, 113, 131, 138
Wright Patterson Air Force Base 9, 10,
        23, 46–7, 97
Wyndham, John 49, 107

Z
Zamora, Lonnie 51
Zeidman, Jennie 74